Steel Dynasty

The Team That Changed the NFL

Bill Chastain

TRIUMPH
B O O K S
CHICAGO

Library of Congress Cataloging-in-Publication Data

Chastain, Bill.
 Steel dynasty : the team that changed the NFL / Bill Chastain.
   p. cm.
 Includes index.
 ISBN-13: 978-1-57243-738-8
 ISBN-10: 1-57243-738-3
  1. Pittsburgh Steelers (Football team)—History. I. Title.

GV956.P57C36 2005
796.332'64'0974886—dc22

2005041821

This book is available in quantity at special discounts for your group or organization. For further information, contact:

Triumph Books
542 S. Dearborn Street
Suite 750
Chicago, Illinois 60605
(312) 939-3330
Fax (312) 663-3557

Printed in U.S.A.
ISBN-13: 978-1-57243-738-8
ISBN-10: 1-57243-738-3
Design by Patricia Frey
All photos courtesy of AP/Wide World Photos except where otherwise indicated.

To Patti, Carly, and Kel

Contents

Foreword

"What you accomplish on these football fields will stay with you forever. What your mark is will be a part of who you are forever."
—Chuck Noll

Who would have thought that what transpired with the Pittsburgh Steelers during the seventies would stand the test of time? Those of us who lived the experience were just happy to be a part of the team, but as we look back, 25 years after our last Super Bowl victory and 31 years after our first, we see that in that six-year period history was in the making. Four Super Bowls in six years, twice back-to-back, has become the standard of excellence in the NFL.

How did it happen? Why did it happen? These questions are still being asked today. The answer, very simply, is that the Steelers were a conglomeration of talent led by Chuck Noll, who had the ability to pull together and get the most out of his players. If you ask Chuck why it happened, he would simply say that it is all about people. That is one very important component, but I have learned that it takes a lot more than that.

So you ask the questions: What makes good teams great teams? What allows them to succeed? The answer, at least for me, can be found in James C. Collins' book *Good to Great*. The components of a great football team are the same components that make up a great company.

Let's take a look at dominant teams from past decades. If you look at the Packers of the sixties, the Steelers of the seventies, the 49ers of the eighties, the Cowboys of the nineties, and possibly the Patriots of 2000, you'll find a commonality. All these teams were built on four pillars: leadership, talented people, vision, and belief. Each of the above teams had a distinctive coach with strong leadership skills at the helm: Vince Lombardi, Chuck Noll, Bill Walsh, Jimmy Johnson, and Bill Belichick. Leadership—both external and internal—guides, directs, and fine tunes the development of the players to reach their full potential.

Leadership may be crucial, but so is talent. As they say, you can't do it without the horses. Think of the above teams, and the names of the great players will roll off your tongue. When thinking of the Steelers, who can forget Mean Joe Greene, Terry Bradshaw, Mel Blount, Jack Ham, Franco Harris, Lynn Swann, John Stallworth, Jack Lambert, and Mike Webster—nine players who all reside in the Pro Football Hall of Fame? Having talented players raises the standard for everyone else on the team.

It is easy to create a vision; we all want to be the best. How to get there becomes a little more complicated. Leadership drives the vision, and talent allows you to become more flexible in attaining it, but you have to get people to believe that it is attainable. Ultimately, that means a coach has to get the right people in the right positions to work together, which is easier said than done.

I asked Chuck Noll, "How do you get a team to play together?" His reply: "By trial and error." I think what he meant is that a coach wants to get self-sacrificing guys who are driven by their own ghosts, whatever they may be, to succeed. You need players who fit within the structure of the team, will do whatever is necessary for the betterment of the team, and, if necessary, subdue their own egos. Ultimately, we had those kinds of guys, and when you do, combined with their unique talent, magical things start to happen, like winning and getting into the playoffs.

A magical moment was the 1972 playoff game against the Oakland Raiders that was the birthplace for one of the all-time great comebacks, known in sports history as the "Immaculate Reception." It was the one play that changed our belief system, the one play that became a stepping stone to greatness, the one play that led us to four Super Bowls.

Looking back at our situation, I realize that in winning our first Super Bowl maybe we didn't get the recognition we deserved even though we won it. The test then was to come back and win the second one. Then you had credibility and were considered to be a legitimate champion. We did it and almost won another one in 1976 but fell short in the AFC Championship Game. The 1976 season became a pivotal year that led to a transitional year in 1977.

Offensively we were a running team in 1974 and 1975, which led to both Franco and I having 1,000-yard seasons in 1976, but we got hurt in the playoffs and eventually lost to the Raiders because we didn't have a balanced attack. So Chuck opted to change the team in 1977, opening up the passing game to utilize the talents of two young receivers who were coming of age: Lynn Swann and John Stallworth.

Most of the success of our young team can be credited to a great defense, which came of age in 1976 by establishing a league record of shutting out five straight opponents. The defense's size, speed, and tenacity became the trademark of the NFL and were emulated by all. They set a standard that was soon to be changed.

As the offense was changing, so were the rules of the NFL. The rules changes were directly related to the play of our defense. When a team becomes too good, people want to change it. By 1978 the game opened up because of restrictions placed on defenses. Chuck saw the changes and adapted accordingly. Why? Because he had the talent to do so.

Whenever I run into people all over the country, they remember our team. Many of them watched us during their own formative years, whether they rooted for us or against us. Some of the names may have been forgotten, along with some of the games, but what they remember is that the Steelers were one of the all-time great teams.

Chuck's prophecy came true.

—Rocky Bleier

Acknowledgments

While attending college at Georgia Tech in the seventies, a Sunday after-noon watching NFL games served as a relaxing escape from school's demanding curriculum. During those days I would sit inside the frater-nity house blowing off my studies to watch the Pittsburgh Steelers dominate the league in a fashion rarely seen. Like other NFL followers, I grew familiar with the names of the bigger-than-life characters wearing the black and gold.

It is not surprising, then, that interviewing those men for this book proved to be a great thrill for me. I particularly enjoyed the discovery of how well most of them have done since leaving the NFL—in jobs and businesses that have little or nothing to do with capitalizing on the fame they achieved during their playing days, other than learning how to be successful. As a group these men came across as intelligent, personable, and, above all else, interesting, and it was my pleasure to talk to them. I greatly appreciate their opening up to me so I could share some of their stories. I would like to give thanks to Jack Ham, Donnie Shell, Joe Greene, Mel Blount, Rocky Bleier, Dwight White, Ray Oldham, L. C. Greenwood, John Stallworth, Mike Wagner, Andy Russell, Bud Carson, and Dan Rooney Jr. In addition, I would like to give special thanks to Chuck Noll, whom I found fascinating and complex. I don't believe he has ever been given the credit he is due for the excellence he achieved.

Others who especially helped this project include Charlie Britton, Joel Poiley, Tom McEwen, Pat Yasinskas, Joe Zalupski, Paul Abercrombie, Jim McNulty, Charlie Dayton, and Joe Gordon.

This book never could have come to fruition without Frank Scatoni and Greg Dinkin of Venture Literary. I am grateful for all they have done and continue to do for my career.

Thanks to my brothers, Tommy—for your interest and PR skills—and Budroe—for always being there; and to my wife, Patti, daughter, Carly, and son, Kel, for tolerating me on the days when I was preoccupied with the "Stillers."

Finally, Mom, thanks for putting to work your Agnes Scott education to help eliminate many of your middle son's grammatical errors. And Pops, don't ever sell out, "There she sits, stately, worldly . . ."

Prologue

"Mean" Joe Greene and Mel Blount carpooled during their playing days with the Pittsburgh Steelers, talking about anything and everything while commuting to work like a couple of Joe Six-Packs. When Three Rivers Stadium came into view, Blount would turn toward Greene.

"See that stadium?" Blount would say. "We kicked a lot of ass over there."

Heinz Field is now the Steelers' home after dynamite turned Three Rivers Stadium into a parking lot. Only the memories of a lost era remain, along with the legacies of Greene, Blount, and the other players and coaches who made Pittsburgh's "Steel Dynasty" of the seventies the glory of their time.

The Dallas Cowboys came to be known as "America's Team" for their popularity in the seventies, but clearly the Steelers were every American's team during the decade. So popular were the Steelers that 21 members of the team had made national commercials by the time the team lined up to play the Los Angeles Rams on January 20, 1980, in Super Bowl XIV. None of the commercials was more memorable than Greene's Coca-Cola ad. The All-Pro defensive tackle looked battered and intimidating when a little boy handed him a Coke. Greene chugged the soda, then smiled at the boy before tossing him his jersey. America loved the fact that Mean Joe had a soft spot for kids, and the ad won a Clio Award.

Greene, Bradshaw, Harris, Swann, Lambert, Ham, Stallworth, Webster, Greenwood . . . these were household names playing for the defending champions, who had won three Super Bowls in five years. But over time, steel had oxidized into rust on this regal NFL product. Ten of the team's twenty-two starters were age 30 or older heading into the 1980

Super Bowl. Among the aging were Terry Bradshaw, Greene, Blount, and Jack Ham. Ham wasn't even suited up for the contest against the Rams after suffering an ankle injury.

Much of the NFL landscape had changed since the Steelers came into prominence earlier in the decade—particularly the rules that made playing defense more difficult every year. Rules were adopted to thwart talented defenses like the Steelers', which had crushed opposing offenses like no team in NFL history. Slapping heads and chucking receivers' running patterns up the field became taboo. Offensive linemen were even empowered to use their hands to block. The success of the Pittsburgh defense initiated the changes that would make their jobs more difficult.

The Steelers' journey had begun in the midst of a depression with a feisty Irishman who loved football. Would their remarkable dynasty culminate with a fourth Super Bowl victory? Sixty minutes of football would answer the question.

A History of
Frustration

Prior to the arrival of the "Steel Curtain" Steelers, professional football in Pittsburgh represented anything but success. Losing characterized Steelers football dating back to owner Art Rooney's entry into the National Football League.

During a period of early growth for the NFL, Arthur J. Rooney, the son of an Irish saloon owner, became involved with semipro football in Pittsburgh. Composing Rooney's team were steelworkers and coal miners; these semipros were hard men—workers by day, drinkers by night, and football players on the weekends because football had always been a way of life.

Pennsylvania's existing blue laws barred the NFL from the state by forbidding Sunday games, prompting towns to form their own squads that played whatever competition they could find.

Rooney hailed from an Irish-American area on the north bank of the Allegheny River near downtown Pittsburgh known as Pittsburgh's First Ward, or "the Ward." Operating from that location, he organized a team known as the Hope-Harveys, for the Ward's firehouse (called Hope) and Dr. Harvey, a local physician.

Rooney's squad proved to be competitive, holding its own against other semipro teams and a few NFL teams during the late 1920s and early 1930s. All along the team continued to show improvement thanks to Rooney's constant upgrading, which included the recruitment of quality college players from time to time.

In 1933, the Pennsylvania legislature repealed the Sunday ban, creating an opportunity for NFL football to find its way to Pittsburgh. Though America was in the middle of the Great Depression, Rooney had the necessary funds to purchase an NFL franchise and plunked down $2,500 to become the owner of the Pittsburgh Pirates, a name selected to mirror the city's immensely popular major league baseball team.

Rooney worked from his office at the Fort Pitt Hotel and hired Forrest "Jap" Douds to coach his initial squad. Though the team did not find success, Rooney managed to stay in business by selling his high-priced talent to other teams and not losing too much money. He understood the economy that dictated the terms for him to stay in business.

Rooney remained a local legend based on his tough upbringing, his leadership skills, and his acumen as a gambler. He had the necessary stones to let a bet ride, which he did in 1936 when he went to New York City with an old Pittsburgh light-heavyweight fighter named Buck Crouse by his side and $300 burning a hole in his pocket. At the Empire City racetrack, Rooney ran his $300 up to $21,000 on a Saturday. Understanding that hot streaks were a phenomenon gamblers had to respect, Rooney paid proper respect to his by heading upstate on Monday for opening day at Saratoga, where he put down $2,000 on an 8-to-1 shot named Quel Jeu, who won in a photo finish. Rooney then placed a $10,000 bet on another 8-to-1 horse in the fifth race, and the horse won by a nose. At the end of the day he had won $256,000. If only Rooney could have passed on some of his gambling luck to his football team!

The Pirates were renamed "Steelers" prior to the 1940 season to reflect the city's heritage with the steel industry. Unfortunately for Rooney and the Pittsburgh fans, the Steelers resembled the same team they were as the Pirates with a 2–7–2 record. At the end of the season a dejected Rooney took stock of his football venture. Here was a man who had been successful in just about every arena he'd entered, yet his team had lost money almost every year since its inception. They made a profit of $5,000 in 1940, but that hardly raised optimism considering the cumulative $100,000 lost during the previous years. Besides the team's dismal fortunes on the field, they did not enjoy a good relationship with Forbes Field, which catered to the Pirates, casting the Steelers as Pittsburgh's ugly stepchild.

Rooney met with businessman Alexis Thompson early in the 1940 season to discuss selling the Steelers. Thompson was just 28 but had the money and desire to own a franchise after inheriting $6 million from a steel fortune at age 16. Thompson attended Yale before assuming the position of vice president for a successful drug company. Rooney did not sell.

Rooney again met with Thompson later in the season and again turned him down. But league meetings taking place the week of the NFL Championship Game between the Washington Redskins and Chicago Bears reopened the dialogue between Thompson and Rooney. On the morning of December 9, 1940, the agreement to sell the Steelers to Thompson for $160,000 was announced but was hardly noticed by the sporting public because the Bears had waxed the Redskins 73–0 the previous day.

Even though he'd sold his team, Rooney couldn't stay away from football. Though accounts are blurred in detail, most agree Rooney bought part of the Philadelphia Eagles franchise for an unspecified amount from his friend, Eagles owner Bert Bell.

By the spring of 1941, Rooney longed for Pittsburgh and Thompson longed for Philadelphia—which was closer to New York, the primary location of his business—so they swapped franchises. Out of this confusion a team under Rooney's control remained in Pittsburgh.

Once again Rooney went into survival mode. Not only did the team compete for dollars, it also had to compete for healthy bodies because almost any man capable of playing football could fight in Europe or Asia in World War II. Teams were forced to select players from men who were 4-F and defense workers, which served up a finite supply. So sparse were bodies to fill the uniforms that in 1943 the Steelers joined with the Philadelphia Eagles and in 1944 with the Chicago Cardinals to form one team. The 1943 team, which combined the Steelers and Eagles to form Phil-Pitt, came to be known as the "Steagles," and the team played its home games in Philadelphia. When the Chicago team joined forces with the Steelers they became the Card-Pitts and played their home games in Chicago. This collection of players played so poorly they were referred to as the "Carpets" because opposing teams would walk all over them. After the war, the Steelers were back at full force for the 1945 season.

The immensely popular coach of the University of Pittsburgh, Jock Sutherland, took over the Steelers' coaching duties in 1946 and brought immediate improvement to the team's fortunes. In Sutherland's initial campaign the Steelers improved from a 2–8 record to 5–5–1. In 1947 the Steelers went 8–4 before losing to Philadelphia in a playoff for the NFL's Eastern Division title.

Sutherland appeared to be the man who could lead the Steelers to an NFL championship. Unfortunately, he died of a brain tumor in the spring of 1948 and the history of losing continued, mixed with occasional splashes of mediocrity.

Typifying the Steelers' frustrations were personnel decisions such as selecting Gary Glick over Lenny Moore (a future Hall of Fame running back) in a bonus draft. And they drafted Purdue quarterback Len Dawson with the fifth selection in 1957, rather than a running back from Syracuse named Jim Brown, whom Cleveland wisely selected with the sixth pick. Dawson washed out with the Steelers before resurfacing with the AFL's Kansas City Chiefs, where he became a star, and Brown is generally regarded as the best player in NFL history. And there was the case of Johnny Unitas, who hailed from Pittsburgh and could have been the team's golden boy.

The Steelers drafted Unitas in the ninth round of the 1955 draft. He'd thrown the ball well during training camp only to have the Steelers' coach, Walt Kiesling, cut him without playing him a down during the team's five exhibition games prior to the 1955 season. Later it was revealed that Unitas carried a label of not being smart enough to be a pro quarterback, a reputation originating from his difficulties taking entrance exams at the Universities of Pittsburgh and Louisville. Typifying Steelers blunders, Unitas went on to Baltimore where he became the Colts' quarterback and enjoyed a Hall of Fame career.

So instead of having a backfield of Unitas, Brown, and Moore, the Steelers settled for a washed-up Bobby Layne complemented by backs Tom Tracy and Larry Krutko. And there is the matter of the Steelers' 1965 first-round choice, which they swapped to the Bears for second- and fourth-round picks in the 1964 draft. Exercising their two choices, the Steelers selected defensive ends Jim Kelly and Ben McGee; the Bears used the 1965 first-round pick acquired from the Steelers to select Dick Butkus, the future Hall of Fame linebacker.

On any given Sunday the Steelers were a franchise of NFL bloopers.

According to linebacker Andy Russell, who joined the club as a 16th-round selection out of Missouri in 1963, the Steelers had a "very good team" during his rookie season. Buddy Parker was the head coach of a team that took a 7–3–3 record into Yankee Stadium to play against the Giants for a berth in the NFL Championship Game.

"We'd beaten them 31–0 during the regular season, so we felt like we had a good chance of winning the thing, or at least winning that game and getting into the Championship Game," Russell said.

The Giants won the rematch 33–17 and went on to lose to the Bears 14–10 in the NFL Championship Game. Russell then left the team to serve a military stint in Germany in 1964 and 1965. In his absence the Steelers posted records of 5–9 and 2–12. Russell returned in 1966 to

4

find S.O.S. signs displayed at Steelers home games; S.O.S. stood for "Same Old Steelers."

"Guys like Ernie Stautner, all the old players that were around in '63, were gone," Russell said. "And they had not done a very good job of drafting, so there wasn't much talent, and we struggled hugely for the next couple of years."

Bill Austin coached the team to a combined 11–28–3 record from 1966 through 1968. Russell laughed remembering the frustration of those seasons, noting they had frequent team meetings in which lengthy discussions were held addressing why bad things continued to happen, what was wrong with them, why they continued to make mistakes, and why they weren't winning.

"We had all been good college players to some degree, so we questioned why this didn't translate to more success at the professional level," Russell said. "We just couldn't figure it all out. Everybody was making mistakes. It was tough. We felt like we were letting down the owners, the fans, and the coaches. We were failing at football, something we all loved and something we had always played well."

Excuses followed. Players complained about anything and everything including the coaching leadership and the ownership; they even squawked about the golden triangle on the shoulders of their jerseys, which they deemed too ugly. And there was Austin's discipline. He had come from the Vince Lombardi school of hard-nosed obedience and struggled with players who disobeyed his stringent rules, some of which were silly and arbitrary, like the rule aimed at players attending a certain Pittsburgh bar. Austin's rule stated you could stand at the bar, but you couldn't sit at the bar. One night the rule came into question when Russell and center Ray Mansfield were at the bar talking to Pat Livingston, a sports reporter for the *Pittsburgh Press*.

Livingston "was always knocking Austin," Russell said. "So we're standing at the bar yucking it up with the hated sportswriter and the next day I'm told that Austin wants to see me."

Russell was a team captain, and he went to see Austin.

"As captain, I want to let you know I'm cutting Ray Mansfield from the team," Austin said.

"Why, what are you talking about?" Russell said.

"He was at the bar last night talking to Livingston," Austin said.

"What rule did he break?" Russell said. "The rule is you can't sit down. You can't cut him."

Russell had his coach on a technicality.

"All right, get the hell out of here," Austin said.

Russell laughed as he recalled the story.

"Ray Mansfield was our starting center," Russell said. "This is a guy who was a very good player."

The conditions in which the Steelers existed were not exactly first class, either.

Steelers headquarters was located on the second floor of the Roosevelt Hotel, and the team practiced at South Park, one of two large county parks in the area. Police horses roamed the field when the players weren't practicing, which added an odor reflective of team performance. An old house near South Park was used for a locker room and offices for the coaching staff. Inside, the kitchen served as the training room, the basement was the locker room, the bedrooms were used for position meetings, and the front porch was the location of the weight room.

During this period, Rocky Bleier joined the team as a 16th-round selection in 1968. He brought youthful enthusiasm to a team filled with lethargy. Bleier experienced this lethargy in his first practice with the team.

"I got to the huddle and I'm like, 'OK guys, let's go,'" Bleier said. "Somebody on the offensive line said, 'OK rook, cut the bullshit.'"

When asked about making the team, Bleier laughed.

"Do you know how I made the team?" he said. "When I ask that question everybody shrugs their shoulders. Then I ask them, do you know who played for the team in 1967? That's how I made the team."

Bleier, who hailed from Appleton, Wisconsin, where his father owned a bar, said his chances of making the team weren't hurt by the fact that he was a "good Irish-Catholic kid whose dad owned a bar, like Mr. Rooney, whose dad owned a bar."

Despite being a member of a team that occupied the NFL's basement, Bleier felt lucky to be in a professional environment. But he added: "What evolved that [1968] season was really a loss of control [and] respect [for] the coaching staff. Specifically the head coach."

Then, in 1969 the Steelers did something right.

Art Rooney had delegated many of his duties running the franchise to his sons, so Dan Rooney and Art Rooney Jr. each assumed significant roles.

Dan Rooney had come into the world the same year as the Steelers and was raised a strict Irish Catholic. Many of his childhood summers were spent at Steelers training camp, where he fell in love with football while learning the business of the sport.

By age 14 he was working as a water boy.

"I did everything, really got to know the business," Dan said. "Jock Sutherland was the coach. He was a very thorough, capable guy. I learned a lot just by observing him."

Having become quite an athlete by this juncture, Dan occasionally participated in team drills.

"I would run with the quarterbacks and beat them all," Dan said with a chuckle. "They would really get mad. They would say, 'Get out of here, you're making us look bad.' And they weren't really killing themselves, which I was of course. I was trying to run as fast as I could. They were trying to loaf a little bit. They were all good friends of mine."

Dan spent a lot of time with the players, which he credits for helping him in later years when he got involved in matters helping the NFL negotiate with the players union. He respected the players because he had been among them. Occasionally he would even travel with the team on the train for road games to Philadelphia, Washington, and New York.

"I would be there and I would take my homework with me," Dan said. "They'd be helping me with my homework. It was just that kind of relationship."

By high school Dan had turned into a good enough quarterback to lead North Catholic High School to the Pittsburgh city championship. All the while he continued to work for the Steelers. During Dan's college years at Duquesne University he became the Steelers' training camp manager, a job that included negotiating player contracts.

"I would sign the players," Dan said. "I would negotiate with the players on their contracts, and I was too young to sign the contracts—I was only 18 or 19 at the time—so I would have to take the contracts in to the coach to get them signed after I worked them out."

When Dan graduated in 1955 with a degree in accounting he went to work full-time for the Steelers, continuing a journey that would see him work at virtually every job available in the organization prior to his father's naming him club president in 1975. By the late fifties he had become heavily involved in league matters as the Steelers' representative, and by the late sixties he began to guide many important team matters, which made him the guy to pick Austin's replacement. Austin had a three-year contract that ran through the 1968 season, and he was not asked to return for 1969.

"I obviously talked to my father [about finding a new coach], but he pretty much left it up to me," Dan said.

Embarking on the task of finding a new leader for the family football team, Dan did extensive research, talking to a lot of existing head coaches about worthy assistants and perusing media guides to read any available information about potential candidates. He carried an open mind into the process, considering former head coaches in the NFL, up-and-coming NFL assistants, and highly visible college coaches. He received a lot of calls from interested candidates and even got used by one college coach, who told his school the Steelers had made him an offer—which they had not—to wrench out a significant pay raise. Included among the candidates was legendary Penn State coach Joe Paterno.

"He considered our job more than he considered any other job," Dan said. "And he just said he was going to stay in college. You can't argue with his decision, but I think he would have done well in the pros, too."

The Baltimore Colts were the toast of the NFL during the 1968 season when they posted a 13–1 regular-season record that featured many lopsided victories. Seeking to emulate such success with the Steelers, Dan examined the Colts' coaching staff for possible candidates.

"I looked at Baltimore and there were a couple of guys there that you would consider," Dan said. "I was pretty good friends with [Colts head coach] Don Shula, so I called him and talked to him. Don said that he thought that Chuck Noll was the guy that should be considered."

Dan asked Shula if he could interview Noll for the job. Shula said he didn't mind if the Steelers told Noll they were interested, but he requested they not talk to Noll about the job until the Colts finished their season. Dan respected Shula's wishes, which delayed the Steelers' initial interview with Noll until the day after the Super Bowl.

Outside of pro football's inner circle, few recognized Noll's name, but he'd spent a lifetime in football and possessed the necessary pedigree for becoming an NFL head coach.

Noll attended Cleveland's Benedictine High School in the late forties, where he switched from running back to tackle when the coach needed a tackle. He turned the position change into a positive, earning all-state honors and beginning his football learning curve along the way.

"My high school coach had a great influence on me," said Noll of Benedictine High coach Ab Strosnyder. "He was very technique oriented and taught a high school kid how to survive football with techniques."

Noll earned a scholarship to the University of Dayton, where he made another position change, moving from tackle to linebacker. Once again the move had a positive effect. Noll became a team captain and played well enough to attract the attention of the Cleveland Browns, who selected him with their 20th choice in the 1953 draft.

Legendary Browns coach Paul Brown, who won four All-America Conference and three NFL championships during his career, knew Noll had been a lineman and converted him into a "messenger" guard on offense, meaning he ran in every other play from the sideline to the quarterback.

"You went in and played a play and then the other guard came in," Noll said. "You alternated plays. I suppose it was a big learning experience."

The late Brown once said of Noll: "After a while Chuck could have called the plays himself without any help from the bench. He was that kind of football student."

Noll learned directly from Brown, but he'd been learning from Brown in an indirect manner from the first time he played football.

"Paul was a big influence throughout the state of Ohio," Noll said. "He influenced my high school coaches, he influenced my college coaches—they were all people who had been influenced by Paul. It was hard to grow up in Ohio and not be influenced by him. Being drafted by him and seeing how he functioned was of course another influence."

Throughout his playing career Noll sought to find his life's work. He attended law school, represented a trucking firm, and even sold insurance. When asked about how good he was at selling insurance, Noll deadpanned: "I coached football."

Noll experienced another position switch when Browns linebacker Tommy Thompson suffered a knee injury. He filled the vacancy and played at that position until he retired in 1959 at the age of 27. He could have continued playing but realized even at this young age that he wanted to coach.

Believing he had a chance to become a coach at Dayton, Noll and his wife, Marianne, thought the timing was right to end his playing career. Though he didn't get the Dayton job, Noll gained employment with Sid Gilman, who hired him to be the defensive line coach with the Los Angeles (later San Diego) Chargers of the fledgling American Football League.

"Sid was a great offense mind," Noll said. "He was offensively oriented, that's what he liked. I went out there as a defense coach. He let me handle the defense, so I was on my own there. It was fun."

Noll remained with the Chargers for six years and noted that he had more exposure to football working with Gilman than he normally would have received in twelve years.

"Sid was one of the game's prime researchers and offensive specialists," Noll said.

Noll left San Diego in 1966 to become Shula's defensive assistant at Baltimore.

"When I was looking for a coach I heard he was interested," Shula said. "I brought him in for an interview, picked him up at the airport, and talked to him for a couple of hours. I was impressed with the overall way he came across intelligence-wise, and [I liked his] sincerity and personality. I liked everything about him. I knew immediately that was the guy I wanted to hire and offered him the job."

Noll felt as if he was going home. Not only was he moving back East, but he also was uniting with Shula, who had played for Brown at Cleveland before Noll arrived. Shula later coached under Blanton Collier, who had been Brown's chief assistant at the University of Kentucky. Noll and Shula spoke the same football language—the language of Paul Brown.

"Because people have different systems it's a language unto its own," Noll said. "So if you go from one to another you have to learn the language. They may be running the same play you run, but they give it a different name. So it takes a while sometimes to learn what you're doing in the whole scheme of things. We put in a lot of hours. That's part of the learning thing, especially when you're joining a new organization. New learning, relearning."

Paul Brown would create a teacher-classroom setting.

"Paul Brown was very good at explaining and diagramming, getting his point across," Shula said. "When you think back, [Noll and Shula] both came from the same school. And that was the Paul Brown school."

Shula described Noll as "quiet and reserved" but said "he did have a great sense of humor. And very bright. He could talk on any subject and also he was a great teacher in the classroom."

Noll's résumé continued to sparkle in Baltimore, where the Colts had just two defensive coaches, Noll and Bill Arnsparger.

"Two pretty good ones," Shula said with a laugh.

The combined efforts of Shula, Noll, and Arnsparger on the Colts' defense culminated during the 1968 season when the Colts tied an NFL record by allowing just 144 points, including three shutouts. The troika implemented a scheme that saw shifting fronts and rotating zones with occasional eight-man blitzes.

"I just think [the key to that defense] was not making mistakes," Shula said. "Knowing what each other's responsibilities were. Not giving up cheap touchdowns. Making teams earn it, then taking advantage of their mistakes."

Veteran Jerry Logan played defensive back for the Colts when Shula brought in Noll, who was an unknown to Logan and his teammates.

"It didn't take very long to see that the work we did in the classroom and the studying we did was a lot different than what we'd been doing in the past," Logan said. "So what that does is it makes you a better student of the game. Everybody [in the NFL] can play, understand that, but that other intangible that Chuck brought to the game and to us was making us better football players because we were smarter.

"Shula was the same. Between Chuck and Don, cerebrally those two guys were kind of ahead of their time as far as preparation, putting you in a position not to get beat. I had physical skills like everybody who comes into the league; those two guys made a difference."

Noll made his defensive players understand the entire scheme of the defense, which was over and above simply understanding their individual positions.

"If you understand the whole scheme of the defense you understand where your help is, where you don't have help, and that puts you in a position where you overplay your strengths," Logan said. "When I first joined the Colts I knew my assignment and didn't really understand where all the linebackers were and where the other defensive backs were. What kind of stunts the linemen were doing. I understood after a little while with Chuck Noll that defense was a team game. Everybody has to know what everybody else is doing. And that makes you a better player."

Logan and the other members of the Colts' defense took to calling their coach "Knowledge Noll" for his instruction and his ability to drive them to think. He conducted himself in a quiet and reserved manner, carrying the aura of a teacher about him.

"He was really dry witted," Logan said. "He'd look at you real funny, then kind of laugh. If you know anything about him or have been around him, he has a real dry personality."

Logan remembered Noll for having outside interests, such as a love for photography and cameras.

"But Chuck was pretty much all business," Logan said. "He knew what it was about and he knew what he had to do to make his players understand what they had to do to win."

Noll perceived himself as a teacher. When asked what he would be doing if he weren't a football coach, his answer remained constant: he'd be a history teacher. Although he had become a teacher to NFL students, he continued to be a student as well. Noll credited Shula with helping him learn organization and attitudes.

11

Baltimore finished its total annihilation of the NFL in 1968 by blitzing the Browns 34–0 in the NFL Championship Game. Remember, this was back when the NFL was perceived to be a superior league to the AFL.

"We had great players, smart players," said Noll about the Colts. "But the other thing we had was an offense that didn't put the defense in a lot of difficult situations. We had an offense that moved the football and controlled it on the field. We had to take the ball away, give it to the offense, let them possess it. Keep our defense off the field, that's a big part of it. That's as much a part of having good defense as what you do when you're on the field."

After dominating the NFL Championship Game, the Colts were huge favorites heading into Super Bowl III, where the Joe Namath–led New York Jets pulled the biggest upset in pro football history on January 12, 1969, at the Orange Bowl in Miami.

Noll met with Dan Rooney the following day.

"Chuck was terrific," Rooney said. "From the very beginning he impressed me. He knew our team. Obviously, playing in the Super Bowl, he wasn't concerned about the Steelers or anything, but when he came in he knew our team. He knew who he thought was good or bad. He had a very good understanding of our players and our situation, which I thought was remarkable for another team's assistant coach. To be honest, we hit it off very well. I remember his knowledge of the game was the thing that impressed me the most, and not just his knowing formations and so forth."

Rooney didn't immediately hire Noll, but he did have Noll come to Pittsburgh to meet his father, and they continued to talk about the job in telephone conversations.

"Every time I talked to him I got more comfortable with him and [became] convinced he was the guy," Rooney said. "I knew from the beginning that Chuck was a guy we had to give a lot of consideration to. Chuck had that same kind of quiet expertise we were looking for."

Noll also received interest from the Buffalo Bills and Boston Patriots; each offered him their head coaching position. He listened to his suitors, but he was not consumed with the idea of becoming a head coach.

"I was happy with what we had done and where I was," Noll said.

But there seemed to be a connection in Pittsburgh and Noll became convinced the Rooneys would be committed to winning.

"In talking to Dan I felt that they wanted to win," Noll said. "It wasn't a question of shortcuts or anything like that. They wanted to win and win badly. They were going to give me what I needed and what I wanted in order to win, and you can't ask for any more than that."

Shula pushed for Noll to get the Steelers job and had no reservations about his assistant taking over a losing franchise.

"It was going to give him the opportunity to be a head coach," Shula said. "And that would be his first head coaching job. And I had great respect, even though they weren't playing that well, for the Pittsburgh organization and the Rooney family."

Rooney hired Noll January 27, 1969, thereby forging a unique relationship between team management and the team's coach.

"He wasn't just tied down to football," Rooney said. "There was never a question about him burning out because he had another life. There was more to him than just football."

But why would Noll possibly want to go to the Steelers? They had been losers for so long that thinking their situation could be turned around would have seemed ludicrous. For starters, the landscape of the NFL had been changing thanks in large part to TV, which had hung its hat on professional football and its increasing popularity. Television—and the NFL—had changed a great deal since the 1951 deal struck between the NFL and the DuMont Network, which had failed to sustain its effort to become the fourth network despite holding such popular properties as *Captain Video, The Amateur Hour,* and *Life Is Worth Living* hosted by Bishop Fulton J. Sheen. The DuMont Network paid $75,000 in 1951 to the NFL—to show its title game only.

The sixties put the NFL into warp drive for a major face-lift. A merger agreement between the NFL and the AFL had been struck in 1966 calling for the two leagues to merge prior to the beginning of the 1970 season. The NFL didn't buck the change that brought a mutual draft in 1967, which eliminated the possibility of drafted players pitting one league against the other to drive up their salaries. And professional football continued to thrive.

During one memorable Sunday in November of 1968, the TV networks—NBC and CBS—attracted more than 100 million viewers to watch four games from noon to 7:00 P.M. NBC, which had sunk in $42 million for its original five-year deal with the AFL, paid out approximately $9 million to the 10 American Football League teams for the

13

1969 season, while CBS paid more than $20 million to 16 clubs. And speculation even circulated that NFL commissioner Pete Rozelle had been considering the creation of an NFL network.

The NFL had an agreement not to televise its games on Friday or Saturday nights, which would have been in competition with high school and college football. So Rozelle decided Monday night would be the way to go. Two Monday night games were shown on CBS in 1969, yet CBS and NBC both declined when Rozelle gave them the chance to show a full season of Monday night games in 1970. Each believed in their existing programming on Monday night and did not want to disrupt a successful lineup. Spurned, Rozelle took his idea to Roone Arledge, then the president of ABC Sports, and Arledge went for it in the hope that the NFL on Monday night could serve as a catalyst for the third-ranked network to advance on CBS and NBC.

Throughout the history of the Steelers' franchise there had been periods defined by financial struggles. Keeping the team in business had been a priority during those years. Now, suddenly, the Steelers, like other NFL teams, had a lucrative revenue stream in TV.

"There was an influx of revenue to pay the bills," Dan Rooney said. "Television money wasn't a lot of money at first, but it was like found money. We were on NBC, and Baltimore, Cleveland, and Washington were on independent networks [in the early days of televised NFL games in the fifties]. Then, of course, the sixties came and television just boomed."

Accompanying the kickoff to Noll's tenure and the NFL's coming boom were the beginning of hard times in the city of Pittsburgh.

Steel had provided the foundation for Pittsburgh's economy dating back to the days when the city's proximity to coal fuel was recognized and deemed an attractive area to create steel. Pittsburgh thrived under the steel industries of Andrew Carnegie, Henry Frick, and Thomas and Andrew Mellon, creating huge employment opportunities and drawing a large population to the city. Sadly, the seventies became the decade in which the steel industry started to shrink. Foreign competition increased, causing many steel mills to go out of business. Steelworkers, who hailed from families supported for generations by jobs within the industry, suddenly were unemployed. The Steelers offered a diversion; improving the team meant something to the community. A new approach was desperately needed. Noll might not have looked like a coach capable of changing the franchise's history, but the wheels of change began to turn immediately upon his hiring.

The task might have been overwhelming to some, prompting feelings of anxiety and self-doubt. Not for Noll.

"No, I never really had any doubts about my ability [when I took the job]," Noll said. "I had what I felt was a good feeling for the game and what it took to win and the techniques that were necessary and the kinds of players we needed, and that's what we tried to go out and get."

Upon accepting the job, Noll immediately began to formulate ideas about what the team needed to win.

Building the Foundation

Chuck Noll had definite ideas about what was needed in Pittsburgh, and he carried a quiet confidence about him that he would get the job done.

"I knew what you had to do to win," Noll said. "Number one, you had to not lose. And that means you have to play good defense. And you wanted an offense that didn't get your defense in trouble. That was our first thought, we had to improve our defense. We have to play good defense and we have to not make mistakes on offense—even if we have to run the ball on every down and punt. Don't get the turnovers. Don't get yourself in trouble giving the ball up at the 20-yard line where they only have 20 yards to score or they're in field-goal range already. You don't want to do that. That's a prescription to lose."

Noll recognized that the landscape of the NFL was heading toward conservative, smashmouth football where ball control would become the mantra for winning teams—stuff the other team's offense, never fumble, kick a couple of field goals, perhaps score a touchdown, and chalk up a victory.

"At that time in the National Football League, the edge went to the defensive linemen," Noll said. "Rushing the passer, a lineman could come in and slap you up the side of your head, grab your jersey, grab your shoulder pads, and go right past you. Offensive linemen had their hands in front of them, and that was what they called protecting."

In contrast to the way Noll saw the game going, others tried to build their teams around offense; the Kansas City Chiefs, for example, preferred a wide-open offense touting radical philosophical differences to old-school trench warfare.

In addition to the idea of fortifying a solid defense first, Noll believed in building a team through the draft—not procuring veteran players from other teams. The calls would come from other teams wanting to trade veteran players to the Steelers for draft choices or the team's young players. Noll balked at the offers, opting instead to adhere to his preference for finding the talent, bringing it in, and then indoctrinating it into his system.

"I'd get all these calls saying, 'Hey, I got this guy or that guy who can help you; give us a draft choice for him,'" Noll said. "I didn't want somebody else's losers. We wanted people we could draft and teach."

Noll believed this would be the prescribed route toward future Steelers success. He taught football, and his lectures were directed toward students wearing the Steelers' yellow and black. He embraced a total team philosophy—one echoed in a message he once posted on the team bulletin board that read: "When geese fly in formation, they travel 70 percent faster than when they fly alone."

However, buying into a team concept and absorbing proper blocking and tackling techniques could take a team only so far. Any successful NFL team needed talent. Noll and the Steelers' penchant for finding young talent began in the first draft he participated in as coach of the Steelers—a draft Shula would have preferred Noll to have participated in for the Colts.

"When the Steelers made the decision that they wanted Chuck, they wanted him right away," Shula said. "I wanted him to stay with me through the draft because he'd done all the scouting for me. But the more they talked to me the more I felt I should let him go, because if I was in that situation I would have wanted to go as soon as possible. So I let him go."

Drafting in the fourth position in 1969, the Steelers watched O. J. Simpson go to the Bills followed by the Atlanta Falcons' selection of Notre Dame offensive tackle George Kunz. The Philadelphia Eagles took Purdue running back Leroy Keyes. The Steelers then selected Joe Greene, a relative no-name out of unheralded North Texas State.

"In the draft [the Steelers] had a high pick and their whole organization wanted [Notre Dame quarterback] Terry Hanratty as the number one pick," Shula said. "And Chuck said, 'No, I know this big, strong defensive lineman from North Texas State by the name of "Mean" Joe Greene.' Then Hanratty's sitting there and they get him in the second round. So they got a bonus pick in Joe Greene because of Chuck's knowledge of him when he scouted him and knowing what an impact player that he could be."

Pittsburgh fans probably scratched their heads in angst at the selection of Greene. After all, he hadn't played at a big program. How would

18

he fare against superior competition? Had the Steelers messed up and brought in another stinker for a head coach?

Inside the confines of the Steelers' offices, the pick elicited a different feeling. Everything Noll did was based on logic he could explain, and he communicated with Dan Rooney every day. He harped on the point he needed to build a line first. Bringing in a star quarterback would not help without the accessories. Even though such a strategy might have been hard to swallow for Steelers fans craving the college players with big names, building from the basics had to get done first.

"I'm not saying [Greene] would have been our pick if we'd had the first pick in the draft," Dan Rooney said. "But he was definitely the guy we felt was going to help us the most. And he did."

Having personally scouted Greene, Noll had seen an intensity that told him he was watching a special player. Greene's ability and his domination of those he played against had impressed Noll. Once Noll talked to Greene he liked him even more. Noll recognized an inner strength and a burning desire to win in the powerful young man from Texas.

"No question he wanted to be the best," Noll said. "And I don't think he was thrilled when we drafted him. Because Joe wanted to win, there was no question about that."

Greene had been a three-time All–Missouri Conference defensive tackle and a consensus All-America pick in 1968 after three years of leading a defensive unit that came to be known as the "Mean Green." Stories about Greene's nasty disposition accompanied his legend, like the Dairy Queen story from his Dunbar High School days in Temple, Texas. After Greene's team lost, he'd gone to a Dairy Queen to bury his mood in frozen goodies. Much to Greene's chagrin, the winning team's bus pulled up to the DQ and began to taunt the obviously miffed Greene. Legend has it that Greene proceeded to board the bus by himself, an act that prompted the entire opposing team—coaches included—to flee to the back of the bus for their safety.

Noll didn't waver in his confidence that he could build a winner in Pittsburgh, and when discussing the 6'4", 275-pound Greene, he had no doubts about the future of his number one pick, telling everyone he believed Greene would be the cornerstone of the franchise's turn-around.

"I had no doubts that he would be a good one," Noll said. "Having seen him, I scouted North Texas State and I saw most every game he ever played on film. There was no question he could dominate a game. I had no doubts he would come in and be dominating. Physically, he

19

had great quickness, which a defensive lineman has to have. And he played with great leverage. He had the ability to rush the passer from the inside, which is rare."

Greene had no idea the Steelers were interested in him, but he knew from visiting the city during his sophomore year of college it wasn't a place he wanted to call home.

"Saying I wasn't excited about going to Pittsburgh was an understatement," said Greene with a deep laugh. "I was really kind of disappointed about it initially. Pittsburgh wasn't thought well of at all at that time. I think the year before they won two ballgames, and the year before that they had won four ballgames. Pittsburgh was a steel city. The steel mills, although they provided an awful lot of work to people, they did kind of put an ugly look on the city with the soot and all of that."

Hanratty had been the sexier pick for the team in the second round, but it was the Steelers' 10th-round selection that personified the franchise's coming years of draft magic. Two hundred and thirty-seven players had been selected by the 26 participating teams when the Steelers pulled the trigger in the 10th round on defensive end L. C. Greenwood from all-black Arkansas A&M (now the University of Arkansas, Pine Bluff).

Greenwood was raised in a family of nine children in Canton, Mississippi. Standing 6'6", he preferred basketball to football, but his father gave him the option of playing just one sport and he chose football because it afforded him the opportunity to get physical. Greenwood's family didn't have the money to send him to college, so he viewed the scholarship he earned to Arkansas A&M as an opportunity. An education would open doors, so he worked hard on his studies while he played football. He figured that his future would be based on what he knew, not what he did on the football field, where NFL scouts told him he was too light to weigh in at the next level.

Greenwood started at tackle and defensive end for three seasons, and by his senior year he was named to *Ebony* magazine's All-America team. During his senior season he hyperextended his knee, which became a deterrent to his being drafted in a higher round. To the Steelers he looked like a projection pick; if he could fill out he might just become a good addition, particularly for a player selected in the 10th round.

The Steelers gathered information on prospective talent through the BLESTO scouting service, which was a scouting cooperative shared by several teams, and by sending out their own scouts. Bill Nunn also became a key to the Steelers' draft-day acumen.

A former football and basketball player for West Virginia State, Nunn became the NFL's sixth full-time black scout when the Steelers hired him in 1969. Noll didn't see color—he saw only wins and losses—and he heaped responsibility on Nunn while at the same time valuing the former athlete's opinion. Noll respected Nunn as an athlete and believed Nunn had the drive to beat the bushes to find him the best athletes.

Nunn was the *Pittsburgh Courier*'s sports editor and covered college football. Each year the *Courier* picked a black-college all-star team and held a dinner to honor the selections.

"They would invite the star players from the African-American schools—the Gramblings and various schools like that," Dan Rooney said. "And he would have this banquet every year, so he got to know all the coaches, all the players, and had a great relationship."

The Steelers hired Nunn to provide an insight into the untapped talent resource of black colleges. Dan Rooney told Nunn the Steelers were hiring him to be a scout, they weren't hiring him to be a black scout.

Rooney said that Nunn was going to be a very important person in the organization and, "He just went on to be one of the top guys."

In Noll's first three seasons the Steelers selected 11 players from small black colleges in the draft; the Dolphins, with 10, were the only team close to selecting this number during the same time period.

Physical talent ranked high in Noll's book, but so did intelligence and character, which became a part of the team's assessment of players ahead of time. Taking a look at a prospect's transcript became a part of the process.

"Because we wanted to see guys who would challenge themselves," Noll said, "we didn't want guys who took woodshop—easy courses they could breeze through so they could play football. I wanted guys that wanted a challenge. Academically, in life, if you're not up for challenges you're not going to do well in professional football because it's a big challenge. So we were looking for guys who were looking for a challenge. There was no question if you look at the transcripts of all the guys we drafted up there, they were taking challenging classes, challenging courses, and did well in them. We also gave them an intelligence test. We weren't interested in guys that did not score well on them."

Adding new talent was one thing. Assessing inherited talent was totally different.

"Fact is Chuck Noll's first speech to us he told us he'd been watching the game films and he could tell us why we'd been losing," Russell said. "You could have heard a pin drop in that room because there were a lot of good guys who tried hard and had good attitudes. He basically said, 'Well, the reason you've been losing is you aren't any good. You can't run fast enough, you can't jump high enough, you're not quick enough, you don't execute quality techniques, and you're just not good enough and I'm going to have to get rid of most of you.'"

Noll laughed when asked about the speech.

"That's Andy's story—he does a lot of public speaking—I didn't really say that," Noll said. "I just said in coming in there we were going to evaluate everybody. We were going to put the best people on the field, and if we had to go someplace else to get them we would."

Noll told the players they needed more talent and that the players needed to motivate themselves—that was not his job. Finally, every player on the team would put the team first or suffer the consequences. Noll conceded that the process of learning how to execute and win would not happen overnight. And he told them they were going to get worse before they got better, but he was going to make them learn to do it the right way.

Noll observed the team going through the primal rah-rah rants and raves prior to the first practice and told them such demonstrations were meaningless. He preferred his teams to have a controlled aggression that could be maintained throughout the game rather than wasting their energy during some mindless emotional displays prior to the game.

"He wasn't into making a bunch of hysterical pep talks," Russell said. "One thing Noll used to say was, 'I'll never motivate you or try to motivate you. If I have to motivate you I will fire you.' Of course, if you make it to the pros you ought to be able to motivate yourself. That was his attitude. And I loved it. I thrived under his system. It always made sense to me.

"He was very stern, very strict. On the other hand, he was very realistic about what the players could or could not do. He didn't wear us out at practice. Sundays were our hard days. To that extent, he was a player's coach."

Painstakingly, Noll demonstrated proper techniques to even the most experienced players and stressed the idea of becoming a complete football player. A complete football player to Noll's way of thinking meant doing your homework on the opposing team, learning tendencies that could give them an edge, or picking up position advantages and reading keys based on the smallest of details.

"He was such a details guy," Russell said. "The first year [under Noll] we didn't have a linebackers coach and he coached the linebackers as a sideline. It was frustrating at times because he was a little too mechanical for me. 'You have to line up exactly six inches out here' and that kind of thing. He was right most of the time, but sometimes it takes some intuitiveness to play the game. Noll obviously was a gifted teacher and wanted you to do something in a very specific way. But he also was smart enough to see if a player did it his way and got the job done."

Russell got beat for a touchdown against the St. Louis Cardinals during a 1969 game at St. Louis that the Steelers lost 47–10. Hailing from St. Louis, Russell felt embarrassed about getting beat on the play and especially so in front of his friends and family. He figured further humiliation would come from Noll, who approached him after the play. Sidling next to Russell, Noll didn't say anything at first. Then he addressed Russell.

"Andy, on the play where we gave up the touchdown, what was your thought process?" Noll asked.

Russell thought it unusual—and to his liking—that Noll didn't berate him with something like "you gave up the touchdown." Rather, he asked what was he thinking, which Russell thought was "so cool."

"Well, my thought process was, they've only showed that formation 10 times in the last five years," Russell said. "And there are only five plays they ever run to my side from that formation. The other five went the other way. And of the five plays that go to my side, four of them are an off-tackle run. One of them was a play-action pass. Why would they run the play-action pass first without first setting me up with the run? Why would they do that?"

Noll remained calm.

"Maybe they know how you think," Noll said. "They think, 'Russell knows about it, let's not set him up. Let's go right to the play-action.' Now don't forget to read your keys. If you'd looked at your postsnap keys, once the ball was snapped you would have seen that the tackle was not firing out. You would have sensed it was a pass. But you were so convinced that you knew by your tendency chart what was right, you overplayed it."

Noll then turned and walked away.

"He was into the thinking," Russell said. "And I loved him. When he walked away I remember thinking, 'I want to play for this guy.'"

Greene made his presence known from the outset, though he didn't exactly endear himself to the locals when he held out for more money before signing a contract, thereby earning the distinction as the first Steelers rookie to be a holdout.

Greene laughed about being a holdout.

"It seemed like it was a lot of money," Greene said. "I think that I read someplace that O. J. [Simpson] signed a contract for $600,000. Now I don't know if it was for one year or four years, but I wasn't even in the ballpark. That's not good enough. I was the fourth pick and he was the first pick, and I said we need to be closer than where I was."

Though having a player hold out wasn't normal, Greene's situation wasn't quite as it appeared.

"Joe had an agent who was trying to make a name for himself," Rooney said. "We finally sat down and got it worked out. I think that guy wanted Joe to be a holdout strictly so he could have a holdout. The agent would get more publicity—not Joe, the agent."

Greene finally arrived at St. Vincent's College in Latrobe on the second day of training camp to a group of Steelers skeptical about his talents.

"We were desperate for a first choice that was any good," Russell said. "We'd had about four in a row that had bombed out, so when Joe was drafted number one I think the headline in the local paper was Joe Who?—something like that because he was from North Texas State; do they even play football? The local writers were just all over the Steelers about that. Not only that, he appears to have a bad attitude right away because he holds out for more money, which was a no-no to the veteran-type guys in those days. So here's a kid you're questioning whether he's really played the kind of football you need to play to really help us. Number two, how important can a defensive tackle be? Can a defensive tackle turn you around?"

While Greene's teammates might have been skeptical of the rookie's ability, Greene had a confidence on par with Noll's.

"In terms of playing football, I can't ever remember lacking confidence in playing the game," Greene said. "I take that back. My first year in high school, when I was in the ninth grade, I probably lacked some confidence. But after that I can't ever remember not believing I could do what I wanted to do when I wanted to do it. Now, that being said, that doesn't mean I always got it done."

Prior to Greene's first practice he had the further audacity to engage in a verbal battle with a team beat writer. Resembling a malcontent, Greene stepped onto the practice field for the first time with all eyes glued on him.

"I'll never forget when he showed up the first day," Russell said. "He was bigger than I thought he would be. He was 6'4", 290—he was big. And we were doing a drill called the Oklahoma drill."

The Oklahoma drill pits an offensive lineman against a defensive lineman, who must fight off the blocker and tackle a running back. Mansfield became the first Steelers offensive lineman called upon to take on Greene in the Oklahoma drill.

"Greene just took Mansfield and destroyed him," Russell said. "Just picked him up and threw him away. We were all in shock. Just in shock. Then he just destroyed the running back. Bruce Van Dyke was next, who was arguably our best lineman. He'd been to the Pro Bowl, a very good player: tough, good technique. Joe destroyed him, and I'm like, 'Oh my gosh, we've got a player.'"

Unlike today's impatient NFL owners, who demand instant results, Noll had the luxury of having a few years to get the Steelers to the lofty perch to which he aspired, a fortunate philosophy for Noll given the outcome of his initial season.

Noll's tenure began with a 16–13 home win over the Detroit Lions; the Steelers then lost their final 13 games.

"You know whenever you come into a situation that hasn't had much success, you know it's not going to turn around like that," Noll said. "First thing is to try and assess the talent, and the only way you can assess the talent is playing games. So maybe about halfway through the season I had a pretty good feel for the talent we had."

Noll didn't say what that feeling was, but the smile on his face could easily be perceived as sarcastic.

Opponents outscored the Steelers 404 to 218, but the team's attitude began to change, thanks to their prized rookie, Greene, who started all 14 games and established himself as a defensive force en route to being named the NFL Defensive Rookie of the Year and earning the reputation as an intimidator and a man opposing players feared.

"No player did more for turning the team around than Joe Greene," Russell said. "Part of it was his extraordinary ability, his quickness, his gut instincts, but also his absolute hatred of losing. This guy just couldn't stand losing. He got thrown out of about four games his rookie year for fighting."

Greene described his rookie season as dismal. He hated to lose.

"That's a fair statement," Greene said. "I've always been that way. When I started playing ball in high school we used to get beaten up pretty good. I probably learned how to fight on the football field before I learned how to play."

In a 38–7 loss to the Bears in the eighth week of the season—the Bears' only win of the season—Dick Butkus participated on the kickoff team and made the mistake of planting Greenwood into the turf in front of the Steelers' bench. Greene didn't like seeing his friend hurting and made a move toward Butkus. Standing toe-to-toe with Butkus, Greene grabbed the NFL's resident badass by the shoulder pads and inched his face mask toward him. Nobody heard the conversation that took place, but Greene removed his helmet and pulled it back as if he were ready to strike Butkus. Before the two came to blows, Butkus turned and ran back to the Bears' sideline.

In week 10 during the fourth quarter of a 52–14 Steelers loss to the Minnesota Vikings, Greene got thrown out of the game for fighting. The Vikings played in Metropolitan Stadium, a baseball stadium that necessitated both teams to stand on the same sideline during games.

"When Joe's coming off the field, [Alan] Page and [Carl] Eller start giving him some shit," Russell said. "Greene doesn't look at them, but he's boiling. He's fuming. You can see like smoke coming out of him. I'm thinking, 'This guy is just a maniac.' He goes over to the trainer's toolbox and gets a pair of scissors and starts charging at them. It was a colossal bluff. I don't really think he would have stabbed them. But they thought he was nuts, and they ran up into the stands. I've never seen anything like it."

Mike Evans, who played center for the Philadelphia Eagles from 1968 through 1973, played against the Steelers three times and said he had a simple philosophy when playing the Steelers: "Hold on tight." Evans remembered Greene getting upset with Eagles guard Jim Skaggs for continually holding him.

"In the NFL, you may not know this, but sometimes we hold," said Evans with a chuckle. "That's basically the only way you could stop Joe. And he went after the guy, 'Stop holding me,' because the refs weren't calling it. And he just grabbed him and let him have it during the play and it's like, 'You want more of that, keep holding.'" Despite Greene's sense of right and wrong, Evans said Greene "wasn't a tough talker."

"If you blocked him and you did a good job he'd say, 'How'd you do that? You weren't supposed to do that?'" Evans said. "His game wasn't intimidation. He was good enough to just beat you; he didn't have to talk any shit."

Greene helped bring about a change in the team's attitude, and Noll remained optimistic.

"We made progress, although it doesn't reflect in the win-loss column," Noll said after the season. "It was progress in areas that are not convertible to win-loss.

"Our ultimate goal is the championship. There is talk [about] 'if we can just be respectable,' but we'll not be satisfied with that. Our goal is the championship, but I don't know when we'll realize it. It's hard to put a time schedule on it."

Noll handled the miserable season by keeping his eyes squarely on the future.

"I have a three-year contract, one of which has passed," Noll said. "I can't allow that to affect my judgment. We're proceeding with the idea of making the right decisions. Can these people win for us? Are they [of] the caliber to give us a championship? If you make the right decisions, you're headed in the right direction. Other problems will take care of themselves."

Even though they had suffered a miserable losing season in 1969, Noll never lost the team.

"I don't know if he got close to losing the team; I don't think he did," Greene said. "I really don't know. He didn't get close to losing me, and he was building the team."

Russell believed the players stayed with Noll for one reason.

"Because he always made sense," Russell said.

Noll had his own theory for why he didn't lose the team.

"I think you lose people when you start blaming everyone," Noll said. "Instead of coming in and saying, 'This is your fault, it's your fault, it's your fault,' we came in and said, 'This is what we've got to do to get better.' And that was the approach. And 'we have to learn how to do this better. It's we, not you.'

"You got that message across and made progress, and you found out the players who couldn't or didn't want to [embrace that philosophy], all they were interested in was collecting a paycheck. Those were the guys we would get rid of."

Noll's approach began to turn the Steelers in the right direction. Their luck in the upcoming 1970 draft would make the Steelers even more dangerous.

3

On the Brink of Greatness

On September 2, 1948, Bill and Novis Bradshaw took home a son, Terry, from a hospital in Shreveport, Louisiana.

Terry Bradshaw grew up in a tranquil Southern setting, where he worked on his grandfather's farm alongside his siblings. Farmwork included tending to the crops of sweet potatoes, watermelon, and cotton in addition to the cattle and hogs. Somewhere during this upbringing, Bradshaw learned how to work like a man. But when quitting time came, out came the football. He threaded many a spiral through a tire suspended by a chain in his backyard.

By the time Bradshaw reached his senior year at Shreveport's Woodlawn High School he resembled a blond-haired Li'l Abner who could throw the bejesus out of anything he put in his hand.

During track season Bradshaw threw the javelin and had been puttering around at distances of 208 to 210 feet until he got to the state meet and changed his approach. Leaving behind all the mumbo jumbo about mechanics, Bradshaw decided to just chuck the thing—let it go as hard and as far as he could. He won the meet and established a national high school record at 244 feet, 11 inches. In the process he learned something about himself: when the pressure was on he had something special that enabled him to elevate his performance.

Great things continued to happen for Bradshaw in the world of athletics.

He remained in his home state to attend Louisiana Tech, a school with an enrollment of fewer than eight thousand students located in Ruston, 75 miles east of Shreveport. Bradshaw majored in liberal arts and excelled in football. During his college career he completed 52.5 percent of his passes for 7,149 yards and 42 touchdowns and led the nation in total offense his junior year. In addition, he had good size and toughness. Part of the Bradshaw legend is the game when he threw five interceptions against Northeastern Louisiana and on all but one of the interceptions tackled the man with the ball. One of Bradshaw's tackles produced enough of a jolt to break the collarbone of the defender. Louisiana Tech wasn't the most visible national stage; nevertheless, Bradshaw got discovered. The Associated Press named him first-team All-America, as did *Time*; *The Sporting News* and United Press International named him to their second teams. He played in the North-South Game and was named the Most Valuable Player for his performance in the Senior Bowl after completing 17 of 31 passes for 267 yards and two touchdowns.

"I saw him in the Senior Bowl, and there was no question about his ability to throw the football," Chuck Noll said. "He was just what I was looking for. He could scramble [and] throw the ball with great velocity and accurately."

Bradshaw appeared head and shoulders above every player eligible for the NFL draft, particularly when compared to the other highly touted quarterbacks such as Purdue's Mike Phipps, San Diego State's Dennis Shaw, and Florida State's Bill Cappleman. Scouts coveted Bradshaw's 6'3", 210-pound frame, his toughness, and the lightning bolt of an arm strapped to his right side—he could routinely fire tight 80-yard spirals. If ever there was an impact player, Bradshaw was it. The Steelers were among the many teams enamored with the blond bomber.

"No doubt, we saw him as the very best athlete in the country," Noll said. "We were somewhat concerned about the competition he'd played against, but when he got down to the Senior Bowl, he exhibited leadership qualities. He was not awed by the competition."

All that stood in the way of the Steelers getting Bradshaw was a coin toss against the Chicago Bears. Football teams don't normally get too worked up about a coin toss because win or lose they'll get the ball kicked to them at the start of the first half or the start of the second. The Steelers faced a toss of a markedly higher significance.

If the Steelers won the toss, they could select Bradshaw, a talent who could become the difference maker for a team trying to eradicate a 37-year run of bad luck. If they didn't, the agony could be prolonged. The Steelers and the Bears had finished the 1969 season with identical 1–13 records, earning them the distinction of being co-worst in the NFL.

"We definitely wanted Bradshaw, and [he] was going to be the guy we took if we won the toss," Dan Rooney said.

Representatives from each team went to the Fairmont Hotel in New Orleans, where the toss would take place on January 9, 1970—two days before Super Bowl IV between the Minnesota Vikings and Kansas City Chiefs.

The quality of any draft can make the difference between the first and second pick insignificant; the 1970 draft would not be so. Bradshaw stood alone as the prize for whichever team drafted first. George Halas' son-in-law, Ed McCaskey, had been designated as the Bears' representative, while Dan Rooney and Noll were there on behalf of the Steelers.

Had Steelers owner Art Rooney been there in person, he would have expressed his philosophy about a game of chance: always defer to the other party when calling a coin toss. Such a move directed the pressure to the guy making the call. You might call this a postulate from the Rooney "school of luck."

Pete Rozelle would be the guy flipping the coin. Everybody knew the NFL's commissioner was close to Art Rooney, which made McCaskey want to make the call. Not knowing his father's stance on how to call a toss, Dan Rooney went with his instincts.

Rozelle pulled out a 1921 silver dollar from his pocket.

"Pete shows us the coin, both sides, what's heads and what's tails, and he said, 'OK, Dan, do you want to call?' I said, 'No, let him call,'" Dan Rooney said.

McCaskey called out, "Heads."

Rozelle flipped the coin in the air. The fate of both franchises would be drastically affected by which side of the coin faced up after it landed.

The coin dropped to the floor. Rozelle bent to examine the result.

"Tails it is," Rozelle called out.

"So [McCaskey] calls it wrong and Pete picks up the coin and says, 'The Steelers got the pick,'" Dan Rooney said. "And he gives me the coin. My father didn't give me advice before I went to New Orleans, but he told me after it happened, 'That was a smart move, always let the other guy call.'"

Later, when Dan Rooney and Noll took their wives to dinner, Rooney passed along the lucky coin to Noll.

"When I gave him the coin I told him, 'This is the start of something big for us,'" Rooney said.

Having the number one pick in their pocket, the Steelers discovered how much other teams coveted the chance to select Bradshaw.

"I'd get a call from some other team and they'd say, 'Who are you going to take?'" Rooney said. "And I'd say, 'Listen, I don't know what we're going to do with this pick. But I can tell you Bradshaw is going to be the first pick.' It was either going to be us keeping the pick and selecting Bradshaw or trading the pick to another team that would then take him."

The Steelers listened to the offers, some of which were phenomenal. The St. Louis Cardinals offered three starters and their first pick. And at least four other teams made serious bids similar to the Cardinals' hoping to pry away the pick.

"But it really was our intention to go with Bradshaw all along," Rooney said. "We sort of listened to some of the other offers to tempt ourselves, I guess. But in reality, even though we had a good quarterback in Terry Hanratty, we always knew we'd keep [the pick] ourselves."

Not trading the pick indicated a different Pittsburgh philosophy. In the past, the Steelers might have done exactly what the Bears did with the second pick by trading it to the Packers for three players: running back Elijah Pitts, linebacker Lee Roy Caffey, and lineman Bob Hyland. All three played a combined two seasons for the Bears; the Packers drafted Mike McCoy, who played 11 NFL seasons.

"When they called me and told me they'd drafted me number one, I just couldn't believe it," Bradshaw told *Sports Illustrated* in 1970. "I mean, all along I wanted to go with a loser. I never wanted to go with L.A. or Minnesota or any good team. I wanted to go someplace like Pittsburgh or Chicago, where if I made it they would make it with me."

Noll felt excited about having Bradshaw, but he understood the realities of the game.

"It takes more than a quarterback," Noll said. "He's got to have a supporting cast. You have to have the receivers. You have to have the pass protection. If you want to throw the football it all begins with protecting the passer—having the time to throw it. And you have to have receivers who get open. So it's not just one guy stepping in to change everything unless you've got all the other stuff in place. And while we were happy to have Bradshaw, it was a question of putting all the other stuff in place. We had to upgrade our receiving corps; we had to upgrade our offensive line so that we could pass protect."

Accruing the rest of the cast continued to be a work in process. Also selected in the 1970 draft were North Texas State receiver Ron Shanklin with the 28th pick of the draft and Southern University defensive back Mel Blount with the 53rd selection.

Blount hailed from Vidalia, Georgia, where he grew up on a dirt farm in a family with 11 children. The youngest of James Blount's seven boys, Mel began working at an early age, loading tobacco onto a wagon in the early morning, hoping to earn the praise of his father while learning the value of hard work, self-respect, and personal responsibility. Following church on Sunday afternoons, the Blount boys played football—tackle football with no pads. From this upbringing and test of survival, a chiseled man of 6'3", 205 pounds arrived in Pittsburgh, unsure about what to make of his situation after being drafted.

"Well basically, I was a little bit disappointed," Blount said. "I was down in Baton Rouge at Southern University, and not knowing any better, I wanted to play for the Saints." Blount offered a laugh at the recollection. "Being a Southern boy, I didn't know anything about Pittsburgh or know anything about the people who were involved with it. But as it turned out [getting drafted by the Steelers] was one of the best things that ever happened to me."

But the North wasn't the South for Blount, who found himself in an entirely new universe. When he went to Pittsburgh, he'd never had the experience of playing with white athletes or being coached by a white man.

"I'm telling you it was a huge adjustment," Blount said.

Blount can't remember his first impression about Noll, but he understood his coach and what he was about.

"He was a young guy; you just went out and played," Blount said. "Chuck came out of that Paul Brown school of thought where the coach was here and the player was here, and he was king. Whatever he said, that's what went and you didn't question it. There was no security. Every play you had to prove yourself. In a way I think that was good because he kept everybody focused."

Prior to the 1970 season, the NFL went to its new alignment of National and American Football Conferences. The Steelers became one of the three NFL clubs (including the Baltimore Colts and Cleveland Browns) to be compensated $3 million for moving to the American Football Conference. Even though the AFL had won the two previous Super Bowls, the move to the AFC Central Division did not please many Steelers fans, which had old-school NFL loyalties.

Accompanying the Steelers' move to the AFC was a change of venues to shiny, new Three Rivers Stadium, a multipurpose stadium—which also played host to Major League Baseball's Pittsburgh Pirates—built on land where the Allegheny and Monongahela Rivers joined to form the Ohio River. The park sat on the approximate location of Exposition Park, which had served as the Pirates' home from

1891 to 1909. Three Rivers also sat on a Delaware Indian burial ground where General George Washington fought many battles while protecting nearby Fort Duquesne. A feeling of rejuvenation accompanied the opening of the $55 million ballpark that sat 47,971 for baseball and 59,000 for football. The Steelers had played at Forbes Field from 1933 to 1957; the team alternated between Forbes Field and Pitt Stadium from 1958 to 1963; and they played exclusively at Pitt Stadium from 1964 to 1969.

"I was so naïve that [Three Rivers Stadium] didn't even faze me," Blount said. "I didn't realize whether that was a new stadium or what. I wasn't aware of their history of playing at Forbes Field and practicing at South Park. It wasn't something I really thought about.

"Looking back on it now, you can see that it was the beginning of a new era, though. Chuck had been here one year, and that wasn't a very good year. Then Bradshaw came and there was a lot of excitement—guy had a cannon for an arm. We were just a bunch of young kids who really didn't know what we were getting into."

On the heels of the Kansas City Chiefs' Super Bowl victory over the Vikings, football experts forecast that the football of the future would be based more on deception and razzle-dazzle rather than the blocking and tackling days of Lombardi. Among the looks employed by Kansas City coach Hank Stram were the "shotgun spread"; the "Kansas City stack," where the linebackers hid behind the defensive linemen; the "triple wing"; the "Kansas City tight I," which was the Chiefs' basic formation; and the "moving [pass] pocket."

Noll didn't buy into any trends, closely adhering to his belief of defense first.

Another major change for the NFL came in 1970 with the advent of *Monday Night Football.* Given the NFL's desire to showcase its game to a national television audience, it sought to give ABC a schedule that included the best contests. The obnoxious and self-important Howard Cosell; the cheeky Don Meredith, a former Dallas Cowboys quarterback; and play-by-play pro Keith Jackson were selected to cohabit in the booth for *Monday Night Football.* Not only would *Monday Night Football* kick off a cultural revolution for American television, it would allow the best teams in the NFL to become more familiar to a national audience than any teams in league history.

Veteran NFL players did not report to camp in July 1970, and on July 30 the National Football League Players Association (NFLPA) voted to go on strike. At the Steelers' camp, Bradshaw used the time to establish himself as the leader of his fellow rookies. The strike was settled August 3, 1970, and the players had a new four-year agreement bolstering the pension fund and insurance benefits by $4.535 million annually in addition to improving other select items. When the veterans returned, Bradshaw continued to play the role of a team leader, even daring to sit with the veterans during dinner on the night they returned. Most important, Bradshaw led on the field with his talent.

Bradshaw played only the second half of the first exhibition game, which the Steelers lost, then led the team to four straight preseason victories. Overlooking the Steelers' youth and the fact they had been winning meaningless exhibition games, some experts forecast great things for the 1970 team, notably *Sports Illustrated*'s Tex Maule, who picked the Steelers to win the AFC Central Division. Alas, their youth also brought an unpredictable flavor to the team, and they were burdened with a streaky nature. They started the season as home favorites over the Houston Oilers only to lose 19–7 in a game that saw Bradshaw complete just 4 of 16 passes, many of which wobbled to open receivers or missed them completely, including one that saw a wide-open Shanklin have to wait for a ball that slipped off Bradshaw's hand. Had the pass been on the mark, Shanklin would have easily scored. Instead, he had to wait for the pass and was tackled 20 yards shy of a touchdown.

Steelworkers inhabiting Pittsburgh bars had long favored an "Imp and Iron"—a concoction composed of a shot of Imperial whisky followed by an Iron City Beer chaser. No doubt the team's opening day performance inspired medicinal servings of the steelworkers' choice of beverages. Losses at Denver and Cleveland followed, which ran the team's record to 16 consecutive losses since they'd won in Noll's first game. But once they returned to Three Rivers Stadium the Steelers began a streak that saw them win four of their next five games. They finished the season by losing five of six.

Newspapers poked fun at Bradshaw for being a country bumpkin when he looked lost on the field. By the middle of his first year he found himself confused and not knowing how to handle failure. A people pleaser by nature, Bradshaw would be torn about what side of his personality to put on display when facing sports reporters. He grew introverted and before long lost confidence in himself, prompting him to call his college coach asking him to send tapes from his senior season at Louisiana Tech so he could watch himself perform successfully. Nothing seemed to work. And Steelers fans weren't exactly enamored with their strong-armed quarterback either.

Mike Wagner, a safety who joined the Steelers as an 11th-round draft choice out of Western Illinois in 1971, attributed some of the negativity toward Bradshaw to the popularity of Hanratty, who grew up in Butler County, just north of Pittsburgh, and had been a big star at Notre Dame, which had a large following in Pittsburgh.

"Then along comes Bradshaw, who was no different than he is now, this goofy, silly guy, who will say and do anything," Wagner said. "He's a small-college kid, Southern boy, country boy, and he's saying all the right things but kind of in a silly way. Like, 'I'm here to win championships and I aim to do this and that,' kind of bobbing his head and stuff—a little different.

"I don't know exactly what it is, but he had so much hype and he didn't really have a team around him. Instead of people saying, 'He's just a silly guy, who works really hard,' people started saying he was dumb and wasn't smart enough. And Terry's the type of person who would laugh it off—nobody likes hearing negative things about themselves, even the most successful people in the world, nobody likes it—and Terry was always trying to win and just struggled. He became a favorite for the fans to criticize."

Blount remembered how talented Bradshaw was, noting, "When he threw the ball you could hear it whistle." He also remembered the abuse his teammate took in the newspapers.

"Almost like the Civil War was still going on between the Southern guy and the Northerners here and they were calling Terry dumb," Blount said.

Finishing with a 5–9 record in 1970 showed improvement, but there were some frustrations.

"To say there were some disappointing times, there was no question about it," Joe Greene said. "There were some heartbreaking times. I recall one ballgame we lost [16–13] to Denver. I was in the corner crying, and there were a couple of other guys with their heads down crying. I think Chuck was probably shedding a tear too. It was kind of miserable."

Despite the team's quarterback becoming a basket case and the season coming to a disappointing finish, the Steelers appeared to have a bright future. Andy Russell, Greene, and Blount were defensive forces, and John "Frenchy" Fuqua had set a record for Steelers running backs by gaining 218 yards in the final game of the season. If the team could just bring in more of the kind of athletes Noll wanted, the improvement would surely continue.

True to form, the Steelers enjoyed another fine draft in 1971.

Grambling's Frank Lewis was the team's first selection. Playing wing-back at the small black school, Lewis had scored 42 touchdowns, averaged more than 10 yards per carry, and clocked a 9.4 in the 100-yard dash. Penn State linebacker Jack Ham was the team's second pick, bringing an abundance of athleticism to the defense. At 6'1" he could dunk a basketball from a standing-still position. Joining Lewis and Ham on that bumper crop of rookies were defensive linemen Dwight White (East Texas State) and Ernie Holmes (Texas Southern), tight end Larry Brown (Kansas), guard Gerry Mullins (USC), and Wagner (Western Illinois).

Wagner arrived at the Steelers' camp as a sleeper with a better chance of making the team than appearances suggested. He'd been educated beyond his years in a womb of football culture beginning at Carmel High School in Lake County, Illinois, which played in a highly accelerated suburban Catholic League just outside of Chicago. All of Wagner's coaches played semipro football. Their knowledge translated to tremendous coaching for the young, impressionable Wagner, who loved the sport.

"To give you an example [of how advanced the teaching was], I was taught how to read pulling linemen in high school," Wagner said. "So it was just the techniques and the situations we were put into. I just learned it at a young age."

Wagner wasn't a highly sought after football player leaving high school, and he received no scholarship offers as a result. He opted to attend Western Illinois where he didn't decide to go out for football until the end of September during his freshman year.

"Football was so bad at Western Illinois at the time that I ended up starting at defensive end," Wagner said, laughing at how he could possibly have earned a starting position on a college team after trying out so late. He played at 185 pounds and took enough of a beating to tell the coaches no thanks when they told him they wanted him to continue playing the position. Wagner told the coaches he'd play safety, and he made the move to the secondary his sophomore season, continuing his quest to quench an insatiable thirst for football knowledge.

"At that point it really became important to me to try and know what everybody on the defense was doing," Wagner said. "When you play in the secondary, you don't always know the lineman's final responsibility, just like the linemen don't know what the defensive backs or linemen are doing. But you try to understand the scheme of things. And you really wanted to know what the coverage was and what the coaches were trying to accomplish with their schemes. Defenses are set to take away tendencies, and you're always trying to figure out how the quarterback is going to attack you, particularly on passing plays. You take care of your responsibility, but you want to be aware of the weakness. You want to be aware of it because if there's a breakdown you can be aware of it right away."

By Wagner's junior year, Western Illinois began to emphasize sports, bringing in a quality coaching staff that taught him how to play pro defenses in the secondary. Wagner also would travel to Forrest, Illinois, to watch the St. Louis Cardinals conduct their training camp. A player on the Cardinals had been a teammate of Wagner's at Western Illinois. Knowing this player's abilities as compared to his, Wagner began to feel as if he could play at the next level. Red Miller, who had once been a Western Illinois coach, was one of the Cardinals' coaches at the time. Miller as well as some of Wagner's college coaches told Wagner they thought he had the size and speed to play in the NFL.

"So those things kind of encouraged me to play," Wagner said.

Working against Wagner, but working for the Steelers, was the fact that Wagner got clipped in a preseason game just before his senior season and badly sprained both of his ankles.

"I limped through most of my senior year," Wagner said. "I won't say I would have been a top draft pick, but it definitely hurt me coming out of a small school."

Wagner went to the Steelers carrying a lifetime allegiance to the Chicago Bears and wasn't thrilled to be heading to Pittsburgh. He knew little about the Steelers other than that they were on par with the Bears when it came to being a bad football team and that they were playing in a new facility. He went to Pittsburgh for the first time in February and found a gray city with smokestacks chugging and an industrial feel. Trimmings aside, Wagner recognized it was an opportunity, which was what he was looking for.

"I was excited about playing pro football," Wagner said.

Dwight White grew up in a black neighborhood in Dallas, Texas, where he said, "Everything I did was black," and he knew to stay on the other side of the tracks.

"There was still that type of separation," White said.

White's first year at East Texas State was only the second year the school had black students on campus. There were 16,000 students and 27 of them were black.

"So when I went to Pittsburgh I'm coming out of a situation that was about as crude and archaic as one could experience unless you were down at Montgomery somewhere," White said.

Despite White's upbringing culturally and his background, he embraced the white Noll when he arrived in Pittsburgh at age 20.

"I don't know how old Chuck was, but he was very much an adult man with family and stuff," White said. "I come from an era where father figures were more prevalent, quite meaningful. That's the way I looked at it then. He was the coach, but he was the leader of the group, like a father figure. He was not warm and fuzzy, but I didn't expect that. I think there's a lot more camaraderie among players and coaches today. I probably subscribe to the earlier, being the employer-employee relationship. It was different back then. While he was a father figure, I took him very seriously. 'This is what Dad is saying we need to do.'"

Ham came to the Steelers with a higher profile than Wagner or White. He grew up in Johnstown, a small town in southwest Pennsylvania. Pittsburgh was within driving distance and had the only NFL franchise anywhere near the town, yet Ham wasn't a Steelers fan.

"I can remember watching games with my father and being frustrated about how they played well for about three quarters or where they were playing a close game then lost in the last two minutes," Ham said. "And my father would be frustrated watching on TV or listening on the radio. I actually preferred watching AFL football, which was wide open and throwing the ball all over the place. So I kind of enjoyed watching that league for the most part."

Ham played linebacker from his grade school days on, evolving into an All-State selection at Bishop McCort High School before moving to Happy Valley where he played outside linebacker for Joe Paterno at Penn State. Ham starred in the Nittany Lions' Orange Bowl victories in 1969 and 1970, and he played in the 1970 East West Shrine Game and the Hula Bowl, where he earned Outstanding Defensive Player honors. His pro potential looked promising heading into the NFL draft.

"[I was] naïve as a guy coming out of college, [and] the San Diego Chargers and the New York Giants both called me the day before the draft and said, 'We're going to draft you number one tomorrow,'" Ham said. "Like I said, being naïve, I believed that. So when I did not go in the first round—I went in the second round to the Steelers—I was disappointed not going in the first round and disappointed being drafted by Pittsburgh. I was not a fan, and they were one of the few teams that

39

didn't even contact me prior to the draft. Thinking about all those years of frustration the franchise endured, I wasn't too happy."

During the summer of 1971 Ham played in the College All-Star Game in Chicago, a game that featured a team of select college all-stars pitted against the NFL champions.

"We were in Chicago for about a month, and all my teammates were kind of feeling sorry for me because I was going to Pittsburgh while they were going to the Los Angeles Rams or some of the other successful teams, and they were like, 'Poor Ham, he's going to Pittsburgh, too bad for him,'" Ham said. "I didn't feel too good about it at the time either."

The All-Star Game was played July 30 on a Friday night in front of 52,289 fans. Soldier Field had just been remodeled, which included the installation of AstroTurf. The Baltimore Colts were the world champions, and quarterback Earl Morrall had a field day against the All-Stars, throwing three touchdowns. One of the few highlights for the All-Stars came when Morrall's replacement, Sam Havrilak, fumbled. Ham recovered the ball and ran 47 yards for a touchdown, which helped make the game seem closer than it was in a 24–17 Colts victory.

Ham traveled back to Latrobe, Pennsylvania, the following day. He'd missed a lot of training camp because of playing in the All-Star Game, so he decided to get an early start, flying into Pittsburgh and then making the hour and a half drive to Latrobe. He reached camp in time to watch an afternoon scrimmage that lasted 30 or 40 plays. At the conclusion of the practice, all the players left camp because they had an off day the next day.

"And I'm like, 'I busted my tail to get here for this?'" Ham said.

Ham felt anxiety pains in addition to those derived from the team's practice schedule.

"They had a lot of veterans on the team," Ham said. "I knew Chuck Noll would be cutting shortly, but I was like, 'This is going to be a long, long year.' And I wasn't sure how much heart I had about playing professional football when I saw the talent on the football team."

What he saw reminded him of bygone days sitting with his father listening to or watching Steelers games.

"If there's one thing I am, it's a realist," Ham said. "The team had never won before, and now I'm a professional in the middle of all this. I was a rookie and would have liked to have high expectations, but I realized it could be a long haul.

"Joe Greene, L. C. Greenwood, and Mel Blount were already there. Terry Bradshaw obviously was there and Andy Russell. But the quality of players was few and far between."

Ham felt the pressure of trying to win a job. Penn State players had not fared well with Pittsburgh to that point. Given that history, he knew there would be question marks about him. He weighed only 225 pounds, which added to the fodder of whether he could step up to the next level. Newspapers covering the team suggested that drafting Ham had not been the wisest of choices. But after intercepting three passes in the final exhibition game against the New York Giants, Ham learned he'd earned a starting spot at outside linebacker for the team's 1971 opener September 19 against the Bears in Chicago.

Ham had been introduced to the Bears earlier in the summer during a scrimmage between the Bears and the College All-Stars and thought the Bears were one of the worst teams he'd ever seen.

"They had Dick Butkus, but they weren't a good team," Ham said. "And I thought, 'I'll tell you one thing, we're going to beat the Chicago Bears.'"

Pittsburgh had a 15–3 lead in the fourth quarter before Butkus caused fumbles on two consecutive possessions, leading the Bears to two touchdowns in the final four minutes and a 17–15 lead.

"We ended up losing that game, a game we never should have lost," Ham said. "And again, I'm thinking, it's going to be a long, long season."

Most memorable about the Bears game were Greene's actions when the final seconds of the game ticked off the clock.

"Joe took off his helmet, I'll never forget this," Ham said. "They were just sitting on the ball to run out the clock. Joe takes off his helmet and whips it to the back of Soldier Field. Fortunately it didn't go into the stands back there. It hit the crossbar and shattered. The whole inside of his helmet came out. And I thought, you know what, I hate that cliché about hating to lose, but this guy actually gets violent when you lose a game. This guy's a competitor. This guy's a helluva player for us. And I'm sure he felt that there was no way in the world we should be losing to the Bears."

While Ham's initial assessment of the team hadn't been glowing, he liked what he saw in Noll.

"I think as a rookie you don't have the opportunity to think about the head coach," Ham said. "All you're trying to do is make a football team and contribute any way you can. But I remember what impressed me most about [Noll] was how thorough and businesslike he was. You're coming into a situation now, professional football, and really it's all about preparation. There aren't a lot of motivational speeches—at least

41

from Chuck Noll—prior to a game or whatever. And I kind of liked that. That's kind of my personality as well. It's very businesslike. I appreciated that. And you just felt like he was a smart guy. If anybody was going to turn that football team, organization around, it was going to be Chuck Noll."

The players also took notice that they were members of a team with a special owner in Art Rooney, who was affectionately known as "the Chief."

"Everybody on the team loved him," Ham said. "He'd come out on the field during training camp or at the stadium when we practiced in Pittsburgh. Everyone had such admiration for him. It was love for him. You kind of felt for everything he'd gone through. He was a tough guy and a sport, too.

"I used to love to go to lunch with my wife and him at the Allegheny Club, which is no longer there now that the old stadium has been torn down, and he would tell stories about the bets he would make on horse racing during the old days. About people from *The New York Times* following him around when he almost broke the track in Philadelphia one Saturday. And you just loved hearing him tell the stories from those days, when he had a hard time making payroll."

Throughout the 1971 season the Steelers grew tougher on defense—aided by Greenwood's ascent to a starting job after serving as the team's fifth defensive lineman since his rookie season in 1969.

"L.C. wasn't quite ready [when he first joined the team in 1969]," Noll said. "He had great vision, great ability. He liked to freelance a lot, which at times would get us in trouble. In order to get the whole thing tied together we were playing some of the other guys but working him in. L.C. was not a real big guy, maybe 218, 220, but he had that great quickness and speed and ability to rush the passer."

A significant sign of improvement came in the third game of the season when the Steelers defeated the San Diego Chargers, 21–17, after twice stopping the Chargers at the goal line. Afterward, Russell added perspective to the victory. "It's a sign we're coming of age," he said. "Two years ago we would have lost this game."

The Steelers lost to Baltimore 34–21 in their seventh game. Don Nottingham, a rookie running back with the Colts in 1971, remembered encountering Greene in that game.

"We used to run this sucker play," Nottingham said. "And you always had to listen to the line calls. Bill Curry was our center, and we had a 'C' call, which meant the center was going to step around the nose guard,

42

who was Joe Greene, and ideally he would say he was stepping around and his next step would be to step into it, which left him wide open for the fullback to come in and basically cheap shot him. It's an influence play, so it gets him looking at the center sliding around. Then the fullback comes and takes him out and the center goes out and becomes a pulling guard."

Setting up the play, Nottingham remembered Curry making the "C" call and Greene yelling, "What's that?"

"The play was on and I knocked the crap out of [Greene]," Nottingham said. "About a quarter later we ran the same play and I wound up about five yards in the backfield. Walking back to the huddle I can hear him telling Bill Curry, 'Thanks for the tip.' Those good ones, you can get them once, but you're never going to get them twice. He was as fast a big man as I ever saw in my life. I thought I did a good job once, and the second time he showed me what an NFL forearm was."

After ten games, the Steelers stood tied with Cleveland for the Central Division lead with a 5–5 record before dropping three of their final four games to fall just short. Tom Mack, the Hall of Fame guard who played for the Los Angeles Rams from 1966 through 1978, remembered the final game of the season when the Rams defeated the Steelers 23–14.

"We beat them, but we're like, 'These guys are going to be legitimate,'" Mack said. "They had developed into the up-and-coming team."

Mack also remembered the game because it was the first time he went up against Greene, which prompted him to wonder why he had the nickname "Mean" Joe Greene. The Rams' offensive coordinator had the idea that he could take advantage of some of his linemen's individual capabilities if he reversed the line. Normally the Rams' formation was right-handed with Mack playing left guard, but when they switched to their left formation, he became the right guard.

"The first time I flipped over on the right side, Joe Greene happens to be the left defensive tackle," Mack said. "He was there in front of me when I got down in my stance, and of course, I was serious. That's just the way I played the game. Obviously he looked at me, and whether he'd heard of me or knew who I was or what not, he looked up at me and said, 'Well, smile.' I didn't say anything one way or the other. He literally got down in his stance and looked up. He was almost lying on the ground and looking into my face mask and saying, 'Well, come on, smile.' And I'm thinking, 'This is a weird guy.' It was clear he was a very good athlete."

Ham's opinion of the team had changed by the end of the season.

"We had spurts all during my first season," Ham said. "Guys were starting to feel like they could play. I'd say by the end of that season the guys probably were thinking, 'This is a young football team; now we have some experience playing.' I think by the end of the year we started to feel that this might become a pretty good football team."

That feeling would be validated the following season.

4

A Title at Last

Leon "Bud" Carson was born and raised in Freeport, Pennsylvania. After graduating from high school he attended the University of North Carolina, where he was a three-year letterman on a Tar Heels team that featured Charlie "Choo Choo" Justice. Upon leaving Chapel Hill in 1951, Carson enlisted in the Marine Corps. Unsure of what direction he wanted to take once his military service was complete, Carson took a job coaching high school football in Scottsdale, Pennsylvania.

Jim Tatum, who coached at Maryland and led the Terrapins to a national championship in 1953, had tried to recruit Carson as a high school player. Tatum coached North Carolina prior to coaching at Maryland, then returned to Chapel Hill in 1956. After compiling a 2–7–1 mark his first season back, Tatum headed to Western Pennsylvania to recruit when he encountered Carson, who had a couple of players on his team Tatum wanted for North Carolina. Already having a relationship with Carson from when he'd tried to recruit him for Maryland, Tatum asked Carson to visit him in Chapel Hill. When Carson made his visit, Tatum offered him a job on his staff.

"That was the break of my life," Carson said.

Carson joined the staff for the 1957 season and remained at North Carolina for eight years—even after Tatum died from Rocky Mountain spotted fever in the summer of 1959. In 1965, Marvin Bass, who had coached Carson in college, became the head coach at South Carolina and wanted Carson to coach his defense. Carson enjoyed coaching at his alma mater, so he agonized over the offer before accepting the job. He coached at South Carolina one season, and then legendary Georgia Tech coach Bobby Dodd hired him as the Yellow Jackets' defensive coordinator.

Georgia Tech put together a 9–1 season in 1966 to earn a slot in the Orange Bowl, where they lost to the University of Florida in what turned out to be Dodd's final game. The timing of Dodd's decision to leave served Carson well. Based on Tech's success and the stellar defensive unit Carson had assembled, he was offered the head coach's position and he accepted.

Carson found out the hard way that filling the shoes of a legend is no small task.

"Nothing was good enough—nothing!" Carson said of his five-year tenure at Tech.

Adding to Carson's anxiety, he was also going through a divorce.

"Those were the days if you did that you were in real trouble," Carson said. "The mothers of a lot of those players you recruited didn't like to hear you were [going through a divorce]."

Carson's Yellow Jackets finished the 1967, 1968, and 1969 seasons with identical 4–6 records before going 9–3 in 1970, including a 17–9 win over Texas Tech in the Sun Bowl. The Tech faithful had been patient and were optimistic they would be rewarded in 1971 for giving Carson some slack. Unfortunately for Carson, Tech went 6–5 in 1971 and lost 28–24 to archrival Georgia on Thanksgiving. The lackluster season earned the Yellow Jackets a berth in the Peach Bowl, quite a letdown after the previous season. Carson understood the magnitude of his situation by this point.

"We were in the Peach Bowl and the players had voted not to go and geez, I knew we were in trouble," Carson said. "They didn't want to go."

Dodd intervened and eventually talked the team into playing in the Peach Bowl in Atlanta against Ole Miss.

"Mississippi was a good team. Billy Kinard was their coach and he was tough, so I knew to really have a chance to beat them we couldn't give a lot of vacation time over the holidays, which wasn't a popular decision," Carson said. "Then we went and got killed. There was a torrential rain to start the game. Crazy things happened. They kicked off and the ball stuck right in the mud. I never saw anything like that happen before or since, and they came down and recovered it. We were losing so bad at the half that Jimmy Carter, who was governor [of Georgia], came into our locker at halftime to try and give us a little boost. He did give us a little boost, because we came back in the second half, and even though we didn't win, we came back a little bit."

Tech lost 41–18, and Carson was fired following the game.

"Like Coach Dodd told me, 'They won't keep you forever; if you don't win you'll be gone,'" Carson said. "And of course he was absolutely right."

Carson found himself in a difficult place after getting fired. He wanted to continue coaching, but he had two children who lived in Atlanta, and he knew his ex-wife wasn't likely to move to accommodate a new coaching position. Carson had to do some soul searching about his profession. He thought he had a shot to be the head coach at Memphis, but that fell through. So with no other college interest, he began to explore the possibility of coaching in the NFL, which he didn't view as such an attractive alternative.

"I remembered [the Steelers] from when I was a kid, vaguely," Carson said. "In those days pro football was something that people didn't pay as much attention to as they do today. People paid attention to college football. Pro football was not like it is today. It was a completely different era."

Carson's status as a divorced man continued to haunt him. He decided he wanted to work for the Dallas Cowboys, but after experiencing what he believed to be a good interview with them, he received a call two days later and listened as a team psychologist told him that he had given a quality presentation, the team liked his ideas, and they would love to hire him, but wouldn't because he had been divorced.

Chuck Noll, whom Carson had never met, then called and asked him to come to Pittsburgh to interview for a job. At the time Carson had one other interview lined up, with the Chicago Bears.

"If I remember correctly, Chuck himself called me and asked me if I would come up for an interview," Carson said. "I called a couple of people and they said there were a lot of good players [on the Steelers] and that someday they were going to gel. But Chuck had been there three years and the rumor was he had one more year to go and if he didn't make it he was gone."

Carson went to Pittsburgh and met with Noll for four hours in his office watching film and talking philosophies.

"We really hit it off," Carson said. "He seemed very intelligent compared to other football coaches I had known. He knew the game, and as I look back on it, I must have felt like if I was going to pro football he'd be a great guy to go with because even if you think you know it all, there's a transition going to pro football."

Carson wanted somebody who really knew the game. In those days a lot of pro coaches were ex-players who never went through the experience of learning to be a coach. Noll obviously had learned to be a coach.

"Plus, we hit it off to the point I thought he would be a friend of mine, and he has been," Carson said. "I was very impressed and he must have been impressed, too, or he didn't have anybody else, because he hired me. He said, 'What job do you want on defense?' I coached the secondary more than anything else, so I said the secondary. He just told me not to visit the Bears. I didn't, and I took the job that day."

For Carson, leaving his children behind in Atlanta took some of the luster off of finding a new job.

"That was one of the real tough periods of my life," Carson said.

The Steelers benefited most from Carson's heartache. Carson threw himself into his work in the NFL, which for him was an entirely new world. Even something as elementary as watching films proved to be a learning experience when judging the talents of the players he would be working with in the secondary.

"I had no reference point to compare the players to," Carson said. "I was just taking it day to day. I hadn't coached pro football before. I had no idea what was going to happen other than I knew I better coach my rear off because there would be no more chances if I flubbed this one up. So it was an intense, get-after-it type of thing for me."

Noll had shored up the coaching with what would amount to be a major hire in Carson. Meanwhile, the Steelers' incredible run of talented players procured through the draft continued in 1972. The team had identified one of their needs as a quality running back. This led to an alleged in-house debate regarding which back to select: Houston's Robert Newhouse or Penn State's Franco Harris.

Harris had taken a backseat to Lydell Mitchell in the Nittany Lions' offense during his senior season. In addition, he'd been suspended before the Cotton Bowl for being late to practice. Was the 6'2", 230-pound fullback a disciplinary case? Would he become a bad influence on the team's chemistry if they selected him?

One story circulating said the Steelers had two different drafting factions that year and that Noll favored the 5'10" Newhouse, while Art Rooney Jr., the director of scouting, liked Harris.

Noll laughed when asked about the story.

"Franco was the guy all along," he said. "We watched film of him and we timed him at the Scouting Combines. I'll tell you how that whole thing came about. When you get into the room with your scouts and you want to find out how strongly they feel about a guy, you throw another guy at them so they have to defend the guy they think is pretty good. I threw Newhouse out there to test the guys on how strongly they felt about Franco."

And what about Harris when compared to Mitchell?

"Franco had size and speed," Noll said. "He was faster and he was bigger. Lydell carried the ball a lot more there [at Penn State]. But when you tried to project what he would do in pro football, Lydell didn't have the size and speed that you're looking for in a back—especially for a first-round choice."

Harris became their choice, but he wasn't necessarily the popular choice. After all, Mitchell had been the All-American, and at Penn State. And he was available for Pittsburgh to draft.

"The question was like, 'What is Noll doing?'" Mike Wagner said. "He'd taken Joe Greene, who obviously was a great player, but he was from a small college and wasn't well known. Bradshaw. Frank Lewis. Then he takes Harris. Very controversial choices instead of taking something safe like a player from the Big Ten. They were somewhat controversial."

Russell called Harris "another draft choice that was very suspect."

"Everybody was second-guessing the choice," Russell said. "The fans might have been excited if they'd gotten Lydell Mitchell, but they got this guy who was sort of a semistarter. And they were not all that excited."

Russell considered himself to be among the nonbelievers regarding Harris at the outset. He'd been a fullback at Missouri and understood the position, which led him to be critical of Harris, who wasn't much of a practice player.

"And he has this funny running style, because he wouldn't hit a hole," Russell said. "He'd bounce around and back up—a unique running style."

Russell eventually became a believer when he had an opportunity to tackle Harris in the open field and Harris made him miss completely.

"After that I could see he had some quick feet on him," Russell said.

Noll liked Harris all along and had no doubt he would be the perfect back to anchor the Steelers' running game. But after watching Harris in practice for a couple of days, even Noll was surprised at his quickness in making his decisions and cuts.

"He'd start up in the hole and he'd be off in another direction in a flash," Noll said. "He had the ability to do that, and there aren't too many who can, especially when you get long striders. Franco would lengthen his stride in the open field, but inside he'd make the choppy steps and make cuts tremendously."

Noll knew he'd once again hit the jackpot with one of his draft choices.

Carson offered insight into Noll's management style by elaborating on what he did while coaching the secondary during his first season with the Steelers in 1972.

"In pro football you made up your playbook the way you were going to present the defenses to the players," Carson said. "And all the strategy involved and the basic strengths and weaknesses of each of the defenses. You went over that and Chuck let you present the defenses in the order you wanted to and apply whatever you wanted to them.

"He was a very good fundamentalist, maybe the best I've ever known, and that was very rare to find in college football and near impossible in pro football with a few exceptions. We had fundamental defenses, but we pushed people and we were all teachers. And that's what Chuck was."

Noll's belief in fundamentals prompted him to hire college coaches for his staff, whom he told to treat the players as if they were freshmen in college. He wanted to emphasize teaching.

"College coaches were teachers, and a lot of the pro coaches that I knew were players and only wanted to administer, and we wanted a teaching staff," Noll said. "You can't assume your players know everything. We thought it was very important that you taught your football and sold it. That's a big part of teaching, the selling part."

Hiring college coaches might have been out of the ordinary for the time period, but it wasn't new for Noll. The staffs in Baltimore and San Diego each had a lot of former college coaches. The fact that the coaches on Noll's staff lacked NFL playing experience did nothing to take away from getting the players' attention and respect.

"Contrary to popular belief, I'm 5'9", and I've shrunk to 5'7" in my old age," Carson said. "When I go out to talk to people in groups, they'll always [say], 'Well it must have been hard to handle those guys.' That was not the case. Very seldom was that the case my whole career. If you knew what you were talking about, people listened. If you could help them, they listened."

George Perles, who joined the Steelers in 1972, and Woody Widenhofer, who arrived in 1973, each came from college coaching.

"I was impressed with these collegiate coaches," Andy Russell said. "It was very interesting for me. He brought in a linebacker coach named Woody Widenhofer, who had been at Missouri when I was a senior—he was a kid holding the dummies. This guy was two years younger than me and now he's my coach? I'll have to say he was really great. He didn't dictate to me; he'd always ask me my opinion. He was very good about that. We got along just fine. He was an excellent coach."

Noll believed in playing the game by the numbers and that success could be found in the details, which perfectly suited the learning climate.

"It isn't all about being a big stallion and hitting people," Russell said. "You better know what you're doing. I agreed with him."

Mel Blount could be counted among the players helped by Carson. Blount had struggled during his early years, prompting fans to shower him with Iron City Beer during player introductions.

"That's probably one of the kinder things they threw at me," Blount said. "I think I came into this league really not prepared for the NFL. I was just a talent; I wasn't a student of the game. It wasn't because I didn't have the ability to learn, it's just, hey, we just lined up and went one-on-one, and I wasn't that sophisticated to read all the different offenses and play the zone coverages."

Carson recognized Blount's immense talents immediately.

"Mel had great talent," Carson said. "You could [not] help but see that. He just needed to be handled and coached and encouraged—one of those things you have to do with people like that. But we had good people. You knew he was going to be a great cornerback, and we had two safeties that were going to be great safeties with [Mike] Wagner and [Glen] Edwards."

The question was: what coverage would they run to best utilize their talented defensive backfield and linebackers?

Cover Two became the answer.

Carson arrived in Pittsburgh and began to watch countless reels of film, and the idea of using the Cover Two kept permeating his thoughts. When he brought up the idea of using Cover Two to the other coaches, he was told Cover Two was a college coverage and wouldn't work in the NFL.

"But Chuck was open to it," Carson said. "He said for us to try it."

Down through the years, several NFL teams had played Cover Two, but they had not really committed to it being the backbone of their defense. For example, the Miami Dolphins used Cover Two, but they played it only two or three snaps per game.

Cover Two is based on a two-deep zone played by the safeties with five underneath zones played by the linebackers and cornerbacks. Given the rules governing defensive play at the time, Cover Two became the perfect complement for the Steelers. Defenders could hit receivers up until the ball was in the air.

"You could jam [a receiver] 20 yards down the field and it would totally disrupt any rhythm to any pass route he had, that was legal," Carson said. "Cover Two was the backbone of our whole scheme. And we shut people down with it. The quarterbacks had no idea what the heck they were throwing into. They'd take a three-step drop, throw it out in the flat, and our corner wasn't playing deep, he was just playing flat, and would intercept it. That happened over and over. I couldn't believe it."

Playing Cover Two called for a different kind of contribution from the linebackers.

"Carson always wanted Ham and me out over the ends, making sure they didn't go off the line of scrimmage," Russell said. "You could jam people back then. He did not want any speed demon running down that field attacking his defensive backs. We spent most of our time preventing an inside release or things of that nature."

Today's linebackers hover around the 250-pound plateau. The Steelers' linebackers were always trying to get lighter in the hope of finding more quickness. And Carson liked for his defense to have a counter defense to what was called by the offense.

After he retired from football, Russell went to a cocktail party at a friend's house in San Francisco. Legendary football coach Bill Walsh was also a guest at the party, where Russell and he began to talk football. Walsh had been the offensive coordinator for the Bengals before gaining fame as the San Francisco 49ers coach. Russell offered background on Walsh's offense before talking about the conversation they had. According to Russell, Walsh would show a lot of different formations to the defense before snapping the football.

"They would come out and show you an I formation, then a full formation, then he'd get to splits, double wing, motion to flood or triple," Russell said. "So he'd show you five formations before he'd snap the ball. Now he might snap the ball while they were in any one of those formations. He might snap it the second time or the third time, but you don't know when he's going to snap it.

"So the strategy originally for offensive coordinators was 'We're going to dictate what the defense does. We're going to make them so confused that we'll force them to play a simplistic zone. Like a two, that's a very simplistic zone. And he wants to know where all those defenders are going to be.'"

Meanwhile, a defense wanted to call the play to best stop the greatest tendency out of every offensive set.

"If they motion to a double wing, you want to play the defense that plays against what they would most likely do out of a double wing," said Russell, noting most defensive coordinators didn't think a defense could change five times before the ball was snapped because it would confuse the defense and lead to mistakes.

"Not Carson," Russell said. "Not only did he have us change every time, we'd be in five different defenses."

Russell told Walsh the Steelers would call five different defenses reacting to the offense followed by another five on the next play.

"[Walsh] said that was impossible," Russell said. "Finally he said, 'I never could figure out what you guys were doing; that's why.' Obviously you had to have some reasonably bright folks to do that. That was Bud Carson. He was a genius. He was doing things other coaches didn't do."

Another part of the Steelers' success using Cover Two was that no other team played it. The warts on the defense had not been exposed by imitation, which leads to offenses figuring out a way to attack a defense.

"Nobody knew how to attack it," Carson said. "We just ruined quarterbacks."

The Steelers' defense also received a much-needed lift from the addition of Harris to the offense, but he didn't get the carries initially when the Steelers began the 1972 season with wins over the Oakland Raiders and St. Louis Cardinals and losses to the Cincinnati Bengals and Dallas Cowboys. Harris carried the ball just 26 times for 79 yards and did not have an attempt against the Cardinals. Then the Houston Oilers came to town, and Harris rushed for 115 yards and a touchdown on 19 carries, and the Steelers won 24–7. The following week Harris had just 11 carries for 27 yards in a 33–3 win over the New England Patriots. Then the Steelers' offense climbed aboard Harris' shoulders and took off.

Harris eclipsed the 100-yard barrier the next six games, and the Steelers lost just once. Having an established running game in their arsenal meant everything to the Steelers' offense, and their defense.

"Having Franco was very important to our defense," Dwight White said. "When I came to Pittsburgh, we looked at the game films and the defense's reel would be, let's say, eight inches in diameter, and the offensive reel would be two inches. What does that mean? It means the defense was on the field a long time. Once the offense got it together they were dominant. We were always fresh on defense. We had time to sit down and go over the previous series of plays."

Wagner marveled at Harris running the football.

"I watched Franco play from the sidelines during game situations, and I'd be like, 'Holy cow, I'm so glad I don't have to play against him,'" Wagner said. "He could run, catch, run over you, run around you, and he could run away from you."

With Harris in the backfield the Steelers' offense had the ability to retain possession of the ball by running it.

"[That] is a big thing," Noll said. "One of the big things you want out of a running back is a guy who is not going to fumble the ball. Franco did not fumble. That was a big key. If you give somebody the ball you want him to keep it, even if [he is] gang tackled and they're trying to strip it. He would not turn the ball over. And he had the ability to make the big play. Those things together made him special. If there was a knock on him at all, especially in the beginning, it was his ability to catch the ball. And that's something that came around."

The Steelers' defense loved the new offense that ground out yardage and killed minutes off the clock.

"[The Steelers' offense] just dominated the football game moving the ball down the field and scoring points," Russell said. "So it was impressive to see that offense and a kid like Franco. He was a game player. When the game was on the line he got it done."

The veterans suddenly found themselves on a talented and young football team.

"It was astounding," Russell said. "All I can say is [Ray] Mansfield and I would drive to the stadium on Sunday morning and we'd say, 'Can we possibly win this? Are we this good? These guys, how can they be this good?' And we couldn't convince ourselves that we were that good, but we kept winning and winning. We'd beaten the Vikings at Three Rivers, we'd beaten the Kansas City Chiefs at Three Rivers, and pretty soon you start believing it. And you just see so much talent around you. Guys making plays everywhere. It was astounding."

Harris had unique features stemming from his Italian–African-American heritage. Underneath his black beard were the chiseled angles of a figure from Greek mythology. Fans embraced him as they had few athletes in the history of the franchise, forming "Franco's Italian Army," which was his own personal rooting section. Harris had equal respect and adoration in the Steelers' locker room.

Wagner characterized Harris as quiet, jolly, friendly, unassuming, and determined—a leader who led by setting an example.

"He was like one of those rumbling volcanoes," Wagner said. "If you're the defense, you just don't want to see him coming out. I was kind of glad we never went live or ever went after him in practice because he was the kind of running back who could really embarrass you."

Another reason Harris fit in so well with the running attack was his understanding of the trap play, which had become a staple of the offense under Noll. The Steelers were so well known for their trap blocking that they were said to begin trapping when they stepped off the bus.

On a trap play a defensive player is allowed to cross the line of scrimmage and then is blocked off as the runner goes through the place the lineman vacated. Critical to the play is the offense's creation of the deception that a defensive player will go unblocked when he penetrates the line of scrimmage. The play comes to fruition when a pulling lineman blocks, or "traps," the defensive player thereby opening a hole for the running back to run through. A guard, a tackle, or even both guards can be the pulling lineman or linemen on the play. Typically, the blocking for a trap play sees a double-team at the hole where the ball goes, and the pulling lineman or linemen make a block on the linebacker, creating a large hole for the running back. The running back needs to read the block on the linebacker to determine whether he takes an inside or outside path.

On inside traps the guard blocks the first man past the defender; outside traps call for the guard to block the first man past the tackle. If a linebacker reads the play properly and reacts accordingly, the trap play can be shut down. If the linebacker does not step into the hole or hesitates, the offensive tackle will have a clean block. When executed properly, trap plays have the potential to turn a routine running play into a touchdown if the blocking falls into place and the running back reads the right hole. Harris had a great feel for reading the right hole.

Among the problems for defenders created by the trap play is reading the pass. Instead of checking the runners, a lineman might rush the pass, which leaves him wide open to fall prey to the trap block.

Houston Oilers linebacker Gregg Bingham cited having a patient running back as the key to successful trap blocking.

"You can not run the trap with a guy like Earl Campbell because he hits the hole too quick," Bingham said. "And Franco Harris was the perfect trap back because he was very patient and he let the hole develop. You have to have some quick offensive linemen. You look back at history and you'll see that the Steelers drafted a lot of guards. They were quick and they were smart and they didn't make mistakes and knew how to adjust. And that's why they [had] all those 50 numbers, 55, 52 [typically numbers worn by centers], because they had a bunch of centers there and you have to have a very patient running back."

Noll learned about the trap play in college from his coach, Joe Gavin.

"Part of it is what you can do," Noll said. "When you have undersized people, you're not just going to go out there and straight block. I was undersized when I played, a 220-pound guard playing against a 270-pound tackle, so you're not just going to knock them off the ball. You have to find ways to do it. Among those ways was to influence and the trap. Pass protection, obviously, was essential, but the running game ended up being mostly traps and influences."

By the end of the 1972 season, Harris had rushed for 1,055 yards, caught 21 passes, scored 11 touchdowns, and was named AFC Rookie of the Year. Newhouse went on to a productive career with the Dallas Cowboys but would be primarily used as a blocking back for featured backs Calvin Hill, Duane Thomas, and later Tony Dorsett.

Harris' boost to the running game and the continued maturation of Terry Bradshaw led to a team-record 343 points. Meanwhile, the defense allowed just 175 points, second only to the unbeaten Dolphins.

"Sometime around the middle of the 1972 season, here I am a second-year player from a small college going, 'Hey man, we can play with anybody; this team is pretty good,'" Wagner said.

Three Rivers Stadium had evolved into a beloved community spot for the blue-collar working class that followed the Steelers. Other playful factions started to develop among the crowd. Besides "Franco's Italian Army" there were "Gerela's Gorillas" (for kicker Roy Gerela) and "Fuqua's Foreign Legion." Foremost, the Steelers were the team with the "Steel Curtain" defense. And their style of play made fans and NFL officials really take notice. Among the key wins during the regular season were a 40–17 thrashing of the Bengals and a 30–0 win over the Browns; both wins came in front of the raucous home crowd, but the 16–7 win over the Chiefs remained etched in Carson's mind for the tone established by the defense.

"Can you imagine my first year at Pittsburgh? Kansas City comes in there—they'd been to the Super Bowl—and we beat them 16–7," Carson said. "Pittsburgh went crazy. It was a great victory, a great football game. The stadium was filled up. They yelled 'Defense! Defense!' It was like being in the Southeastern Conference. People loved the game. But pro football, the powers that be, would decide in the next couple of years that they wanted it to be an offensive game. But in those days, geez, it was not that way. It was a defensive game."

On December 17, 1972, the Steelers clinched their first-ever division title in the 40-year history of the franchise when they defeated the Chargers 24–2. The victory gave the club an 11–3 record—the franchise's best ever—and put them in their first playoff game since 1947. The team's "Steel Curtain" defense looked primed for the playoffs after allowing just one touchdown in the team's final four games; additionally, the Steelers' defense finished first in the league with 28 interceptions and fourth in sacks with 40.

While the Steelers' season ranked high on the list of the NFL's top stories in 1972, the landscape had other compelling images. The Dolphins finished the season with a 14–0 record accrued by an intelligent and talented defense and an offense that reflected the changing NFL. The Dolphins gained 2,960 yards on the ground to set an NFL record. Larry Csonka and Mercury Morris rushed for 1,117 and 1,000 yards respectively, and Jim Kiick added 521.

The Dolphins' running game served as the perfect microcosm for a rules change that moved the hash marks—officially known as "inbound lines"—which are the guides that show the official where to mark the ball near the sideline or out of bounds. The hash marks were moved inward toward the middle of the field to 23 yards, one foot, nine inches from each sideline. The hope for the rule had been to get offenses to open up their passing games more—which is what the NFL believed the fans wanted to see. Instead, it freed up play calling once restricted by short- and wide-side-of-the-field calls and, in effect, ushered in an era of conservative football. Prior to the change teams would either be left-handed or right-handed depending on whether the official placed the ball on the left hash mark or the one on the right side of the field. With the change in effect, teams could send their backs wide to either side of the field due to the extra space, and they took advantage of the change in a season that came to be known as the "Year of the Runner."

"When the hash mark was wide and the ball was over there, you'd put your whole defense to the wide side of the field because there wasn't any room to do anything on the short side," Noll said. "When you moved the harsh marks in, they were thinking passing game, but the running game now was almost like being in the middle of the field wherever you were. So you had the whole field to work with. And that helped the running game probably more than it helped the passing game."

Noll laughed when asked if coaches knew this would be the effect of the change.

"The coaches don't make those rules," Noll said. "The competition committee does. Pete [Rozelle] wanted a lot of scoring because they could sell that, it was exciting. It wasn't like that college game, three yards and a cloud of dust, the old Woody Hayes stuff. They wanted to see the ball fly through the air, exciting, right? They were trying to promote that. But one thing Woody said, and he was right, when you pass the ball, bad things happen in two out of the three possible results. It was set up to help the passing game, but it helped the running game.

"Personally, I always thought the most exciting games were defensive struggles, when it came down to the last minute. When you're scoring every other play and you get 50 points, that wasn't really exciting."

Redskins running back Larry Brown became the marquee back of the NFL, gaining 1,216 yards in twelve games before sitting out the final two games of the season due to bruised knees. Brown's absence from the lineup allowed Buffalo's O. J. Simpson to win the NFL rushing title with 1,251 yards. In a season dominated by running backs, 10 running backs surpassed the magical 1,000-yard plateau—and there would have been 11 had Atlanta's Dave Hampton not lost 6 yards on his final carry of the season to drop to 995 yards. And even though offenses became more conservative, NFL teams exceeded the previous year's total points by 324.

While several teams seemed headed in the right direction, Steelers fans could look around at the rest of the NFL and see few teams that came close to them in overall talent, and no team in the league had so much young talent.

5

The Immaculate Reception

On December 23, 1972, a powerful earthquake devastated Managua, Nicaragua; heavy American bombing of North Vietnam continued; and Charles Atlas died. But in Pittsburgh, no world event ranked anywhere near what would happen on the synthetic Tartan Turf of Three Rivers Stadium when the Oakland Raiders met the Steelers in the AFC playoff semifinal.

Art Rooney became everyone's favorite uncle during the week leading up to the game. The Steelers' 71-year-old team president had waited 39 years for the Steelers to have a postseason.

"I figured we'd win if I lived long enough," Rooney told *The New York Times.* "But I did get kind of worried as it got late in my life."

Pittsburgh players wanted to win for "the Chief," but extra incentive came in the promise of bonus money for progressing through each tier of the playoffs. Players would receive an extra game's salary for participating in the first round of the playoffs. If a team reached the conference title game, players on the winning team would each receive $8,500 and the losers would get $5,000. The Super Bowl breakdown would be $15,000 for winners and $7,500 for losers. So, a run through the playoffs followed by a Super Bowl win would earn approximately $28,000—which included the extra game's pay plus being paid for the game against the College All-Stars the following summer.

A raucous crowd of 50,350 crammed into Three Rivers Stadium, bringing an infectious enthusiasm, but the task at hand for their Steelers would be enormous.

Oakland had a roster that showed a nice blend of youth and veterans that had speed and could play smashmouth football. The Raiders' offense—consisting of seven Pro Bowl nominees—would present a huge challenge to the Steelers' defense. Quarterback Daryle Lamonica could throw the long ball; wide receiver Fred Biletnikoff and tight end Ray Chester were the tops at their positions; tackle Art Shell, guard Gene Upshaw, and center Jim Otto anchored a solid line; and running back Marv Hubbard had gained 1,100 yards during the regular season and ran with a bruising style that reminded everyone who watched him that football was a violent game.

The Raiders' offense thrived on running a conservative offense. While Lamonica threw for just 1,998 yards after throwing for 3,302 three seasons earlier, he seemed even more dangerous as he completed 53 percent of his passes and was intercepted just 12 times.

But Oakland's offense could do nothing against the Steelers' defense. Pittsburgh led 3–0 after three quarters and 6–0 with a little over a minute left in the game. At this point Hubbard's 10-yard run was the Raiders' longest of the day, and they'd completed just 12 of 30 passes for 78 yards. The Steelers had recovered two Raiders fumbles and intercepted two passes.

Pittsburgh had shut down the Oakland offense so decisively that the Raiders brought in backup quarterback Ken Stabler at the beginning of the fourth quarter in the hope of making something happen.

"We'd played great defense the whole game," Andy Russell said. "We'd really shut them down. Lamonica had started, and we'd intercepted him and we'd really held him back. They probably put Stabler in to see if he'd give them a spark. Lamonica was not going to run the ball. And that's what hurt us."

Stabler could run the football—but not without a little help from the Steelers.

Oakland had the ball at the Steelers' 30 when Dwight White had to be replaced by Craig Hanneman due to a leg injury. After reading a blitz, Stabler circled left to the outside to elude Hanneman, and Russell was taken out of the play. A heartbeat later Stabler found the end zone, sending a hush over the once-enthusiastic crowd.

"Yeah, it wasn't a fun time," Noll said. "But I don't think it took the wind completely out of our sails. We were able to go back out and try to make something happen."

The Raiders had a 7–6 lead with just a minute and 13 seconds remaining.

"The play preceding Stabler's touchdown I got injured and came out of the game—one play," White said.

One of any defensive end's first responsibilities is outside containment.

Containment "is a lot about the angle you take when you're rushing the quarterback," White said. "Going into that game we had gone over that a billion times. Craig Hanneman was the backup for L. C. [Greenwood] and myself and comes in for me, they go back to pass— guess what, Craig doesn't contain. Stabler pulls the ball down and runs the damn thing in for the touchdown. I couldn't believe it. Nobody could believe it."

Hanneman didn't contain, but where was Russell?

If the Raiders showed a certain formation, Russell knew to call a stunt where he went inside and the end went outside, which would protect the flank.

"And I called that out, even slapped [Hanneman] on the butt, that's sort of what I'd do with Dwight to make sure he understood what was happening," Russell said. "Anyway, I go up the middle and I get blocked by the guard. Stabler rolls out and there's just nobody outside, and he goes 30 yards for their only touchdown."

When the Steelers' offense went back on the field to try and get into field-goal position, Bradshaw threw three straight incomplete passes to leave the Steelers facing fourth down on their own 40 with 22 seconds remaining.

Inside the Steelers huddle Bradshaw called "66 Option," meaning his first option would be a pass to Barry Pearson; running back Frenchy Fuqua was his second. If he could complete one more pass, the Steelers would be within kicker Roy Gerela's range.

"I remember standing there with Glen Edwards and Glen was bitching about our offense being so bad that day, we'd only scored a few points," Russell said. "I always tried to be positive, pull for the offense. Never criticize them. So I'm like, 'Something can happen.' Because the game seemed like it was over."

Up in the owner's box, Art Rooney began his journey to the locker room to console his team. About the time Rooney set foot into the elevator, Bradshaw walked to the line, took the snap from center, and drifted right to avoid the charging Raiders line.

Throughout the Raiders' team history they had been cast as NFL rogues, the curious blend of finesse and smashmouth football played by outcasts. Their players had talent but could not follow the conventional rules employed by other franchises. Their brand of football tended to make the opposing team want to fight or cower. Standing up to the Raiders demonstrated that the Steelers' collection of youngsters indeed had backbone.

Sensing danger, Harris strayed from his pass-protecting assignment and headed up the field to give Bradshaw an alternative target. Bradshaw elected to throw the ball up the field to the Raiders' 35, where Fuqua hooked then awaited Bradshaw's bullet. The ball and Raiders defensive back Jack Tatum converged on Fuqua simultaneously, which sent the ball ricocheting back toward the Steelers' line.

"That last play with Bradshaw scrambling around, when the ball was thrown I watched it thinking that Frenchy might catch it," Russell said. "When I saw the ball deflected backward, I just looked down. I thought the season was over."

Now down on the turf, Bradshaw thought the play had been broken up, and he slammed his helmet in disgust.

Trailing the play, Harris saw the ball pop in the air, and he moved toward it, somehow managing to scoop it up inches before it hit the ground and run untouched the rest of the way. His 42-yard scamper into the end zone put the Steelers on top 13–7 and had them headed for the AFC Championship Game.

"I saw the ball and thought I could catch it, but I felt someone hit me from behind," Fuqua told reporters. "Next thing I knew, Franco went roaring past me, and I wondered what was going on."

Harris sounded equally mesmerized by the play.

"I wasn't even supposed to be out there [as a receiver]," Harris said after the game. "But I saw Terry in trouble, and I figured I better get out there if he had to throw it to me. But he threw it deep."

Russell, who thought the game was lost, went from dejected to euphoric in an instant.

"I heard this roar and there's Franco streaking down the field," Russell said. "I did see the hit that Tatum put on Frenchy. And the big thing was whether the ball hit Tatum or hit Frenchy's chest.

Rooney missed the play entirely but became privy to the controversy that ensued.

Tatum screamed at Fuqua, "Tell them you touched it! Tell them you touched it!"

Had Fuqua touched the ball, the prevailing rule would have judged the play an incomplete pass because two offensive players had touched the ball consecutively.

"I didn't see the ball bounce away," Bradshaw told reporters. "I just saw Franco take off. I thought, 'Man! It must have hit him right on the numbers!' I've played football since the second grade and nothing like that ever happened. It'll never happen again. And to think it happened here in Pittsburgh in a playoff!"

Noll described the scene after the touchdown.

"After it happened it was pandemonium," Noll said. "People were all over the place."

Though it is believed instant replay was used in determining the right call, the NFL denied reviewing the play.

Jim Kensil, the NFL's executive director, explained the situation afterward as follows:

"When Franco Harris crossed the goal line after catching the batted pass, an official signaled that it was a touchdown.

"The referee wanted to be sure that it had been a legal play, so he contacted the umpire, Pat Harder, who usually has the best view of such a play. He also went to Adrian Burk, the back judge, and he agreed with Harder that both Jack Tatum and the intended receiver, John Fuqua, had touched the ball.

"Oakland was apparently arguing that the two Steelers had touched the ball successively."

Referee Fred Swearingen contacted Kensil and Art McNally, a league supervisor of officials, to tell them the touchdown was legal. Kensil said that was all they needed to hear up in the booth and that instant replay was not used to clarify the on-field ruling. But reports said that McNally, who had access to the instant replay on TV, asked Swearingen how he ruled, and when Swearingen replied "touchdown," McNally told him, "That's right."

The ruling went the way of the Steelers, giving birth to the "Immaculate Reception" and leaving Raiders coach John Madden frustrated.

"The officials told me they didn't know what happened," Madden later said to reporters. "And they were going to check upstairs to see what it was. The referee went in to use the dugout telephone, and when he came out he called it a touchdown.

"I saw McNally at the airport and he told me there was no doubt Tatum touched the ball. But then I saw Jay Randolph of NBC television and he told me there was no way to make a positive decision off the TV replays. Those are the same films McNally saw."

Noll wryly commented: "We're putting the play in tomorrow."

Later, when Fuqua was asked whether he had touched the ball, he answered, "I cannot tell a lie. No comment."

To this day Fuqua has not revealed the truth. Russell laughed at Fuqua's stance.

"We're in the locker room afterward, and it's chaos as you can imagine," Russell said. "Then they let all the sportswriters in and Frenchy's locker is next to mine—I'm No. 34 and he's 33—and the first few writers go over to him and ask, 'Did the ball hit you or did it hit Tatum?' And he said, 'I tried to catch it, the ball bounced off my chest.' Well I knew the rule that that can't happen, so I grabbed him around the shoulder and said, 'Now what you meant to say was the ball really was above your shoulder pads and it hit off of Tatum.' He's like, 'That's right, that's right.' Then all the sportswriters came over and he got it right. See, I don't personally think he knows. I honest to god don't think he knows."

Russell said longtime Steelers analyst Myron Cope saw a revealing view of the "Immaculate Reception" that one of the local stations had on tape.

"He's never been able to find the tape again, but he saw a tape that proved the ball ricocheted off Tatum's shoulder pads and back to Franco, who did catch it before it hit the ground, so it was a totally valid play," Russell said. "Myron had no reason to say that. This was 25 years later. He didn't need to make that up. He said he saw it for sure. I asked him why didn't somebody dig that out of the archives and prove it. He said they couldn't find it, but he swore he saw it."

Pittsburgh's win moved the Steelers to the AFC Championship Game in Pittsburgh against the undefeated Miami Dolphins.

The Dolphins defeated Cleveland in the first round, which gave them their third win against teams that had finished the season with winning records—lending fodder to accusations that the team had played a weak schedule. And the Dolphins had played their previous 10 games with 38-year-old quarterback Earl Morrall at the helm after Bob Griese, the Dolphins' regular quarterback, broke his ankle October 15 against the San Diego Chargers. But the Dolphins looked like a team with something to prove after playing in the previous year's Super Bowl and getting embarrassed by the Dallas Cowboys in a 24–3 loss.

Miami's determination did little to curb the enthusiasm of Pittsburgh fans, who now felt their team was destined to go to the Super Bowl and win. How could they not feel that way after the Raiders game and the "Immaculate Reception"? Everything looked to be coming up black and gold—even the schedule favored the Steelers.

The Dolphins had not lost a game all season. In today's NFL, if a team had no losses and another team did, the undefeated team would earn the home-field advantage throughout the playoffs. Not so in 1972 as the undefeated Dolphins had to travel to Pittsburgh to play the Steelers to get to the Super Bowl.

"We looked at the Steelers as every bit an equal," said Dolphins center Jim Langer. "But can you imagine today being undefeated and having to go play the AFC Championship [Game] at Pittsburgh? That was unbelievable. Of course they've changed the rule since then. But to go into the Steelers' stadium, we were scared to death because we thought this is a very dangerous game, much less having to go into Three Rivers. Bradshaw and all those guys—Franco Harris—they had the big game with Oakland."

Dolphins coach Don Shula didn't think much about having to go to Pittsburgh at the time.

"Because the procedure back then was to alternate championship games from one conference to the other, year in and year out," Shula said. "So that's just the way that it fell. Now when you look back and think about it, 15–0 and you've got to travel. If that happened in this day and age it would be unheard of."

Dolphins linebacker Nick Buoniconti knew the Steelers were no Cinderella team.

"They weren't an up-and-coming team," Buoniconti said. "They were a very good football team. That team was more than up-and-coming. We knew it was going to be very tough going into that ballgame. That was a good football team.

"They were a well-rounded team. They could throw the football. That was a team that you went to sleep the night before and you woke up in the middle of the night and said, 'How the hell are we going to stop that offense?' And that was true. They were a very well-balanced team, so you couldn't just sit back and play run or pass. They mixed it up pretty well. That [Steelers] team was both physical and smart. Like our team, they didn't make mistakes and neither did we."

An intriguing element to the game lay in the history between the two head coaches. The teams had similar defenses with similar nomenclature.

"One of the things we tried to do was disguise by lining up the same every time, then once the ball was snapped, we'd adjust or move," said Dolphins safety Dick Anderson. "We choreographed false steps. We used to run what we called a 'weak safety zone' where I'd go to the deep middle and [safety] Jake Scott would go to the deep outside. We'd roll up the weak cornerback. And we would both take a false step as if it was going to be a safety zone. And then wheel. So when their quarterback was reading the two safeties, he's saying, 'Oh shit, the strong safety is going to be deep outside,' and I end up in the deep middle. Or we'd do that with the strong linebacker. On the strong side in a basic safety zone I could put people in three different zones, except for the linebacker going deep outside. But that's the kind of thing we did and Pittsburgh did a lot of the same thing."

The Steelers' basic numbering systems and passing routes were similar to the Dolphins' because both rivers flowed from the same source, Paul Brown.

"And I'm sure their defensive schemes reflected that in their game plans as ours did," Langer said. "I think both Noll and Shula were smart enough. I think one of the great things they possessed was taking the players they had and maximizing their skills.

"And the other thing, having the quarterback call the play. They would get feedback from players on the field—they're still the best people to see what's happening. Noll and Shula were two chess masters going at one another with players who could think on the field, like a Joe Greene, and they could see stuff and adjust to it. Then go back to their coaches and say this is the adjustment they're doing."

A lot of things looked similar when the Steelers lined up against the Dolphins.

"There were no surprises, let me put it that way," Noll said. "So [the game] was all going to come down to execution: how well your people are going to execute."

Anderson believes the offenses were similar but different in the fact that Bradshaw had one of the strongest arms in the NFL and Harris brought a different element to the running game than the Dolphins' backs, but that the Dolphins had a better offensive line and a better overall running game. In addition, the Dolphins had wide receiver Paul Warfield.

"Nobody was better than Warfield," Anderson said. "He is extremely underrated [in pro football history]. He was the most magnificent receiver I've ever seen. He was disciplined. He was precise. You hear the stories about [Hall of Fame Baltimore Colts receiver] Raymond Berry being precise. Well, Paul was Raymond Berry with speed. And he was the most graceful individual you'll ever see. He was a phenomenal receiver. Now Randy Moss is probably taller, faster, bigger, but certainly didn't have the brain or the intensity that Paul did. You've got to remember that Warfield played when you could hit receivers. And today they can't hit the receiver."

Warfield could burn defenses deep when they crowded the line of scrimmage to try and stop the likes of Csonka, Kiick, and Morris. He brought an X factor to the Dolphins' offense.

Despite some of the challenges presented by the Steelers' offense, the core principles of the Dolphins' "No-Name Defense" would remain the same.

"Our defenses were designed where you don't let them get outside," Anderson said. "We played against O. J. [Simpson] 18 times and he made 100 yards once, I think, because we kept him boxed inside. If he ever got outside, that's where he was really dangerous. That's where he excelled. Or, if he caught a pass out in [the] open, it would be difficult to tackle him. If you kept him boxed up, he wasn't that hard to tackle. My job on the run was to turn the play in, and that's where Nick would come in and make the tackle."

Dolphins defensive coordinator Bill Arnsparger had an innate ability to design defenses around the players he had so they were in a position to succeed and rarely left in a position that exposed their weaknesses.

"All of our systems were designed to know where your help was and know who you could give help to," Anderson said. "So the only time you were really naked was on a blitz and we didn't blitz all that much. Bill was a brilliant defensive coach. So we always had total confidence that he would put us in the right place at the right time. And I'd come off the field sometimes and I'd say, 'Bill, they got second and long, why don't you run this defense because I think they're going to do this, this, and this.' And he'd say, 'Well, do you have this, this, and this covered?' And I'd say, 'Yeah.' He'd [run the suggested defense] and I might get an interception."

The Steelers did not fear the Dolphins, a team that historically has never gotten the recognition it deserved. Some felt by beating the Raiders, the Steelers had already cleared the biggest hurdle blocking their path to the Super Bowl. Even if the Dolphins were undefeated, they didn't have intimidating players and Morrall was their quarterback. How would they possibly contain the likes of Greene, White, Greenwood, and Blount?

The Dolphins checked into Pittsburgh's William Penn Hotel where they were targeted for an air raid from the legions of Franco's Italian Army, who dropped two thousand leaflets over the hotel. The message on the leaflets guaranteed safe passage out of town to any member of the Miami Dolphins if presented to a member of Franco's Italian Army. The note concluded with: "Surrender now and enjoy life with your loved ones rather than face destruction on the field of battle at Three Rivers Stadium." Accounts of the episode say the leaflets never found their mark due to a foul wind or a poorly executed drop.

If the errant leaflets weren't bad enough karma for the Steelers, the weather struck an even crueler blow on December 31, 1972. Instead of Three Rivers Stadium being covered by a blanket of snow and ice with freezing temperatures, players faced a balmy day in the 50s with the sun shining for the 1:00 P.M. kickoff.

"It was terrific," Buoniconti said. "It was an ideal football day. I think they would have rather had something below zero and in the snow. The gods were shining on us—every once in a while, the right thing happens for you at the right time. That weather hit us great. You go from hot to cold, you can never warm up."

The Dolphins usually played in the sunshine in the Orange Bowl, where they normally watched another sort of weather take its toll on opposing teams.

"First, when they'd come down they'd be on the visitor side and the sun would be hitting them all day," Buoniconti said. "It would be about 100 degrees and the sun would be beating down on them so by the fourth quarter we had a major advantage because we trained in that every day, versus going up to play in the cold. I think teams who are winter weather teams are much more prepared to play in that than Southern teams. If there is an acclimation that takes place it's with throwing the football, holding on to the football, tackling, all that stuff is a lot different when you're really cold and you can't get loose. It's a big difference."

Shula remembered the weather making everyone on the Dolphins' sideline feel better. "We felt like it was going to be our day," he said.

A raucous crowd greeted the Dolphins when they ran onto the playing surface of Three Rivers Stadium.

"Gerela's Gorillas were up there screaming and yelling, wearing their gorilla masks, hooting at us and booing us and everything else," Buoniconti said.

And the noise built when everything appeared to be going the Steelers' way. Early in the game the Steelers took the ball 48 yards on the ground toward the Dolphins' goal line. Bradshaw tried to cap the drive by running the ball in himself.

"I remember Bradshaw was taking it in for a touchdown and Jake [Scott] hit him and knocked him out and he fumbled the ball into the end zone," Anderson said.

Gerry Mullins recovered the ball in the end zone for a Pittsburgh touchdown and a 7–0 lead.

"I said, 'Oh no, not one of those days,'" Buoniconti said.

The Dolphins' defense had done more than force a fumble. Bradshaw went to the sidelines in a woozy state. He'd spent two nights in the hospital that week recuperating from a virus, which might have been a contributing factor to his state as well. He went back into the game for the next Pittsburgh series, which lasted three plays, before Terry Hanratty replaced him.

"I don't know what happened [on the play]," Bradshaw told *The New York Times*. "I blanked out. I thought I was in [the end zone], but I was just laying there out cold."

In the second quarter with the Dolphins punting from the Steelers' 49-yard line, the game turned. Punter Larry Seiple received the snap and noticed all the Steelers had turned away from him to drop back to block for the return, which left the middle of the field wide open. Seiple took off running.

"Larry, I think being the type of player he was, had talked to the coaches about the possibility of a fake punt if it presented itself," Langer said. "That's what good players do, they think out there. And one of the great things about Shula was if he got to a point where he trusted your judgment you could do those things. Larry just saw the play developing, and he'd seen it on film, that they were turning very quickly and they were trying to get a big return, so he just took advantage of it."

Seiple made it to the Steelers' 12 before getting dragged down.

"Seiple's fake punt was the most important play of the game," Anderson said. "Shula's rule was don't get caught. If it's there, take it. But it's not a designed play. He had the opportunity and they peeled off and he just said 'oh shit' and took off."

Seiple's play got the momentum back on the Dolphins' side and took the crowd out of the game.

"I think it caught them a little back on their heels," Langer said. "And our defense was playing a great game the entire game."

Two plays later Morrall completed a nine-yard scoring pass to Csonka to tie the game at 7.

Shula thought his offense looked stagnant in the first half and weighed his options. Morrall had been the good soldier, filling in admirably during Griese's absence. The Dolphins would not have been undefeated had Morrall not played so well. But the Dolphins needed a spark. Shula believed Griese could provide such a spark, so he started Griese in the second half.

"Griese had been my quarterback and the guy I was going to build my football team around, but I was able, and fortunate enough, to get Joe Robbie to let me bring in a guy like Earl Morrall as the backup quarterback at $90,000 a year," Shula said. "When Griese went down, Earl came on and did a magnificent job for me. The week prior to [the Pittsburgh game], Griese returned to practice and looked like he was sharp and didn't seem to have any ill effects from the broken ankle that he had.

"I knew that Griese was back to form from the way that he practiced. So when it looked like Earl was struggling a little bit and we had back— in my mind—a healthy Griese, I made the decision in the second half to go back to my starter from the beginning."

Griese and Morrall were totally different quarterbacks. Griese was the consummate field general who excelled at moving the team down the field. Totally unselfish, he loved the running game and the play-action pass. Morrall was more of a wide-open, offensive-type quarterback. When Morrall took over after Griese got hurt the Dolphins' offense actually opened up more than it had with Griese at quarterback.

Shula looked at Griese prior to the start of the second half and asked him, "Are you ready?"

Griese replied, "Yes. I'm ready."

Griese quickly validated Shula's faith in him when he faced third-and-long early in the third quarter with the Steelers leading 10–7 and the Steelers' crowd gaining steam. Warfield lined up in the slot on an "81–1" play and found Russell covering him from his right linebacker spot. Russell excelled in forcing receivers to go to the outside. Having done his homework on Russell, Warfield stared him in the eyes and looked outside then broke outside, and Russell bought the fake, which allowed Warfield to cut back inside. Griese hit Warfield perfectly in stride and the speedy Dolphins' receiver covered 52 yards before Mike Wagner brought him down. Six plays later Kiick scored on a 2-yard run to put the Dolphins up 14–10.

"I think bringing Bob in was a lift at the time because every player on the team knew that we had to do something," Langer said. "I mean the whole season was on the line here. God knows Earl got us that far; we knew Bob was ready for weeks. And of course, the guy Shula was, he let Earl play because Earl was winning. But it was clear at halftime we were not going to win that game.

"We needed to give them a different look. Bob certainly brought to the table different skills than Earl had. They were totally stuffing us. We just couldn't get any breathing room. And they were playing a hell of a game. I think when Bob came in they hadn't prepared for it and he opened the game up a little bit. It was just enough of a lift, when Bob came back in, and we felt like we'd pulled the ace out of our sleeve."

The Dolphins added another score when Kiick went in from three yards out to make it 21–10.

The Dolphins' defense effectively dealt with the Steelers' dangerous trapping.

"What they try to do is let the defensive linemen get across the line of scrimmage and bring a guard or a tackle around to knock them out," Buoniconti said. "They were very good at that, but we had the best defensive coach in football in Arnsparger, and we knew what they were going to do.

"They still were very effective, but I think we pretty much controlled that game. We had a great coach who put us in the right situations. But their trapping, everybody knew they were a trapping team. Everybody knew Franco was going to get the carries. And they had a terrific offensive line with guys like Ray Mansfield. But I think if you prepare enough for it, they're going to have some successful plays. But I think we had more than they did."

On the Steelers' sideline, Bradshaw remained dazed.

"I thought I knew what was going on, but I really didn't, I was pretty loony," Bradshaw told *The New York Times*. "I kept looking at the plays in our game plan and they were Greek to me. They didn't look like anything we had practiced. I could have sworn the game plan was somebody else's. I kept looking at the heading to see if it was some other team's. Then Terry [Hanratty] kept quizzing me and telling me stuff and I didn't know what he was talking about."

Bradshaw reentered the game with just over seven minutes remaining and threw a 12-yard scoring pass to Al Young with five minutes to go to cut the score to 21–17, which is how the Steelers' season ended.

"Earl Morrall had led us most of the way during the season, but Earl had a tough going in the beginning against the Steelers," Buoniconti said. "You've got to hand it to Shula for making the change to Griese. He came in and was terrific. That sparked the team. I think that was the biggest difference in the game."

Buoniconti noticed a difference in the crowd he'd seen prior to the game and took satisfaction in how deflated the stands seemed when the Dolphins ran off the field victorious.

"At the end of the game all you could see was the 'Gerela's Gorillas' sign hanging off the upper deck," Buoniconti said. "They no longer had their gorilla heads on, and they were sitting there in shock. I think that's the one thing I remember most about that day."

Harris was held to 76 yards on 16 carries and Fuqua had 47 yards on 8 carries to account for most of the Steelers' offense on the day. The Dolphins' running game, which had averaged 211 yards per game, had been held to 193—or 156 after Seiple's fake punt yardage was subtracted—and they had completed just 10 of 16 passes for 121 yards, yet they still won the game.

"I walked away from that game with the Dolphins and I kind of learned something," Jack Ham said. "I'm thinking to myself, 'Wow, we should have beaten them,' which is the way I'm sure a lot of teams felt after losing to them. But you know what, they made plays. They were a smart football team; they didn't make mistakes. They forced you to make mistakes. We'd been one game away from going to the Super Bowl, but walking off that field, I think we felt like we now understood what it was all about to win playoff games and to be in pressure situations and what it takes to be a championship football team. And even though we lost that game, I think we drew a lot from that game. I know I did, and I think a lot of the other players did as well."

The Dolphins went on to defeat the Washington Redskins 14–7 in Super Bowl VII at Los Angeles to complete a 17–0 season, the first perfect-record regular-season and postseason mark in NFL history. Approximately 75 million people viewed the NBC telecast of the game.

While the Steelers did not make it to the Super Bowl in 1972, the NFL's popularity had kicked into warp speed, and the Steelers were becoming a darling of fans.

6

Raiders Revenge

Progress sometimes occurs by taking one step forward and two back. The 1973 Steelers arrived at training camp with the goal of winning the Super Bowl, and anything short of that goal would mean failure.

But injuries hampered the team throughout the season. Franco Harris had a bad knee, Frenchy Fuqua suffered a broken collarbone, Terry Bradshaw separated his shoulder, and Terry Hanratty had broken ribs.

The Steelers' defense again played a dominant brand of football, allowing just 210 points in 14 games while the offense scored 347 points.

L. C. Greenwood led the team with 8.5 of the defense's 33 sacks, which made fans remember the fashion statement he made. Some Steelers wore white shoes during that era; others wore black. But after an ankle injury team doctors told Greenwood he needed to wear a high-top shoe if he wanted to play. High-tops were not popular at the time, so shoe companies weren't making them, which made the prospect of finding a pair for Greenwood to wear a difficult proposition.

"The equipment manager went to one of his friends and got some old high-top black shoes from Rydell that they had, and they brought them in and asked me to try them on to see how they fit," Greenwood said. Then came the conversation between Greenwood and the equipment manager that would add a little color to the Steelers' lineup.

"They fit pretty good, but they're ugly," Greenwood said of the size-14 shoes.

"You want me to paint them white?" the equipment manager asked.

"No, Joe Namath wears white," Greenwood said. "I won't wear white high-tops."

"You want me to paint them?"

"Paint them gold," Greenwood said.

Greenwood said he had just been kidding.

"Because I would have worn them black, it didn't matter to me," Greenwood said.

Greenwood should have known. Someone standing 6'7" normally gets what he asks for, which he discovered when he got to the locker room before the game and found two pairs of gold shoes in front of his locker.

Greenwood's lack of conformity did not sit well with the NFL and fines followed.

"I don't think the Steelers paid; the shoe company paid them," Greenwood said. "Initially the shoe company was paying a hundred dollars a game for me wearing those shoes. Then [the NFL] grandfathered in the shoe after that and I was allowed to wear them."

Opposing offenses feared those yellow shoes, but they did nothing to help the injury-riddled Steelers' offense. With Bradshaw and Hanratty on the shelf, Noll turned over the Steelers' offense to Joe Gilliam, a young black quarterback who had been an 11th-round draft selection from Tennessee State. The list of black quarterbacks to have played in the NFL to that point could be counted off on one hand: Willie Thrower, Marlin Briscoe, and James Harris.

Gilliam possessed one of the best arms in the league but was prone to throwing interceptions, which he did in abundance during one of the more memorable games of the 1973 season on a Monday night against the Dolphins in Miami.

"*Monday Night Football* was big," Dick Anderson said. "There was no cable and there was no *SportsCenter.* That was the only time you'd see the highlights from the Sunday games. So the highlights at halftime with Howard, that was big time. Everybody watched *Monday Night Football.*"

Anderson intercepted three Gilliam passes en route to a four-interception night. He returned two for touchdowns.

"That was all in the first half," Anderson said. "I almost had a fifth one in the third or fourth quarter, and my legs cramped and I couldn't get to it. I think the thing I remember most was after the fourth interception. I'm coming off the field and [Bill] Arnsparger comes up to me and hugs me and I'm just laughing, not believing it. The only thing more bizarre was the way the game ended."

Late in the game with the Dolphins leading by six points, Don Shula called for an intentional safety rather than risking a turnover or having a punt blocked. With colorful commentator Don Meredith completely confused in the TV booth—he thought Miami was trying for a first down—Bob Griese assessed his situation and surmised that the difficulty of Shula's assignment came down to winning a race against Greenwood and Joe Greene to the end zone. He did, and the Dolphins won 30–26, handing the Steelers their third consecutive defeat.

Though beaten up, the Steelers managed to regroup the next week, taking a 33–7 win against Houston in front of a disappointing Three Rivers Stadium crowd of 38,004.

Bradshaw continued to play quarterback. Young and strong, Bradshaw drilled the football with little touch during his early years, leading Noll to encourage his quarterback to throw the ball down the field. Good things could happen when Bradshaw threw the ball down the field—and it protected the receivers.

"When he threw short passes, our receivers would come back with slits in their fingers," Noll said. "Seriously, they'd go to catch the ball and that thing would come in there, it was coming so hard and spinning so hard that early on in his career, especially, we had to send [the receivers] down the field. We used to call them cancer shots, bruises on your chest because they couldn't catch it with their hands so they had to catch it with their chest and it would leave them black and blue."

Bradshaw had shown glimpses of brilliance during his four seasons with the Steelers, but he had not yet convinced Noll he could get the job done.

"There was never any question about his ability," Noll said. "It was a question about his dedication. How much he learned. What kind of example he was setting for the rest of the squad. Terry was a good time guy. It was a lot of those things he had to overcome."

Noll rode Bradshaw, which got under Bradshaw's sensitive skin.

"I knew [Bradshaw was sensitive] and I'm sure I got into him pretty good, because we had some of our offensive linemen who used to take him aside and calm him down and say don't pay attention to that guy, we'll be together, which was no bad thing," said Noll with a laugh.

Rocky Bleier said Bradshaw "wasn't Chuck's kind of guy."

"Meaning that Chuck would like to have a guy that's like Chuck—a guy that catches on quickly, understands defenses, and would be like, 'What about this Chuck? What if we ran this?' kind of guy," Bleier said. "That wasn't Brad. Brad was kind of a gunslinger. He dealt from emotion. I think it would be interesting if Chuck ever would admit it—though he never will—that to get the best out of Bradshaw he needed to give him hell."

Pittsburgh finished the 1973 season in San Francisco with a 37–14 win over the 49ers to give them a 10–4 record and earn a position in the playoffs as the wild-card team.

Winning their final two gave the Steelers a lift, but in the first game of the playoffs they would have to travel to Oakland to play the Raiders, who were riding a four-game win streak and still had the "Immaculate Reception" burning fresh in their minds.

Oakland had successfully made the transition from having quarterback Daryle Lamonica run the offense to Ken Stabler. But the Steelers would have Bradshaw back—and the knowledge that they seemed to have the Raiders' number.

Six weeks earlier the Steelers had met the Raiders in Oakland and came away 17–9 winners despite the fact that the Raiders' offense had doubled the Steelers' offensive output. In the playoff game the Raiders' offense continued to pummel the Steelers, only the outcome was different this time around.

In the first quarter, Marv Hubbard plunged over the goal line from a foot out to cap a 16-play, 82-yard drive and put the Raiders up 7–0. A George Blanda field goal of 25 yards pushed the lead to 10–0 before Preston Pearson hauled in a 4-yard touchdown pass from Bradshaw in the second quarter to make it 10–7 at the half.

The fact that the Raiders had dominated the game but led by only a field goal at the half fueled the Steelers' hopes for more magic like what they had found the previous year. In the other locker room the Raiders felt like they needed to put away the Steelers to such an extent that they could even handle a freak play such as the "Immaculate Reception."

Leaving no room for miracles, the Raiders continued to pound the Steelers on both sides of the ball in the second half. And Bradshaw, who managed to throw for 167 yards and two touchdowns, made a costly mistake.

With the Steelers trailing 16–7, a play-action pass was the call for the Steelers' offense. Bradshaw failed to preread the Raiders' coverage and threw a sideline pass to Pearson. Raiders cornerback Willie Brown was coming up off a zone and didn't make up his mind to go for the ball until the last instant. Darting in front of Pearson, Brown tipped Bradshaw's delivery in the air, juggling the ball once before hauling it in and racing 54 yards for a touchdown to put the Raiders up 23–7.

"It was the turning point of the game," Noll told United Press International afterward.

When time ran out, the scoreboard read Raiders 33, Steelers 14.

How thoroughly did Oakland dominate the game? On the ground the Raiders had 232 yards to the Steelers' 65; Harris and Fuqua combined to run for just 42 yards; the Raiders ran 74 offensive plays to 42; and the Raiders had the football approximately 42 minutes of the 60-minute game.

Oakland lost 27–10 the next week in the AFC Championship Game against the defending Super Bowl champion Dolphins, who went on to beat Minnesota to claim their second-consecutive Super Bowl victory.

While the Steelers were disappointed in their early exit from the postseason, the organization managed to regroup nicely during the 1974 draft—which Hall of Fame coach Bill Walsh would call "the best draft ever."

7

Amazing Draft

From the outset of Chuck Noll's tenure the Steelers made drafting the right people appear to be a foregone conclusion. Granted, high draft choices are the residue of poor performance, but even after the Steelers drafted lower the organization's propensity for finding talent continued to defy logic. And when the Steelers drafted in 1974, the result would be astounding.

Unbelievable as it seems, the Steelers drafted the following players using four of their five picks in the first five rounds: Lynn Swann, Jack Lambert, John Stallworth, and Mike Webster.

Following their playing careers, each would be elected to the Hall of Fame.

Based on the Steelers' 1973 won-lost record, they tied with four teams for the 20th draft choice, forcing a coin toss to determine draft position; the Steelers came away with the 21st draft position.

When the time came for the Steelers to draft in the first round, Swann was available and intrigued the Steelers.

The acrobatic receiver from USC had caught 95 passes, more than anybody in the school's illustrious football history, and he was the Trojans' third-best punt-return man of all time. He also earned a letter in track and field, once long-jumping 24 feet, 10 inches; his best 100-yard-dash time was 9.8 seconds. Swann, whose mother named him Lynn due to her desire for a girl rather than her third boy, took ballet lessons as a youngster. Those ballet skills would be cited as a contributing factor for the graceful leaping moves he developed.

But the Steelers had concerns about Swann's speed.

"He didn't have a real good time in the 40," Noll said. "We went out and got a 4.6 on him, and BLESTO had him like 4.8. But I could not believe he wasn't faster because on film he was outrunning these defensive backs and doing all these things."

Noll discounted the use of the stopwatch for complete accuracy.

"Sometimes if the situation's not right you don't get the right time, or if the scout doesn't give you an accurate time because of the way he handled the watch, either starting it too fast or too slow," Noll said.

The Steelers finally decided the evidence weighed in Swann's favor and made him their first selection.

When the Steelers approached their second pick they were cautiously enamored with Lambert.

Lambert had a body like no linebacker in the NFL, standing 6'5", 210 pounds. He appeared to be too lanky and tall and lacking the necessary weight to play the position. When the Steelers took a firsthand look to see Lambert for themselves, they were shocked at his size, which clouded their interest.

"In person, he did not look like a football player," Noll said.

But within that lean frame beat the heart of a champion. Lambert above all else was a football player, and his body was deceptively strong dating back to all the summers he'd worked on his grandfather's farm. If his body didn't support the fact he had been born to play the game, the gap where his front teeth had been suggested otherwise. The vacancy of his front choppers had come via a collision with a teammate during basketball practice at Crestwood High in Mantua, Ohio, and left Lambert with a menacing look that complemented his spirit on the football field.

Don Nottingham had been a senior at Kent State (now known as Kent University) when Lambert was a freshman. Even then you couldn't help but notice the rangy youngster.

"Jack was about 165 pounds," Nottingham said. "Just tough as nails, but really skinny—mean as heck and tough. They had him playing defensive end as a freshman. I remember my whole senior year they'd run the other team's defense and he'd come roaring in and you'd knock him ass over tin cups and he'd come roaring in the next time."

Lambert became Kent State's starting middle linebacker with three games remaining in his sophomore season, but he was slated to return to defensive end as a junior until the starter quit the team right before the season began.

"The rest is history," Nottingham said. "He was your good, northeast Ohio football player. That's what we like to do. We like to be physical."

The Steelers continued to review films. Frame by frame Lambert's productivity and determination continued to scream out.

"He was something special," Noll said. "You looked at him on film and there was no question this guy knew how to play the game."

A story from a Kent State practice helped sway the Steelers toward making Lambert their second pick. Kent State's football field had been too muddy to practice on the day a Steelers representative visited, so the team practiced in a nearby parking lot. On one particular play Lambert tried to tackle a ball carrier and dove on the parking lot. In the process he absorbed a painful dose of cinders to his body. Disregarding the pain, Lambert reported to the defensive huddle picking out cinders while he waited for the next play.

The Steelers had traded their third-round pick, which brought them to Stallworth. If ever a player personified the Steelers' proficiency at finding talent, he was the guy. Chuck Noll and the scouting department were so enamored with the wide receiver from Alabama A&M that they almost selected him with their second pick.

Growing up in Tuscaloosa, Alabama, Stallworth had a unique perspective shaped by a frightening experience when he was nine. After playing outside one day, he came home feeling feverish. His fever progressed to the shivers and culminated in his becoming paralyzed. His parents feared their son had polio.

"And they could not find out what had gone wrong," Stallworth said. "I went through a battery of tests, and all I could do was just sort of sit in that hospital bed looking out. I know I scared my parents to death.

"I remember one time when I got up to go take an x-ray and I sort of passed out on the floor. And my mom couldn't look at me because I knew she was to the point of tears and she didn't want me to see her crying. When she finally looked at me that look on her face is something I carry with me today. But I remembered being in there and seeing her, and really looking outside and thinking if I ever get out of this bed I was going to do something to be remembered, that if I had to leave this world that I need to do something where people will remember John Stallworth."

Turned out Stallworth had a viral infection.

"That was a tremendous motivating factor for me—coming face-to-face with my own mortality and trying to handle that at nine years old," Stallworth said.

Stallworth attended Tuscaloosa High School where he played football on the same team with one of his best friends, whose father had played football for Alabama A&M. The University of Alabama was not recruiting a lot of black athletes at the time, so his friend's father recommended Stallworth to Alabama A&M, and Stallworth ended up attending the school. Stallworth's friend was Sylvester Croom, who went on to play football at Alabama and would become the head coach of Mississippi State in 2004, thereby becoming the first black head football coach in the Southeastern Conference.

Stallworth excelled at Alabama A&M, and observing that excellence was Bill Nunn.

"Bill was *the* black college scout," Stallworth said. "He was known throughout the black colleges and conferences as *the* scout. Bill also named an All-American team for the *Pittsburgh Courier*, everybody knew that, and for us that was *the* black All-American team to be named to. We didn't make the big ones. We were never on Bob Hope's show. So if you made [the *Pittsburgh Courier's* team] that was the pinnacle for us."

Whenever Nunn sat in the stands the players knew. That would be big news, more for his picking the All-American team than for being a Steelers scout.

Nunn liked what he saw in Stallworth, and Noll fell in love with the idea of pairing Stallworth with Swann. Whether other teams didn't like what they saw, or they lacked the necessary information to properly evaluate Stallworth, they weren't enamored with him when they had the chance to select him in the first three rounds.

"When I was still in college, I had some bad times in the 40, and Bill [Nunn] had seen me play a couple of games against some teams he had respect for, and I had good games, which probably made him think, 'This kid's running faster than the times would indicate,'" Stallworth said. "So he came and got me out on a better field than the ones I had had the times on before. And I came up with a better time. He was the only scout that had that time on me."

Stallworth said his time in the 40 was deceiving because of his lack of technique.

"There's a technique for running the 40 to get your best time," Stallworth said. "If you come out of the blocks well, you can do well. I did not have that technique. I actually ran track in high school. But I ran middle distances, so starts were not something I concentrated on. You need to stay low coming out of the blocks."

Times in the 40 could not measure game speed, a facet of speed the evaluators of talent might or might not take into consideration.

"I think there is such a thing as game speed, competitive speed," Stallworth said. "There are certain guys when they're in that situation they run a little bit faster. Just running a straight line and trying to reach a certain point as fast as you can doesn't really motivate certain players.

Chuck Noll arrived in Pittsburgh with the firm belief that a solid defense would be the foundation upon which to build a championship team for long-suffering Steelers fans.

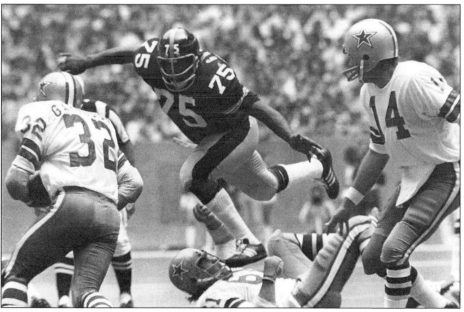

With that in mind, Noll made a relatively unknown defensive lineman out of North Texas State by the name of Joe Greene his top pick (fourth overall) in his first draft in 1969. Greene proved to be a playmaker from day one.

Greene was named Defensive Rookie of the Year and helped bring some respectability to Pittsburgh's defense despite a miserable 1–13 record in 1969.

What would become Noll's and the Steelers' trademark for working draft magic was even more evident in their 10th-round selection in 1969: an even lesser known defensive end from Arkansas A&M named L. C. Greenwood (No. 68). *Photo courtesy of Focus on Sports/Getty Images.*

When the Steelers first selected him, Greenwood was considered a projection pick by most, but he wound up playing in six Pro Bowls as a Steeler. *Photo courtesy of Focus on Sports/Getty Images.*

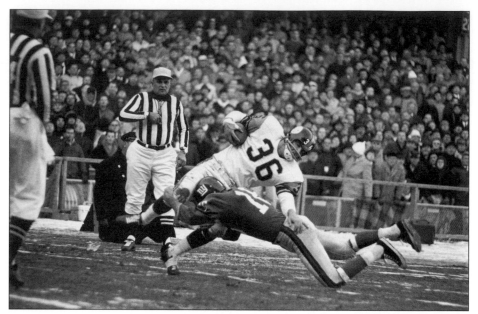

Linebacker Andy Russell (No. 36), shown here returning an interception against the Giants, was one of the veterans Noll "inherited" when he arrived in 1969. *Photo courtesy of Bettmann/Corbis.*

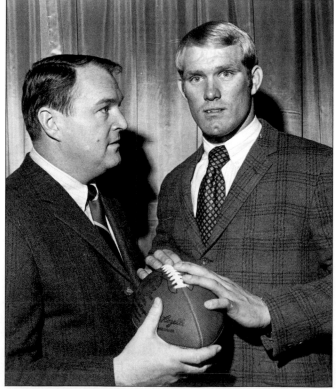

Noll's and the Steelers' fortunes really began to turn in 1970 when the flip of a coin resulted in their earning the first selection in the draft and the right to choose a cannon-armed quarterback from Louisiana Tech named Terry Bradshaw.

Bradshaw said he'd hoped he would get drafted by a struggling franchise all along, where "if I made it, they would make it with me."

Mel Blount, a cornerback from Southern University, was another product of the 1970 draft and became one of the cornerstones of the vaunted Steelers defense.

Jack Ham (left) and
Dwight White (No. 78,
below) both joined the
team in 1971, a season
that saw the young
Steelers show some
signs of what the future
potentially held.

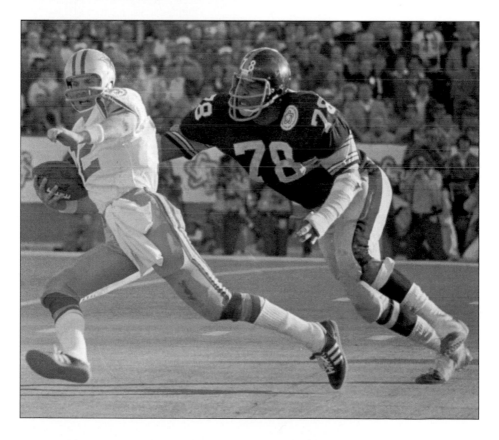

Noll made another "suspect" draft choice when he took Franco Harris ahead of Robert Newhouse and Lydell Mitchell in 1972. Harris, however, excelled in his rookie year, and the rest of the team jelled enough to finish the season 11–3. *Photo courtesy of Getty Images.*

And it really didn't motivate me. But again, I think my situation was more a lack of technique for running the 40."

Stallworth learned only recently that his college coach had given Nunn the only game film they had featuring Stallworth with the promise Nunn would pass along the film to other organizations. Nunn fessed up by telling Stallworth, "John, I never did that, so I want to apologize to your coach."

"I told him it turned out OK," Stallworth said.

Had other organizations known about Stallworth, he could easily have been selected in the first round. Some might have been disappointed in not getting drafted until the fourth round; Stallworth wasn't.

"I really didn't have any expectations about where I might get drafted," Stallworth said. "I didn't have anybody to talk to. There wasn't a former Alabama A&M player in the league who was in the NFL that I could ask what he thought.

"I had some folks who said I was going to go high, higher than four. In the back of my mind I'm thinking maybe round two. Yeah, a part of me thought going in the fourth round was maybe a little bit of a downer. But as far as coming out of Alabama A&M is concerned, we had never had a guy get drafted in the fourth round, or the fifth round. I was the highest draft choice to come out of that school. I was kind of happy about that."

Noll remembered that neither Swann nor Stallworth had great times in the 40.

"But when we got them in we got better times on them," Noll said.

When it came time for the Steelers to make their fifth selection of the 1974 draft, Noll and company remembered a performance by an undersized offensive lineman from Wisconsin that had caught their eye while watching film.

"We looked at film of All-Star games," Noll said. "I think it was the East West Shrine Game and then the Hula Bowl. And [Webster] was supposed to be questionable size. He wasn't tall enough. Six feet. Wasn't real big—at that time he might have weighed 225. But he was playing center and there was a tackle from UCLA playing opposite of him, who was rated real high, who weighed about 290. Everybody thought he was the greatest thing. Mike took him and knocked him five yards up the field, just crushing him. I said, 'If this guy's a first-rounder, then what's [Webster]?"

Webster became the Steelers' fifth selection.

Webster had grown up on a dairy farm in Harshaw, Wisconsin, where daily chores in the early morning preceded his attendance at Rhinelander High School after an 18-mile bus ride. Rhinelander's football coach noticed Webster and asked him to go out for the team his junior year only to be told Webster had work obligations to the family and there was the bus commute to and from school. Wisely, the coach offered to drive Webster home from practice, and just like that Webster became a football player.

The Steelers drafted Webster in the fifth round. He would gain 30 pounds and become the poster child for the rugged Steelers offensive line. A generation of football fans would grow to recognize Webster's beefy biceps when he grabbed the football and prepared to snap it.

Art Rooney Jr., the Steelers' player personnel chief at the time, would say of the team's four splendid selections among the twenty-one selections they had in the 1974 draft: "We got out of the right side of the bed that year. The stars were lined up."

Nunn called the 1974 draft "the draft that set the foundation."

Stallworth had no idea at that point that he had been a critical selection in what is still considered the greatest draft in NFL history.

"None," Stallworth said. "I knew nothing of Jack Lambert and Mike Webster. I knew something of Lynn because of USC and he played in the Rose Bowl. And I think he caught a big pass in the Senior Bowl. He was on the North squad and I was on the South. He caught a big pass in the end and they won that game. But I never heard of the other guys.

"I don't think any of us had a sense of how that draft was going to turn out. Even after one season you can't tell. The test of a player comes two, three years down the road. Your expectations as an organization are that your number one is going to help you right away, your number two, maybe a little less than that. Getting to four and five you're drafting for the future. For Webster and me, we came in and we were able to get some valuable playing time in that first year."

In addition to the Fab Four selections, the Steelers signed two free agents who became standouts for the team in Donnie Shell, who became a five-time Pro Bowl strong safety, and tight end Randy Grossman.

Why would a free agent choose the Steelers? In Shell's case, it came down to Denver, where a friend of his already played, and Pittsburgh, an organization Shell's South Carolina State coach had told him about.

"He had a little bit of a relationship with [Nunn]," Shell said. "He told me a little about the organization—they were a fair organization, hard-working people, and they'd give you a fair opportunity. So instead of going to Denver with my buddy, I chose Pittsburgh."

Noll conceded the obvious about the Steelers' drafts. "It's nice to be lucky," Noll said. "You never know how it's going to turn out. Fortunately, we got some guys who wanted to produce."

8

Super Bowl Season

The 1974 season began with several incidents outside of the Steelers' control.

First, never failing to look for ways to tweak its game and increase its popularity, the NFL had made several rules changes prior to the 1974 season. Goal posts were moved to the back of the end zone from where they once rested on the front of the end zone; a sudden-death overtime period was added to regular-season games; missed field goals kicked from a distance outside the 20-yard line were given to the opposing team at the original line of scrimmage after the miss; roll blocking and cutting of wide receivers was eliminated; holding penalties were reduced from 15 to 10 yards; wide receivers were no longer allowed to use crack back blocks below the waist; and the amount of downfield contact by the defense to receivers was restricted.

Second, in 1974, a new professional football league came into being.

The American public's appetite for football was seen as insatiable, and the World Football League was formed. Franchises were put in 12 cities, and in mid-March 1974 the WFL held a draft of NFL players. Any players not under contract or those players whose contracts were about to expire were fair game. The WFL's presence as a competing faction forced the NFL to loosen its purse strings in regard to player salaries. Many NFL veterans, including Oakland's Ken Stabler and Miami's Larry Csonka, Paul Warfield, and Jim Kiick, could be counted among the more than 50 or so players who said they would jump leagues when their NFL contracts ran out. The three Dolphins eventually signed deals totaling $2.7 million to play for the Toronto Northmen beginning in the 1975 season.

By season's end, the WFL found itself in dire financial shape. There were stories of players and coaches not receiving paychecks and of equipment and uniforms being impounded to take care of some of the teams' debts. Mercifully, the WFL's season ended on December 5, 1974, when the Birmingham Americans defeated the Florida Blazers in the WFL's "World Bowl."

Finally, and perhaps most immediately significant, with plenty of foreshadowing, the players went on strike without having a new contract between their union, the National Football League Players Association, and the league.

"There were rumors of a strike even at the time of the draft," John Stallworth said. "We got letters—at least I think most of the draftees got letters—from the union saying don't go. And we got calls. But I think most rookies felt like they hadn't made the team yet, so they all reported."

The strike began July 9 with the major issue being free agency. Free agents were players who did not sign new contracts with their teams when their current contracts expired. Once the contract ended, any team could bid for a player's services. The owners would not agree to a free-agent system.

Camps opened anyway.

"Mostly rookies there," Stallworth said. "There were a couple of veterans, but they were the guys who felt their careers were kind of borderline as far as whether they would make the team. We didn't get the chance to see the frontline guys. We went through two-a-days and never saw the veterans. We played a preseason game in New Orleans, and Mel Blount, who was living in New Orleans, came to the game, so Mel was the first Pittsburgh Steeler of note that I saw."

Stallworth immediately bought into Chuck Noll and the way he conducted business.

"He was the head coach, that was my first impression of him," Stallworth said. "From my history with head coaches I knew he was the guy who was going to lead the team as far as preparing us for what we need to do. I always thought Chuck was very meticulous.

"I came from an environment in college where you went out to practice and you didn't know what you were going to do that day. You just knew you were going to be there until the coach said it was time to go. With Chuck I found the way he ran practices very refreshing. He would outline everything we were going to be doing every day. At practice, we would be doing this for five minutes, this for ten minutes, and this for fifteen minutes. Go over here for another ten or fifteen minutes. Add it all up and our plan is to be out there two hours and fifteen minutes or somewhere in there. And this is why we're going to do this or that. We hope that doing this we'll get better at this, better at this. He also talked a lot about his philosophy of winning—what it meant, where the emphasis was going to be. He talked about going through the course of a week. You put the game plan in and go through the repetitions of the plays you're going to run and why you're going to run them. By Friday's practice we should not be making any mistakes. Chuck made it very clear where we were going and why we were going there. What he thought it was going to take for us to win and be successful. And I thought that was great because I had never experienced that before."

Stallworth went to camp housing insecurities about how someone from Alabama A&M would stack up against players from the bigger schools. In the back of his mind he had no way of knowing if indeed a major difference existed between the caliber of talent at the level of football where he had played and the caliber of football they played at Ohio State and USC; he just didn't know. He did know the other players in camp were human, and he knew that every once in a while he would drop a pass here or there. So he didn't feel the pressure to an extent that if he missed a pass he would get cut.

"I did not feel very comfortable how my talent played against theirs until I got to orientation camp with the Steelers and I got the chance to see Swann," Stallworth said. "I got the chance to see guys who went to bigger schools. And I quickly realized, and it was no slight against them or their talents, but I felt I could play as well as they could. Everything was new. I sort of committed myself to doing the things I could do to make the team. And everything else was out of my control and I just decided not to worry about it."

Pittsburgh coaches were afforded more time than normal to watch their rookies play. Normally coaches don't have the luxury of spending much time evaluating the rookies because they have to get their teams ready for the season, meaning unless you were a high draft choice, you had better make a quick impression. Because of the strike, this wasn't the case in 1974.

"We were able to see what [some of the rookies] could do," Noll said. "When the veterans came in, [the rookies] were very competitive, and as a result we had a lot of rookies make our football team that year."

Stallworth and the other rookies felt the benefit of the extra attention.

"The fact the veterans were not there when we first got there helped a lot," Stallworth said. "I got more reps with the first team of guys that were there and playing time in the games. Gaining more experience in the pre-season sped up my development. The guys that were veterans, Frank Lewis and Ron Shanklin, if they had been there, maybe [neither] Swanny nor I would have gotten as many reps and developed as fast as we did."

Joe Gilliam, who had been in the league only since 1972, was one veteran who was an exception. He didn't feel his career to date afforded him the luxury of going out on strike, and he reported to the Steelers camp along with the rookies. The strategy paid off for Gilliam.

On August 13 federal mediator W. J. Usery asked the players to return to their teams for a two-week cooling-off period. Believing they were unified in their resolve, the players agreed. When the two weeks were up, the NFLPA voted twenty-five to one to call off the strike even though they didn't have a final agreement in place. The NFLPA took the case to federal court and eventually won most of their demands; however, that did not happen until 1976.

Sports provide an escape for many fans, so any time the real world intrudes on the fantasy, most fans are left with bitter feelings. The 1974 strike was credited for a downturn in the NFL's popularity, interrupting what had been an unprecedented growth—and profit—in the sport. Stadiums experienced "no-shows"—empty seats where fans that had bought tickets did not attend. The national economy wasn't in great health; gas prices soared due to the fuel shortage, which contributed to others opting not to purchase tickets to NFL games that would set them back anywhere from five dollars to fifteen. Declining ticket sales and TV ratings hit the NFL where it hurt most—in the wallet.

In the midst of this downturn, Pittsburgh romped undefeated through their preseason with Gilliam at quarterback filling the air with footballs. Gilliam looked terrific, and Noll named him the starting quarterback prior to the opener against Baltimore, which made for a tumultuous beginning to the 1974 season.

Gilliam's starting role came six years after Marlin Briscoe of the Denver Broncos became pro football's first black starting quarterback, and the Steelers demolished the Colts 30–0 in the opener. The man known as "Jefferson Street Joe" for a boulevard near his Tennessee State alma mater, Gilliam led the Steelers to four wins, a loss, and a tie in his first six starts. Quarterbacks called the plays for the Steelers at the time, and during a game with the Denver Broncos in the second week of the season, which went into overtime and ended in a 35–35 tie, Gilliam had continued calling passes and had ignored Franco Harris and the running game. When the game was over Gilliam had thrown a team-record 50 passes and had earned the scorn of Noll, who did not care for Gilliam's play calling.

The following week Oakland played Pittsburgh at Three Rivers Stadium. Gilliam threw two interceptions while completing just eight of thirty-one passes in a 17–0 Raiders win. By the end of the game, many Steelers fans were chanting for the return of Bradshaw. A racial tone could be felt within the chants. Gilliam soon began fielding hate mail and death threats. And Noll continued to have a hard time accepting Gilliam's wide-open style of playing quarterback, which conflicted with the percentage football he favored.

Noll reinstated Bradshaw on October 28, and the Steelers rolled in a 24–17 win over Atlanta, a game that saw Harris rush for 141 yards.

Noll's track record indicated he was color blind in regard to race. He had grown up in a racially mixed neighborhood in Cleveland.

"There was no 'You're black and you're white,'" Noll said. "We were all the same and we tried to treat all of our people the same. All we were doing was evaluating football players and what they could contribute to the team. It didn't really matter whether they spoke English, what color they were, or whatever."

Gilliam, however, felt the demotion was racially motivated.

"I was shocked," Gilliam told *The Tennessean* in a 1999 interview. "I thought if you played well you got to play. I guess I didn't understand the significance of being a black quarterback at the time."

Stallworth said there was a realization by most of the players on the team that "Joe had issues."

"And that we saw them," Stallworth said. "We saw the effects of them. And we knew long term that was not going to be good for the team. The public looked at that as here we are, we've got a black quarterback, and we know nobody wants a black quarterback. Most of the fans want the other guy in there. Get the black guy out of there. I don't know that as a team that ever entered our mind, that we ever thought that Joe was being replaced because he was black."

Suggesting Noll had any racial motive in benching Gilliam had no foundation according to Stallworth.

"We knew, for those of us who knew Chuck, we mostly all did, that the reason Joe was not there was because of some habits he had that were detrimental to him as an individual and certainly detrimental to us as a football team," Stallworth said.

But opinions did vary on Gilliam, producing a situation that could have divided the team. Andy Russell called the situation "complicated."

"Gilliam was a brilliant player," Russell said. "I mean absolutely, astoundingly good. His arm was as strong as there was. He was an awesome talent. He could throw it a long way. He was just an awesome talent. Was he better than Terry? In some cases yes, certainly other cases no. He got himself in trouble with drugs. The drugs ate him up. Once that happened he's done. He wouldn't do what Noll told him to do and he got benched, even though he had just been on the cover of *Sports Illustrated* and even though he was this brilliant player, leading the league in passing. And Noll benches him.

"The danger is it being seen as a racial kind of thing. But it clearly wasn't. It was a coaching decision that I think had to be made. When that decision was made I think it was strictly because he wasn't doing what Noll wanted him to do, which basically was, on third-and-5, give the ball to Franco. You know, it's not hard. Joe wanted to throw the ball."

Gilliam joined the Steelers during a period when black quarterbacks were not fashionable. Many were converted to defensive backs, wide receivers, and running backs, but the unspoken opinion said black quarterbacks didn't have the mental faculties to play quarterback in the NFL.

"When Joe Gilliam came to Pittsburgh we had Joe Gilliam, Terry Bradshaw, and Terry Hanratty," White said. "Bradshaw was young; he was getting up the learning curve, but he was playing terrible. Terry Hanratty, so-so, lukewarm. Then here comes this young black quarterback. He is hell-bent on being a quarterback. 'I don't want to be a wide receiver. I don't want to be a punter. I want to be a quarterback.' Came from a good family, great father, who was a coach. Great team, Tennessee State, came up here. Make a long story short, actually played better than Bradshaw, OK. He was on the cover of *Sports Illustrated* opening up the season. This was big news."

White sounded perplexed about why there was any sort of quarterback controversy given the fact the Steelers were winning with Gilliam playing the position.

"You remember that old rule of thumb, if it ain't broke, don't fix it?" White said. "You don't want to break up a winning combination. Well that didn't apply here."

A public opinion poll that ran in the newspaper asked Steelers fans if they wanted Gilliam or Bradshaw as their quarterback.

"It was the *Pittsburgh Post-Gazette*, you sent it in and they tallied the response," White said. "And after that poll—obviously the votes came out for Bradshaw—I remember us being at a meeting room and Chuck

Noll going to the chalkboard and he said, 'Brad, you're up this week.' And the rest of us looked at each other like 'Ooohkaay.' And of course the basis of this was 'Bradshaw was always my starting quarterback.' My point is that was like pulling the rug out from under Joe.

"We came out of a period where good guys wore white hats, you work hard you earn it. We thought, Joe thought, he had earned the job. We were winning. He got screwed. Joe was never the same after that— never the same. And I'm not supporting his behavior, because he should have handled the situation differently. But when you're a young kid and you're high-strung like that, when you look at your whole dream and you thought you've succeeded, and then you get a knife in the back so to speak, he kind of went off."

Mike Wagner said the team was lucky Gilliam's situation didn't fester and "become more of an explosive thing."

"I loved Joe Gilliam," Wagner said. "His locker was near mine. I saw a lot of the exuberance, but also some of the pain that Joe suffered off and on the field. It was a very hard time for Joe in Pittsburgh. He had some extreme highs and some extreme lows. I think it was kind of a situation where if you look back on it in a historical sense, it was Bradshaw's destiny to lead the Steelers to a number of championships. Terry was a quarterback of destiny. Roger Staubach was a quarterback of destiny. Joe Montana. These guys had tremendous skills. They had the tools. It might have been better for [Gilliam] to play somewhere else."

The Steelers had great depth. Players sitting on their bench, like Gilliam, could easily have started for other teams; Mike Webster did not start until the final game of 1975, and Donnie Shell didn't start until 1977.

"When Noll, and his staff, and Rooney, accumulated this kind of talent on the team, it's got to be really, really hard for players who could be starting and performing at a high level for other teams but they were still here in Pittsburgh," Wagner said. "And I think that was Joe's situation. You want to have that kind of talent at backup from a team standpoint, player standpoint. But from a friend standpoint, it was tough."

Gilliam did not see much playing time during the 1975 season and was cut the following year amid speculation about his drug use. He caught on with the New Orleans Saints but was dismissed for breaking team rules. Gilliam never played in the NFL again, and his addiction to heroin and cocaine left him homeless and living on the streets from time to time. Three years after apparently staying clean, Gilliam died of a heart attack in 2000 at age 50.

"Looking back at the situation from Joe's perspective, he was really crushed," White said. "I make no excuse for what he did; I even told him, 'Joe, you handled this poorly,' but from a human resources standpoint, the Steelers and Joe could have handled the situation better, differently.

"Most times all you hear about it, 'Joe Gilliam was this and that and he was a drug head, blah, blah, blah,' but then things happen in people's lives that make them react foolishly, sometimes irrationally, and sometimes stupid. And that was probably a combination of all three with Joe. The question is, what was the catalyst? We may never know. But if you understand what I said, that's my take on Joe Gilliam. As far as I knew he didn't have any problems [early in the 1974 season]. It kind of all bubbled up. Just like 'oh screw it.' He started doing everything that was the antithesis of what he should have been doing. You didn't handle it right, I'm not defending you Joe, but if I had a human resources hat on, yeah, you got kind of screwed around. Yes you did. Nobody wants to talk about that. They want to go right to the drugs."

White said he didn't want to get into it but that there were "some other things that happened, other than the drugs, prior to that."

"There were a lot of things that happened on that football team over the years, and [with] the success that we had, the bad stuff people sweep under the carpet," White said. "But just like any corporation or any business, you've got some skeletons. It's just not a real popular thing when everybody is winning and everybody is at the party, for you to put a turd in the punch bowl. But there was a lot more good than bad."

Until Bradshaw went through the benching, his teammates viewed him as a star up on a lofty pedestal in relation to the team's pecking order. They had seen Noll ride him hard, but he remained the team's Joe Namath, an outgoing guy who talked well and got all the media attention. Within the locker room Bradshaw was perceived—fairly or not—as someone who didn't know what it meant to earn his spot. The Gilliam ordeal changed that. When Bradshaw didn't play he could have sulked and felt sorry for himself, or he could put on his best face. Bradshaw chose the latter, joking about his situation and keeping up a good face. As a result, his teammates began to see Bradshaw as more vulnerable than they had in the past, which made him more of a regular guy in the clubhouse.

In addition to the key rookie additions to the 1974 squad, the Steelers welcomed running back Rocky Bleier to a starting role.

Late in Bleier's rookie season the army drafted him, and by 1969 his moves were confined to those made as a specialist fourth class in

Vietnam, which is where he nearly lost his life near rice paddies outside Heip Duc, approximately 200 miles north of Saigon.

Bleier first took a rifle bullet in the left thigh.

"When I got shot I thought somebody was behind me and threw a rock at me to get my attention," Bleier said. "When that initial impact didn't go away I knew I'd been shot."

Gauze was wrapped around Bleier's wound, but he could not be sent to a hospital for further attention because his platoon remained engaged in battle. Bleier's commanding officer did have time to tease him that he had received the "million-dollar wound."

"Meaning they might send you home, but at the very least you're out of the field for a while, or you might get duty in the rear, who knows," Bleier said.

During a firefight later that day, a grenade flew into the area where Bleier and his commanding officer had taken cover.

The grenade "hit my commanding officer on the back and it didn't go off," Bleier said. "It bounded toward where I was. I just reacted and tried to jump out of the way."

The grenade exploded under his right foot, leaving shrapnel in his big toe and instep. Bleier's platoon and the Vietcong continued to fight, which added to the delay in Bleier's receiving medical attention.

"We had guys dropping here and there," Bleier said. "The medic came by and he'd already been wounded; he had a bandage around his throat where he'd been hit. He cut off my boot and took a look, wrapped a sterile gauze around it, that's the best we could do. We were in a firefight. You got your adrenaline pumping. You've got all this action going on. They ended up dragging me out of there. Guys dragged me and carried me, seemed like forever, probably a four-hour trek out of there. When the adrenaline wore off the pain started to hit."

Throughout his time in Vietnam, Bleier thought about resuming his NFL career when he returned home. So understanding the reality about the chances of a running back with combat wounds playing football accompanied his thoughts while he recovered. Three days after Bleier received his wounds he found a blessing in the hospital.

"Right across from me in this little ward was a triple amputee," Bleier said. "He'd been there a while—this was still 'in country'—I hadn't been flown to Tokyo yet. This guy would get out of his bed in his wheelchair and he'd wheel himself over to each of the guys and he'd say, 'How you doing? What's your name? They're good docs, they'll take care of you.'

"I thought to myself, wow, if anybody should be pissed off about the results of war it should be this guy. Yet he chose to have this attitude. It was sort of an infectious thing. You tell yourself, I'm not that bad off. I've got everything in place. You still go through the pain, you still go through all the steps of 'why me' depression. But at least I'm here."

He left Southeast Asia a decorated war hero having been awarded a Bronze Star and a Purple Heart. Once he returned stateside, operations on his foot for bone spurs and scar tissue followed. Throughout his painful ordeal, Bleier still harbored the dream of returning to the Steelers by training camp in 1970. Art Rooney had sent Bleier postcards during his tour of duty, and Bleier was determined to play once again for the Chief's football team. When he did show up for training camp, his less-than-blazing speed had dwindled.

"Rocky worked very hard to overcome all the physical problems he had trying to come back after the wounds," Noll said. "When we first timed him he did not run very fast."

Hanratty had been Bleier's teammate at Notre Dame and told his friend he might want to consider attending law school. Pro football looked like a pipe dream. Bleier would not quit even after Noll cut him in the final cut for the 1970 team. Bleier received a call from Dan Rooney the next day telling him they wanted the Steelers doctors to take a look at him to see if they could do anything more for him. He was placed on the injured-reserve list.

"They paid me a salary, let me heal, and I was able to hang around," Bleier said. "At least hanging around wasn't the end, you're outta here.

"The fortunate thing was I had no responsibilities; I wasn't married; I didn't have a family. I didn't have to provide. I didn't know what I was going to do with my life except I wanted to come back and try to play something I enjoyed. That was my focus. I could be pretty selfish in my own comeback."

Bleier was placed on the team's taxi squad in 1971.

"That let me hang around another year," Bleier said. "Then I made the team in '72."

Bleier was used on special teams during the 1972 season, and by 1973 he was used sparingly as a blocking back in short-yardage situations. Bleier continued to work hard.

"In the off-season he spent a lot of time conditioning, weight training, and otherwise, and when he came back he went from like a 4.9 40 to a 4.6 40, and that caught the coaches' eyes," Noll said. "And he was stronger and more durable, and ended up being a helluva blocker, pass receiver out of the backfield."

In the fourth game of the 1974 season against Houston, Bleier's efforts began to pay off. Harris had gotten banged up and the other backs weren't having good days, so Noll inserted Bleier and Preston Pearson in the backfield. By the end of the game, Bleier had 48 yards on the ground—which was monumental considering his career total going into the Houston game was 70 yards—and the Steelers had a 13–7 road win. The next week the Steelers played the Chiefs in Kansas City and Bleier started for the first time. In the aftermath of the game, Noll gained Bleier as one of his believers.

When the team met to watch the films from the game, Noll congratulated them on beating the Chiefs, who still had marquee players such as Willie Lanier, Buck Buchanan, and Bobby Bell. Then he began to talk about the importance of basics, fundamentals, and creating habits. Noll pointed out that players experienced a gradual period of decline when they didn't create those habits and didn't pay attention to the details. As an example he cited Kansas City's left guard, whom the Steelers had gone through like a turnstile to sack Mike Livingston numerous times.

"He told us in practice it was so easy to let teammates slide through one way or the other then [tell] yourself, 'I'll stay in front of my player in the game; in the game I won't do this,'" Bleier said. "He said in the game, when it's hot or cold and there's a blizzard or it's raining and you're tired and you've been beaten up, you don't think, all you do is react. And the only way to react is with the habits you've created.

"From my point of view, I'm like, 'holy shit, if [Noll] is going to take this whole win that we had and boil it down to an opponent's position, I've got to respect this guy. He knows his shit.' For me, that was that one little instance. Afterward, I'm like, 'I'm on board. I understand.'"

Two games later Bleier started in the backfield alongside Harris, who gained 156 yards. Bleier tallied 78.

"We were using him as a blocker for Franco," Noll said. "He was a good halfback blocker. We were running what we called the 'special inside,' and he had to block the defensive end. He did a great job of it and it really contributed to Franco's success."

Bleier's presence as a blocker in the backfield helped the running game, which ran behind a diminutive offensive line. The Steelers' offensive line averaged 247 pounds at the beginning of the 1975 season, making them one of the smaller units in the league. Size aside, the Steelers' offensive line got the job done.

Integral to the unit's success were several tricks employed by the offensive line coach Dan Radakovich. Because of their smallish size, Steelers offensive linemen were tossed aside on occasion by opposing linemen. To help fight the grabbing, the equipment manager's mother-in-law tailored all the offensive linemen's jerseys so tight that they could not be grabbed. A healthy application of double-sided tape to his linemen's shoulder pads made clutching their jerseys nearly impossible.

Radakovich also introduced area blocking, a technique that saw Steelers linemen bounce opponents around like pinballs. And he instructed his linemen to fire out their arms at their opponents like punches, which led the Steelers' offensive linemen to wear padded gloves to help protect their hands while using this technique.

Still, the real strength of the team remained the defense, which had developed into the best in the NFL. Adding Jack Lambert's athleticism and attitude provided the final piece of the puzzle.

Shortly after Lambert learned he had become property of the Steelers, he began to make weekend trips to Pittsburgh from Kent State to begin learning the defense, going over countless reels of tape with linebackers coach Woody Widenhofer.

"He really impressed me," Jack Ham said. "I just thought, 'Boy that's the kind of guy who understands what it takes to be a player in the National Football League. The preparation he's doing, he's way ahead of time.'"

During training camp, with most of the veterans out on strike, Lambert played outside linebacker. Ham's return and an injury at middle linebacker prompted Lambert's move to the middle when the incumbent went down with an injury.

"[Lambert] was a tall, raw-boned, skinny guy," Russell said. "They actually tried him on the outside as well as the middle. They weren't sure where he would fit in. We had a middle backer, Henry Davis, and he had gone down in the first exhibition game. There had been a strike that year, which meant that some of the rookies had gotten more playing time because the veterans didn't come. And then when we came in, the starter went down. Lambert got this big opportunity to get in there, and [he] took over."

Lambert did well from the beginning, as if predestined to succeed.

"He wasn't any more devastating against the run than [Dick] Butkus, [Tommy] Nobis, or [Ray] Nitschke [prominent middle linebackers of the era]," Russell said. "He'd still make the same plays, but he made more plays because he was faster. And he rarely missed a tackle. He may not have been as explosive a hitter since he wasn't as heavy, but on the pass side, which was 50 percent of the game even then, he was dramatically different."

The Steelers could play defenses other teams couldn't dream of because of the things Lambert allowed them to do. He could cover the first back out on the weak side, which allowed Ham to go out on the out end and ignore the back. Or Lambert could cover the tight end. He could do things other middle linebackers could not in part because he could run a 4.7 40. Because of Lambert's size, speed, and intelligence, the Steelers were able to play more complex pass coverages when most teams would have to use a simple zone. He had to play Cover Two, which required him to run down the field chasing a tight end or a running back or settling in a zone to make it difficult for a quarterback to throw the ball.

Lambert also added fire to an already accomplished group.

"I'll say Jack changed the personality on the team," Wagner said. "He was the guy who came in here and was very vocal, very demonstrative, had all his antics before, during, and after a play."

Lambert came in and immediately challenged the veterans to elevate their play to a higher level. Though the veterans might not have known how to take Lambert's attitude, he won their respect with his play. He was willing to do whatever was necessary to step up his play. He wasn't big, but he was willing to sacrifice his body when the defense needed to make a big hit.

"But the key thing I think Jack brought was a discipline for the position," Wagner said. "Up to his arrival there, we had Henry Davis. He was an older player, an experienced player; he had some real strengths. But Jack was able to fill in and kind of balance it all out. He made few mistakes. He was a great person at that position."

Though Lambert weighed in at less than most playing the position—6'4", 220 pounds—his missing front teeth gave him a vicious appearance. Not only did opposing quarterbacks see the famed Lambert scowl, they had to look over the Steelers' defense while Lambert barked the signals with his arms and legs shaking in anticipation of another play.

"Jack has a reputation as being a wild and crazy guy, and he certainly is, but I don't think he gets enough recognition for being a smart football player and a smart guy," Jack Ham said. "And that's what made him a great player. People don't realize he was the middle linebacker making all the calls for our front four and also to the secondary—as a rookie."

Finding weaknesses in the Steelers' defense taxed some of the NFL's great minds. Teams had difficulty running with any consistency on them, and if they tried to pass with a seven-step drop by the quarterback, he might get protection briefly, but the Steelers' linebackers and defensive backs would knock receivers off of their routes.

Residing inside the Steelers' locker room was an interesting cast of characters; the team probably led the league in nicknames. White was "Mad Dog" for his style of play; Roy Gerela hailed from Canada, making him "Cannuck"; Bleier, an avid bodybuilder, was "Boulder"; L. C. Greenwood, who harbored dreams of becoming an actor, was "Hollywood Bags" as his bags were packed for when the call to the silver screen came; center Ray Mansfield, the oldest starter, became "the Old Ranger"; Ernie Holmes, formerly known as "Fats," had evolved into "Arrowhead" after buzzing the hair on top of his head late in the season to form an arrow that pointed forward; and last, but not least, was John "Frenchy" Fuqua, who called himself "the Count," claiming that in reality he was a French count who had spent so much time in the sun on the Riviera bronzing his body that his tan would never leave him.

The Steelers clinched their second AFC Central Division title on December 8, 1974, when Harris rushed for 136 yards and Swann made an acrobatic touchdown catch in a 21–17 win over the Patriots. The season-ending 27–3 victory over the Bengals gave the Steelers a 10–3–1 record. For the season the defense allowed 115 yards per game rushing, 105 yards passing, and 13.5 points. On top of that, they had 52 quarterback sacks, intercepted 25 passes, and forced 38 fumbles, recovering 22.

The Buffalo Bills were the Steelers' opponent in the first round of the playoffs at Three Rivers Stadium, meaning the Steelers' ability to stop the NFL's premier running back, O. J. Simpson, would likely determine the winner of the game.

Looking to step up their run defense, the Steelers added a new wrinkle to the defensive line that saw Joe Greene pinch in on the center almost to the point where he had a sideways stance in front of the guard.

"Pro football did not have any great running teams back then the way I remember it," Bud Carson said. "The idea was you had to stop people's passes [and] then [stop] the run. But to make a long story short, we tried to come up with something in our 4–3 defense."

Noll had learned the stunt in high school that could clog up the middle if performed successfully.

"Because of Joe's quickness, we'd play him in the gap between the center and the guard, and actually, they would have to commit two people and he had a linebacker right behind him," Noll said. "That freed up our linebackers. If they didn't double-team Joe he would make the play. He was all over the place from the inside, sideline to sideline."

Greene remembered practicing the alignment for most of the season without using it.

"We should have been doing other things, but we were messing around with that," said Greene, noting that the Raiders had "killed us running the football" during their 1973 playoff game.

"We knew we had to play better run defense if we were going to beat them," Greene said. "At the beginning of that '74 season, we played them at Pittsburgh and they shut us out 17–0 and they still ran the ball on us pretty good, and right after that, I think we played the Bills and the Juice [O. J. Simpson], and Juice put 200 [yards] on us. [Editor's note: This game was actually played in 1975.] And we just started tweaking that thing. It was out of desperation, you know. We had to do something to stop the run."

Greene said the alignment allowed him "to play the position more firmly and solid."

"And I'd get hooked, overblocked, by the center, and I could take two people just by the alignment if I did that properly," Greene said. "And Jack [Lambert] did a great job of taking advantage of it when they did double me. If they didn't double me, I was in the backfield; if they doubled me, then he was in the backfield on running plays."

Another motivating factor for using the defense was to protect Lambert from getting his lightweight body pounded by the larger offensive linemen. Out of the fray at the line of scrimmage, the sure-tackling Lambert could swoop in to make the stop.

The Steelers used the prescribed inside stunt to prevent the Bills guards from pulling on power sweeps for Simpson, and they went into the game with a mind-set of not being too aggressive. Simpson had a unique ability to haunt teams that played too aggressively by taking advantage of open running lanes to cut back. And the strategy worked. Simpson gained just 49 yards on 15 carries, and the Steelers' offense received a standout performance from Bradshaw, who completed 12 passes in 19 attempts for 203 yards and a touchdown in a 32–14 rout. Bradshaw called the game his best as a professional and credited the improvement he'd shown over the course of the season to his finally being relaxed after five NFL seasons.

The game proved to be a coming-out party of sorts for Swann, too.

Swann, who babysat Simpson's two children during Swann's senior season at Southern California, caught just 11 passes during the regular season. But he showed what a versatile threat he could be against the Bills by gaining 25 yards on an end-around that proved critical in the Steelers' second touchdown drive. He followed with a diving 35-yard catch that helped lead to his team's third touchdown.

The victory moved the Steelers into the AFC Championship Game in which they would travel to Oakland to play their old nemesis, the Raiders, for the right to play in the Super Bowl.

Since Harris' "Immaculate Reception" the Raiders had beaten the Steelers both times they played in California, including a victory during the third week of the 1974 season.

The Steelers arrived for their Sunday game against the Raiders on Friday night. They were six-point underdogs, based at least partially on the fact that in the previous ten playoff games the home team had won nine times. Noll understood the notorious Raiders fans, noting during a press conference the day before the game, "We know we will be playing in a hostile atmosphere; we've been here before."

During the same press conference a reporter told Noll, "The Raiders have a motto, 'Pride and Poise,' which they plaster over everything." The reporter followed by asking the question, "Do the Steelers have pride and poise?"

Noll, who had served as an assistant coach on the Chargers with Raiders owner Al Davis—which had clearly produced some bad blood—quipped: "Not on our stationery."

The Raiders clearly did not occupy the warm part of Noll's heart.

The Raiders had beaten the Dolphins in the first round of the play-offs, snapping the Dolphins' chances for a fourth-consecutive Super Bowl appearance and a third-consecutive Super Bowl win. In the aftermath of the Raiders' win, a lot of talk circulated about how the Super Bowl would be an anticlimactic affair, as if the real Super Bowl already had been played between the Dolphins and Raiders. Although normally even-tempered, this drew some emotion from Noll, who told his team following the Buffalo game: "The Raiders think they can't be beat. But we're going out there and kick[ing] their butt."

Greene characterized Noll as not really being excited when he addressed the team.

"His voice level just got stronger and got elevated," Greene said. "He was just letting us know that the Super Bowl hadn't been played yet and

100

the best team in the National Football League was sitting right there in the room.

"Chuck hit the mark for sure. He hit the mark when he said that. That's really the gist of the entire thing, the fact he never used emotion. No matter how he was prior or how he was afterward, it was a great statement. But it was even better because it was out of context for him in terms of the way we had been dealing with him."

Shell remembered Noll being "really fired up that week, which was unusual for Chuck."

"He didn't have that personality," Shell said. "Normally we didn't see emotion from him, but we did that week when we started prepping for that game, and that really got us fired up. We're like 'Oh man, Chuck is fired up for this one.' Seeing his emotional side was very rare to see, but that was good. He got us fired up."

A Steelers victory would earn the team its first-ever trip to the Super Bowl, which is the kind of burden sports teams fold under every year. The Steelers didn't seem to feel the pressure. At Sunday's breakfast the day of the game, Bradshaw told Art Rooney Sr. he needed to be ready after the game because everybody was going to be asking him about what it felt like to go to the Super Bowl. The attitude seemed prevalent even prior to the start of the game when Greenwood could be seen outside the locker room in a tunnel watching the NFC title game between the Minnesota Vikings and Los Angeles Rams on TV. When someone asked him what he was doing, he said he was watching to see which team the Steelers would play in the Super Bowl.

Throughout the week leading up to the game, Holmes heard an earful from his peers on the Steelers' defensive line about what Raiders guard Gene Upshaw was going to do to him. Greene laughed recounting the story.

"Ernie is a great guy," Greene said. "And we had been geeking Ernie up all week. We'd had battles with the Raiders before, and they'd beaten up on us. Ernie played in front of Gene, and we were telling Ernie that Gene was going to beat up on him. Ernie just didn't take kindly to us teasing him. I think he'd done pretty well against Gene, but we made it like Gene had kicked his butt."

The teasing got a rise out of Holmes, who vented after the opening kickoff.

"We kicked off to them to start the game," Greene said. "I don't know what yard line they were on, but our defense was standing up next to the ball. The Raiders were in the huddle and Ernie stepped across the line, across the ball, and he called out Gene's name several times, screamed it out. Uppy was in the huddle trying to get the call, obviously, and finally he turned around and Ernie said, 'I'm going to kick your ass!'"

The Steelers were dominating the line on both sides of the ball, but the score stood tied at 3 at the half after a controversial call took a touchdown away from the Steelers.

Just before halftime, Stallworth ran a route down the sideline and caught a pass that appeared to be a touchdown.

"They ruled him out-of-bounds," Greene said. "But he caught that ball in his left hand over his shoulder in the end zone, [Raiders defensive back] Nemiah Wilson held his right hand, and John kind of crossed his feet over to stay inbounds and made a one-handed catch, beautiful catch. And they ruled him out-of-bounds. And that was just before halftime.

"There wasn't any complaining about that. It just gave us more impetus to beat that football team. And when we walked off that field, going across to the locker room at halftime, to a man we knew we were going to win the ballgame even though [the score was tied] at halftime. And I recall years later, Mr. [Al] Davis was saying he recalled that moment too, and he said, 'We had you, didn't we?'"

After three quarters, the Raiders held a 10–3 lead on a 38-yard scoring pass from Ken Stabler to fleet-footed receiver Cliff Branch.

The touchdown didn't have a deflating effect on the Steelers; rather it seemed to invigorate the team like a frigid blast from a Pittsburgh winter. Bradshaw led the team on an eight-play, 61-yard scoring drive capped by an 8-yard Harris touchdown to tie the score at 10 early in the fourth quarter.

Stabler, who had three passes intercepted on the day, threw his second one to Ham minutes after the Steelers' touchdown. Ham had intercepted Stabler earlier in the game; this time he returned the ball 25 yards to the Raiders' 9-yard line. Bradshaw then connected with Swann from six yards out to give the Steelers their first lead of the day. Raiders kicker George Blanda kicked a 24-yard field goal to cut the lead to 17–13.

When the Raiders got the ball back, Stabler was sacked for a 9-yard loss, but Steelers cornerback J. T. Thomas was called for holding on the play, giving the Raiders a first down at their own 32 and planting a seed of hope in the minds of Raiders fans. Stabler wasn't called the "Snake" for nothing—he knew how to steal a game by throwing the football, running it, using guile, or a combination of all three.

The Steelers' defensive unit took turns telling Thomas to not let the officials get into his head.

"We told him to keep playing aggressively," Russell said.

Positive lip service paid off handsomely when Stabler escaped from the Steelers' defense just in time to snap off a floater and Thomas snatched the pass for the Steelers' third interception of the day, returning the ball 37 yards to the Raiders' 24. Harris put the game away when he busted loose on the Steelers' second play for a 21-yard touchdown run, and the 24–13 upset was complete.

"I realized I was going to my first Super Bowl with four or five plays left in the game," Ham said. "It's a great feeling, number one, for Pittsburgh to beat the Raiders, and number two, doing it on the road."

Bradshaw had played it close to the vest, hitting 9 of 17 passes for 95 yards, while Harris gained 111 yards and Bleier had 98.

Ham laughed remembering Greene's antics in the waning moments of the game after being held by a Raiders lineman.

"This is Joe Greene, who had a very short fuse," Ham said. "He tries to kick the guy. He tries to kick this offensive lineman, I forget who he was. And I just walked over to Joe and said, 'Joe, you can't do this right at the end of the game because we need you for one more game, the Super Bowl.' And he had that big Coca-Cola smile, 'You know, you're right, Jack.'

"I think that was probably the only time he listened to me his entire football career." Ham paused to enjoy a chuckle. "I think the fact we were going to the Super Bowl hit us at the same time. It was a great feeling. It meant a lot to Joe and me, and that's something I'll never forget."

Greene fondly remembers the game that saw the Steel Curtain defense limit the Raiders to just 29 yards rushing in 21 attempts.

"Not so much because of how I played," Greene said. "But the game [and] the climate before, during, and after was probably my greatest experience on a football field."

New Orleans and Super Bowl IX sat on the horizon for the Steelers. They would play the Minnesota Vikings, who had defeated the Los Angeles Rams to earn the franchise's third trip to the Super Bowl after losing in their previous two appearances.

9

Super Sunday Finally

With two weeks sandwiched between their respective championship games, the Minnesota Vikings and Pittsburgh Steelers employed different approaches for preparing for the game. The Steelers conducted light workouts in Pittsburgh, while the Vikings took the week off; both teams flew to New Orleans the Sunday before the game.

Heading into the game the Vikings carried a lot of historical baggage. They held the dubious distinction of being the only team to lose its first Super Bowl game and not win in the sequel. Baltimore, Dallas, and Miami all won in their second trip following initial losses. At the other end of the spectrum, the Steelers were making their first Super Bowl appearance and would be trying to become the third team to win its first appearance; Green Bay and the New York Jets were the others.

Looking at the ledger chronicling past Vikings Super Bowl defeats brought to light the team's meager rushing totals. When they lost to the Kansas City Chiefs in 1970, they gained just 67 yards on the ground; against the Miami Dolphins in 1974 they ran for only 72 yards. A hint that the Vikings' ground game futility still lived came in the NFC Championship Game when they ran for just 21 yards against the Rams in the game's first 25 minutes. Vikings quarterback Fran Tarkenton finally opened up the running game with his passing, and they finished with 164 yards on the ground in their 14–10 win.

The Vikings did not say so, but they had to be concerned about the Steelers holding the Raiders to 29 yards rushing.

Tarkenton gave the veteran Vikings a wild-card at quarterback. He could pass, scramble, or just improvise, which made him a dangerous man to defend. On the other side of the ball the Vikings had a defense known as the "Purple People Eaters" spearheaded by a line that boasted veterans Carl Eller, Jim Marshall, and Alan Page. If the Steelers were to win their first Super Bowl, they would have to defeat a veteran team that had played in many big games.

Perusing the statistics prior to Super Bowl IX, only one favored the Vikings—their NFL-leading 7.3 yards average per pass attempt. The number personified Tarkenton's acumen for finding deep threat John Gilliam and running back Chuck Foreman circling out of the backfield. However, the Steelers had put up 3.7 yards allowed per pass attempt average. Could the Steelers stop the Vikings' pass attack? Perhaps even more to the point: could the Vikings stop the Steelers' blossoming offense which had led the AFC in rushing and had Terry Bradshaw, who finally seemed to be coming into his own?

"I think 1974 was his key year," Chuck Noll said. "In 1973 we were still trying to find our way. I was a lot more confident in our protection and with the receivers."

Every Super Bowl has its story line. In the early years of the game it was legendary Packers coach Vince Lombardi against the AFL, or the Jets' Joe Namath guaranteeing victory against the Colts in Super Bowl III. Lovable Art Rooney stood at the forefront for Super Bowl IX. Everybody wanted to see the 73-year-old Steelers owner finally get a championship. The Chief collected friends. So when the Steelers got their allotment of twelve thousand tickets to the game, Rooney secured close to two thousand for his legion of friends, who revered him. But they weren't the only ones. Rooney became the warm and fuzzy face of the Steelers, making him the sentimental favorite for a nation of professional football fans.

In preparation for the big game, Noll, ever the teacher, proved he could be a student as well. Learning from his experience with the Colts in the 1969 Super Bowl, Noll had surmised that a contributing factor to the Colts loss had been the fact that they had been wound too tight. He'd seen the tight-jawed expressions on the faces of the heavily favored Colts, and he didn't want to see those same expressions on the Steelers sideline. Noll's approach to handling New Orleans and notorious Bourbon Street was simple: don't fight it.

Instead of setting curfews and having bed checks, Noll set the Steelers free to go out on the town.

"We weren't guys looking for trouble," Andy Russell said. "We were just out to see the city. That was Bourbon Street, the whole French Quarter. Essentially we just found a nice restaurant that had oysters and tried to eat as many oysters as we could and match 'em with a drink;

then [we] walked around to various establishments, some with music—and other things of interest."

Russell recalled getting tired and leaving Ray Mansfield at 2:00 A.M. their first night out on the town. "I told Mansfield, 'I gotta go to bed,'" Russell said. "He said 'leave me the car.' We had rented a car. I said 'OK.' The next day I said, 'Ray, where's the car?' He said, 'What car?' He'd forgotten all about it and when we went back to where it had been it was gone."

Mansfield forgot he'd driven the car somewhere else.

"We did find it," Russell said with a chuckle.

The team quickly got its fill of New Orleans and returned its focus to the business of winning the Super Bowl.

In the Minnesota camp the Vikings weren't extended similar privileges to roam Bourbon Street. Instead they were ensconced in the team hotel, leaving Vikings tight end Stu Voigt unimpressed.

"Our practice facilities were kind of crappy," Voigt said. "At the time you're sitting there going, 'This is the biggest sporting event in the world, a one-day event.' And we basically stayed at a hotel like you'd stay at on the road like in Cleveland. So you're asking yourself, 'Is this all there is?'"

Daily news leading up to the game dealt primarily with the bumps, bruises, and illnesses both teams were experiencing.

Tarkenton had a sore right shoulder and wrist, prompting stoic Vikings coach Bud Grant to use backup quarterback Bob Berry for most of the repetitions in the Wednesday practice—a situation the Vikings did not consider dire.

In 14 NFL seasons, Tarkenton had never missed a game due to injury. He'd even played through a shoulder separation during his tenure at quarterback for the New York Giants. Tarkenton said the injury wouldn't affect him, and Grant went further to note that he liked his quarterback having a minor injury. He told reporters: "It isn't serious, I even like it. I'm sure he'll have a great day. When a player gets a little nick, he seems to perform even better on game day."

Franco Harris had a head cold but was expected to be ready. The forecast for Dwight White wasn't as optimistic. White checked into the hospital when the team arrived on Sunday. The Steelers said the defensive end was dealing with a viral infection and back pains.

"Sick might be an understatement for the way I felt," White said. "I had viral pneumonia and pleurisy. I got sick the first night I got into New Orleans. That was a Sunday night. We practiced in Pittsburgh the first week [after beating Oakland]; it was a real nasty winter here then. Winters seemed to be a lot worse back then, but it was snow and cold. And then we left that Sunday after that first week's practice to go down to New Orleans to play the Super Bowl. I guess it was combination of change, the humidity and stuff—you know you play a football season. You practice in the rain, snow. Your body's tired and you're susceptible to a lot of stuff. A lot of guys were sneezing and coughing. And I guess I had this and it really didn't bother me as a whole until I got down in that humidity. I couldn't breathe. I got down there and I couldn't breathe. I had an infection in my lungs. But I'm sucking it up practicing every day.

"Once you start hacking up phlegm, that's the way it is and you go about your business. But that didn't work down in that heat and humidity down in New Orleans, because the night we got down there I had an attack. I stayed in the hospital. They had me on breathing treatments for a whole week. I lost 20 pounds in one week. Imagine that, 20 pounds. Regularly I weighed 250, maybe 245 at the end of the season. I was probably around 220 by game time."

Bud Carson was concerned.

"We didn't know if Dwight would make it or not," Carson said. "I never thought that he would make the game."

White showed up at Thursday's practice and lasted about 15 minutes before returning to the hospital; Steve Furness would start if White wasn't able to go.

John Stallworth had a sprained thumb, which didn't seem to matter that much because Frank Lewis and Ron Shanklin had been the starting wide receivers all season. But Noll planned to get a lot of use out of his rookies, Stallworth and Lynn Swann.

"They made things happen, so we needed [Stallworth]," Noll said.

Despite the looming possibility of not having White, the Steelers were confident of their chances against the Vikings.

"I thought we would get them," said Carson, who now lives in Sarasota, Florida. "I was going through some scrapbooks before all of these hurricanes [hit Florida in late summer and early fall of 2004] and decided what we were going to lose and what we were going to save. I saw an interview with Jesse Outlar, who was a sportswriter with the Atlanta paper. He was a friend of mine from when I was at Georgia Tech. He was interested in doing a story on Tarkenton since he was a University of Georgia guy, so he called to ask me about him.

"In the column, and today you'd never say this, but I did say it to him and he wrote about it. I was very confident that we were going to win the football game. There's no way Tarkenton—he was more of a rollout passer than he was a drop-back passer—I said he's got to roll toward L. C. Greenwood. And L. C. Greenwood is probably faster than any quarterback in the league. So he's going to have a hard time. And if he comes back the other way he's going to have to deal with Dwight White, who had just outstanding speed for a defensive end, so he's going to have to throw from the pocket. I said I don't think he can beat us. Jesse wrote a big article about that. When I talked to Tarkenton five or six years later, when I was with Los Angeles, we were in the playoffs, I went up to say nice game and he wouldn't talk to me. I think he read that article and still was mad."

White lay in a hospital bed the night before the game considering the prospect of not playing in the Super Bowl.

"I'm thinking, this is unconscionable; how can you do this?" White said. "That was probably what drove me more than anything. I'll be damned if I'm going to miss this. There ain't no way I'm going to miss that. We played for something other than money back then.

"We played for a town that had been an armpit. Their team had been identified as a loser that would always find a way to lose a game. Then we started winning and we brought a winning atmosphere to Pittsburgh. I saw a whole community come together and develop such pride in their football team. Thirty years ago, goddamn it, I saw people proud to be from Pittsburgh."

White rose from bed the next day and dressed.

"I'm feeling like death warmed over," he said.

White's clothes were literally hanging on him.

"I'd lost all that weight and my appetite was shot," he said. "So they come over and get me. Chuck says, 'We want to see how you feel. Let you warm up.' I know they're thinking there's a 90 percent chance this guy's going to have to be gurneyed off during pregame warm-ups.

"I don't think [the coaching staff] really thought I'd show. I figured they were thinking they'd let me come out Sunday morning, you know, I had really been involved in the whole season, and after 40 years we're at the Super Bowl. And you really don't want to disappoint this kid; he played his heart out for you all year. Then he gets down to the Big Dance and gets sick. So I really think the idea was to patronize me; they're humoring me by letting me get dressed and being on the field to see if I fall down."

Greenwood said the team didn't really know White's condition had been so bad.

"Of course they rolled him out of the hospital Sunday morning for the game," Greenwood said. "It was pretty evident he was in rough shape. He hadn't had anything to eat and they were feeding him intravenously for a couple of days. They just kind of brought him to the football field in the ambulance, rolled him out of the ambulance, taped him up, and he went out on the field to play football."

After all the buildup, the time had come for the upstart Steelers to play the veteran Vikings in Super Bowl IX before a television audience of 75 million people and a crowd of 80,997. Originally the game had been scheduled to be played at the New Orleans Superdome, but construction of the building had not yet been completed, so the game was moved to ancient Tulane Stadium, hardly the palace worthy of hosting football's ultimate prize. The Steelers didn't care about the accommodations, though.

"We could have played that in a cow pasture," Jack Ham said. "It wouldn't have mattered for us. Your whole career you're trying to get to that game. You're trying to be the best that year in the National Football League. No, it didn't matter where we were playing that game."

An early-morning storm waterlogged the field, leaving players and fans to brave the cold and damp weather, easily the worst weather conditions for a Super Bowl to date.

"It was an ugly day—rained all day, the rain kept coming down," Ham said. "It didn't dampen it for me or any player on our football team, what we were trying to do, why we were there, or what we were trying to accomplish. No, that didn't matter one bit."

Russell "loved the weather that day."

"It probably froze most of the spectators," Russell said. "Of course it was very invigorating for the players."

Outside Tulane Stadium it was a buyer's market. Scalpers tried to peddle $20 tickets for $5 with little luck because of the biting weather. Approximately one thousand tickets went unused.

The windchill factor was 20 degrees below zero. A man actually died in front of the Steelers locker room before the game, even though the Steelers did not know that at the time.

White got dressed, went through warm-ups, and then joined up with the defensive line.

"We're going through everything like it's a normal game," White said. "They said, 'OK Dwight, do you think you can make it?' And I'm like, 'Yeah, I can make it. Start the game.'"

Addressing the team during his pregame remarks, Noll remained stoic, telling his players the Super Bowl was a team reward for a championship season and that they needed to keep their intensity up and execute. He closed by telling them to go out and "have some fun."

The Steelers established the tempo early with a solid running game led by Harris, who appeared to be fully recovered from his cold, and a healthy dose of Rocky Bleier, who went 18 yards up the middle on a "sucker play" the Steelers would use successfully throughout the game.

Noll and his coaches had done their homework in the film room noticing the aggressiveness of Vikings defensive tackle Doug Sutherland.

"Sutherland was very quick," Bleier said. "The Vikings had their big-name people, Alan Page, Jim Marshall, and Carl Eller, but Sutherland was probably the quickest and the most disciplined."

Exploiting that discipline, Noll noticed Sutherland would likely bite on a fake sweep to the left, which would leave the hole between the center and the right guard open after the guard pulled.

"We'd never run a counter before," Bleier said. "I'd take a little step to the left then back toward the [opening]. We ran that the first play of the game and I pick up [18] yards. Franco would have scored."

Pittsburgh moved the ball early, but their two deepest drives resulted in botched field-goal attempts. On the Steelers' first drive, Roy Gerela missed a 37-yard field-goal attempt when he hooked the kick and the ball flew left of the goal post. On their second drive, holder Bobby Walden bobbled an errant snap from center and tried to run before getting thrown for a 7-yard loss. The misses didn't seem to matter. The Steelers were physically handling the Vikings, allowing just 27 total yards and one first down during the first quarter.

"We knew they were going to be tough to run on with the two big guys right in the middle, Fats Holmes and Joe Greene, but you've got to mix things in and we were going to try that," Voigt said. "We had Chuck Foreman, so we were going to try and run outside a little bit."

White played well, while Holmes proved particularly effective in hampering Tarkenton, either by lining up over center Mick Tingelhoff and attacking him directly or by looping around tackle Joe Greene and participating in a double-team.

The Steelers' loose sideline reflected confidence through the easy smiles and laughter. The Vikings, who tried to run the football, didn't cross their own 35-yard line in the first quarter.

"We were surprised they tried to run the football because we had just stuffed a very good Oakland attack," Russell said. "We kind of thought they'd try to do a lot of rollouts with Tarkenton, and we certainly didn't expect them to run at our strength. They attacked the middle of our line and that went nowhere. Joe had a big game. L. C. Greenwood had a big game. Tarkenton liked to roll to his right, which was our left; L. C. had a big day coming up field, knocked a bunch of balls down."

Carson cited the weather as a contributing factor to the Vikings' dedication to the run.

"You were not going to make a living throwing the football in that game and that weather," Carson said. "I don't care who you were, on a field like that. Minnesota wasn't really a running team, but they tried to run the football anyway. That day they had to run the football."

Once again the Steelers employed the single stunt off a basic 4-3 defense that had worked so well against Buffalo and Oakland in the playoffs. Against the Vikings, Greene and Holmes lined up pinched in on Vikings center Mick Tingelhoff.

Tingelhoff said the Steelers' "pinching in on center" didn't really make a difference.

"They brought up a lot of that stuff," Tingelhoff said. "But that wasn't it. We just never got started. On that particular day it seemed like we never got started. I've watched that damn game film: we just didn't play very well at all. Nothing went right.

"They had a very good defensive line. We knew it was hard to run up the middle on them. They were big and mobile up there. We just ran our same offense that we'd been running and had been successful with against other teams. It just didn't work out."

When people talked about Pittsburgh prior to the game, they brought up the lack of experience playing in Super Bowls and the fact that the Vikings had been to the Super Bowl so many times. But this Super Bowl proved to be one of those games where experience didn't matter. The Steelers' linebackers, who normally made most of the tackles thanks to the defensive line taking care of business up front, weren't making many tackles because the Vikings kept trying to run inside only to be stopped by Greene or Holmes.

"I'm not an offensive coordinator, but I would have tried something a whole lot different against us than trying to run against that stunt we had with Joe Greene turned toward the center," Ham said. "And they try to run the football inside with offensive linemen who could not dominate those two big guys in the middle.

"[The Vikings game plan] just didn't make any sense to me. First, if you're in a stunt 4-3, you should try to throw the ball on first down; don't try to pound the ball up the middle, which is truly the strength. Because you have two guys in there plus Lambert and you're not going to move Ernie Holmes—who at that period of time was probably playing his best football—and Joe Greene. So I always questioned whether it was [Vikings coach] Bud Grant or the offensive coordinator, or whomever; I would not have had my offensive game plan built around trying to pound it up the middle against our defense."

Despite the Steelers' stellar defensive effort, the Vikings were hand delivered a scoring opportunity when Rocky Bleier fumbled early in the second period and Randy Poltl recovered to give the Vikings the ball at the Pittsburgh 24. But the Steelers' defense stuffed the Vikings as they had on their previous four possessions, and the Vikings had to settle for trying a 39-yard field goal. Vikings kicker Fred Cox missed.

Lambert sprained his ankle in the second quarter, and Ed Bradley replaced him. Suddenly the Vikings were attacking the middle, but Bradley came through.

"Bradley came in and played well," Noll said. "He made all the plays."

Late in the second quarter the Vikings had the ball near their own goal line when a handoff between Tarkenton and running back Dave Osborn was muffed. The ball fell to the ground where Greenwood's gold high-top kicked it backward into the end zone. Tarkenton fell on the ball and Dwight White touched him to record the first safety in Super Bowl history and give the Steelers a 2–0 lead with 7:11 remaining in the first half.

"That was going to be a handoff to Dave Osborn," Voigt said. "But for some reason the handoff wasn't made; Tarkenton got stuck with the ball. That was a play designed to be a handoff; straight ahead, we were at the 2 or 3, and that was the Vikings' luck in the Super Bowls. We had the same deal against the Dolphins [in 1974]; Oscar Reed fumbled in the end zone. Later we played the Raiders [in 1977] and same deal: block a punt, get the ball on the 1 and first play, Brent McClanahan fumbles. That was our mistake. I'd like to say that was caused by the Steelers, but it was caused by a mistake by the Vikings offense. That cost us. And, although that was only two points, I think it took us out of our game. It was a key play."

The Vikings mounted another challenge before the half, moving from their own 20 to the Steelers' 25 using Tarkenton passes and Foreman runs. The clock showed 1:17 remaining in the half when Tarkenton looked to the 5 and spotted Gilliam, who had been engaged in a two-quarter-long feud with Glen Edwards.

Gilliam hauled in the pass, but the Steelers' safety unloaded a vicious hit on him that forced the ball into the air. Mel Blount alertly made the interception in the Steelers' end zone. Had Gilliam held on to the pass, the Vikings' worst scenario would have been first down at the 5. Instead they came away with no points again, and the Steelers led 2–0 at the intermission.

"They were driving the ball and Gilliam came across the middle," Blount said. "That was a turning point. Glen Edwards made just a tremendous hit on John Gilliam, knocked his helmet off. I was able to make the play because I hustled across the field running toward the ball—because the play really took place across the field. When you look at the film, I saw the ball being thrown and just took off running that way. Glen Edwards made what was, in my opinion, one of the all-time hits. He made a big-time hit. Pound for pound there wasn't anybody who could hit like Glen Edwards on the football field. He was a tremendous hitter. But anyway, he shook the ball loose and it popped up in the air. It kind of hung up there for a while, and that gave me a chance, because I was moving toward the ball. And it was a big play for us."

Mike Wagner said of Edwards' hit: "The rest of that game John Gilliam did not want to run over the middle."

Noll told the team at the half: "Keep on doing what you're doing and we'll win."

In the other locker room the Vikings could take solace in their situation. They hadn't played well, yet they trailed by just two points.

"We weren't big on adjustments," Voigt said. "They use Polaroid pictures now and all that; you make some adjustments; some things are working, some aren't. We're like, 'If offensively we can just execute our plays and hang onto the ball.' And, 'Hey we're in good shape. We've been in tight games before.'"

While the Vikings made no adjustments, the Steelers made an important equipment adjustment. Steelers equipment manager Tony Parisi had anticipated the artificial surface at Tulane Stadium being slick if it rained. Taking a proactive approach, Parisi called the weather bureau for a long-range forecast and was told there would be a lot of rain before the game. Parisi remembered what the Miami Dolphins equipment manager had told him about how to deal with such conditions after the Dolphins had defeated the Steelers on a wet field four years earlier. Parisi also had read about a special type of shoe in Montreal that had not yet been put on the market. He ordered 75 pairs of the nonskid rubber shoes, which arrived on Wednesday before the game.

Russell, Harris, and Bradshaw were among the key players who wore the shoes in the second half upon Parisi's suggestion.

"We had worn Adidas with a little stubby spike, not the big cleats, because we played on Tartan Turf in Three Rivers and that had pretty much worked for us," Russell said. "But this was an artificial turf that was soaking wet. We were all slipping and sliding. We're all falling down. It was very disconcerting because I could not plant my foot to drive off of it. And you can't play like that."

Parisi, who served as an assistant trainer as well, hailed from Canada and played hockey. He would tape the players' hands, and he carried himself with the tough-guy confidence of a prizefighter.

"He asked us to try these shoes, thought they'd do a little better," Russell said. "There were more cleats, a little bit spikier and taller. So we all tried on these shoes and we went out and had no problem. So it went from a big problem to no problem. Tony saved the day. I don't know if the Vikings had those shoes. I don't know what kind of difference it would have made if they had them."

Gerela must have taken a pass on the shoe change, for he slipped on the second-half kickoff, squibbing the ball to Bill Brown. The veteran Vikings running back couldn't handle it, and Marv Kellum recovered for the Steelers at the Vikings' 30. Harris went around left end for a 24-yard gain then got thrown for a 3-yard loss before finishing off the drive with a 9-yard touchdown run around left end. The score was 9–0.

The Vikings put together a modest threat in the third quarter, reaching the Pittsburgh 47 before Greenwood deflected a Tarkenton pass and Greene intercepted, returning the ball 10 yards to the Minnesota 46.

Earlier in the quarter, Greenwood, who batted down three Tarkenton passes on the day, deflected one of the passes back into the Vikings quarterback's hands. After catching his own pass, Tarkenton reloaded and threw to Gilliam for a 40-yard completion. Alas, you can't throw two forward passes on the same play. The Vikings were called for an illegal second pass, which nullified the play.

Opinions varied about Greenwood's ability to knock down passes.

"I'd be going out for a pass and L. C. Greenwood, who was completely blocked by Ron Yary at the line of scrimmage, kept knocking down passes," Voigt said. "A couple of those were headed to me when I felt like I was open. That was one of those deals where L. C. was getting blocked, but he was tall and he could jump up. There's a situation, what do you do when a guy is at the line of scrimmage and he can jump up and get a piece of the ball? Ron was doing his job. He's got the guy at the line of scrimmage."

Wagner commended the job Greenwood did knocking down the passes. He also wished his teammate had not been quite so proficient.

"From a selfish standpoint, L. C. had this wonderful game knocking down these passes, but our secondary was so good back then, I think if L. C. lets some of those balls go through we would have had a few more interceptions," Wagner said. "We had those guys pretty well covered."

Greenwood laughed about Wagner's comment and at the suggestion Yary handled him.

"Fran Tarkenton wasn't that tall and I'm 6'7"," Greenwood said. "My objective was to try and stay in front of him. I didn't want to let him get outside of me. I thought that I had a chance of getting my hand up in his face, and that's what I wanted to do because I knew he was going to try and sprint out. I knew that the tackle I was playing in front of knew that I could stay in front of him or do what I needed to do with him. That's what I did. I just sort of [kept] him in front of me, and fortunately when he threw the ball I was able to just get my hands up and knock the ball down. That was the objective going into the game—not to let him run the football. I think I accomplished that. I know that in some instances, defensive backs and linebackers were screaming because they were sitting there waiting to pick the ball off. But it was too late then. I was trying to do my job. My job was to keep him from scrambling. Keep him in front of me so the other guys could get there and make the tackle that's necessary for a sack, but not to let him get around the corner."

Russell suffered an injury in the third quarter and had to leave the game.

"I leg whipped a guy and my leg went numb and I took myself out of the game," Russell said. "I was going to throw Foreman for a loss of about three yards; I had him. Then he makes this unbelievably quick move inside, and I'm going to miss him unless I leg whip him. I just throw my knee at his knees and I caught him dead center of his thigh, made my whole leg go numb."

Loren Toews replaced Russell, who pleaded with his coaches to put him back in the game. The thought of finishing the game on the sideline ate up Russell, but when the coaches asked him how he felt, he figured he'd better tell them the truth. He didn't want to be alone on Foreman or Gilliam and have one of them beat him for a touchdown in the close game.

"So we had two backup linebackers playing the fourth quarter when the game was still on the line," Russell said. "And they attacked Loren Toews and he did great. They ran some screens against him, and he came up and made the plays. We weren't just 11 good players: we had a helluva team."

The ledger showed the Vikings had gained just 23 yards rushing while the Steelers had gained 192 by the end of the third quarter. Even if it didn't feel like it, the Vikings still had life.

Early in the fourth quarter Paul Krause recovered Harris' fumble at the Pittsburgh 47 to set up a Tarkenton-to-Gilliam pass that produced a pass interference call that moved the ball to the 5.

"Pass interference, I was upset about that," Wagner said. "Put the ball on the 5-yard line in a close game. That's a questionable ruling there. I had position on that receiver. If I had been standing still and that receiver ran into me, would that be pass interference? It would be like basketball charging. He said, 'Well, you didn't make an effort for the ball.' Well I'm standing there running down the sidelines and the receiver wants to run over my back."

Foreman fumbled on the next play, and Greene fell on the football. But four plays after the fumble recovery, Vikings linebacker Matt Blair blocked Walden's punt and Terry Brown recovered in the end zone for a touchdown. Cox missed the extra point, but the lead had been cut to 9–6.

In a display more suitable for a veteran team like the Vikings, the Steelers showed poise in a situation where another young team might have panicked.

More than 10 minutes remained in the game when the Steelers began a time-consuming drive from their own 34. Bradshaw looked composed, completing three third-down passes for first downs on the drive. The biggest of these came on a third-and-2 when he passed to tight end Larry Brown, who made the catch for a 30-yard gain. Bradshaw capped the 66-yard drive with a 4-yard touchdown pass to Brown. On the play, which had been suggested by Joe Gilliam, Brown made a smart move. He stopped running toward the corner of the end zone and then started again. The stop-start move forced middle linebacker Jeff Siemon to commit himself, and Bradshaw rifled the ball to Brown. Gerela connected on the point after touchdown to end the scoring, and the Steelers had a 16–6 win.

Harris ran six times on the final touchdown drive. His last carry of the day, which produced a 15-yard gain, gave him 158 yards rushing, eclipsing the record of 145 yards set by Larry Csonka in Super Bowl VIII.

Tarkenton finished with just 11 completions in 26 passes for 102 yards with 3 interceptions and 4 deflected passes.

"Our front four put on too big a rush to permit Tarkenton to have success throwing the football," Carson said. "The way I remember it, the biggest thing we had to deal with was Russell and Lambert getting hurt. We didn't know how their replacements would do, but Bradley and Toews did good jobs."

The Vikings knew they had been outplayed.

"Their defensive line outplayed us," Yary said. "They beat us with their defensive line. They beat us with their linebackers. They beat us in our secondary. Today our defense played well enough to win, but our offense didn't do the job."

Grant sounded embarrassed about the quality of football played.

"It wasn't a very good football game, and that's a shame because this is football's showcase," Grant said. "The kicking game was not good, with three missed field goals, some fluke interceptions, some penalties. It was not the type of game either team played to get here."

Voigt was surprised at the Steelers' offense being effective.

"I thought, quite frankly, that they would not be able to do much against our defense," Voigt said. "But Franco Harris had a nice day and they got the safety. And I think the surprise was how tough their defense was. No question they shut down the Vikings. We had good talent, Tarkenton, Foreman, Gilliam, the linemen. They pretty much dominated the line of scrimmage and made the plays when they had to. It was surprising, I think we took a lot of heat for that, but history would say that was a pretty good defense."

While Voigt credited the Steelers for their play, he said the Vikings played poorly.

"Don't get me wrong that I'm not giving all the credit in the world to the Steelers, but the weather and everything, nobody was doing anything," Voigt said. "I'm talking about the Steelers, too, on offense. It was a hard-hitting game, and both defenses were excellent.

"If you had come back and read the accounts of the game, it would say Minnesota lost the game rather than Pittsburgh took it from us. Pittsburgh played well enough to win, but when you can't score points in the Super Bowl and when you have your chances and you can't do much with them. . . . I'm not sure Tarkenton had his best game either. In looking back, maybe that wind and all that with an aging quarterback, arm strength might have been a factor throwing into the wind."

Tarkenton made no excuses: "They deserved to win. They did it. We didn't."

Surprisingly the Steelers locker room lacked the raucous celebration scene that usually plays out after a Super Bowl victory.

"You only get excited when you surprise yourself," Noll said afterward.

Art Rooney—the beloved "Chief"—finally had the NFL's best team.

As defensive captain, Russell stood in the front of the team prepared to give away the game ball to the day's best defensive player, and the past flashed through his mind.

"It was just awesome," Russell said. "I got real emotional at the time. The Chief had been wonderful all during those losing years."

Russell remembered the 1963 season when the team had been a contender, one step away from the NFL Championship Game, but had lost to the Giants on a frozen field in below-zero temperatures. Though disappointed, Rooney walked around the clubhouse after the defeat, patting players on the back, telling them they had great years and to have a good off-season. Such a family atmosphere—and Rooney was a classy gentleman. The thoughts continued to rattle around in Russell's mind while he prepared to present Greene the game ball. Russell felt like Greene deserved the award for being the defense's strength on a day when the Vikings had tried to play smashmouth football and had gotten humiliated.

"I'm standing there and I see the Chief standing back there against the wall, out of the spotlight, and then it hit me, I had to give it to him," Russell said. "He was the man. It was the right thing to do. I think Joe would have agreed with me 100 percent."

Russell's eyes met Rooney's.

"Chief come up here, this is your ball," Russell said.

Minutes later, Rooney stood next to Pete Rozelle, and the NFL commissioner awarded him the Lombardi Trophy signifying his team had reached the pinnacle of professional football. Clutched in Rooney's arms was a pigskin that had affixed a glow on his face.

"Getting that game ball meant more to him than getting the trophy," Dan Rooney said. "That was something very special to my father."

Asked to remember the special moment, Ham said of Chief: "I don't think he liked the idea that people thought, 'Gee, I wish he could win a championship. He deserves one after being the owner of a team for 40 years and could not get over the top.' Now he had his championship."

Rooney tried to dodge the attention in his typical understated fashion.

"I didn't want to accept the trophy. Dan Rooney and Chuck Noll deserved it," Rooney said. "I guess they just wanted me to be a big shot for a day."

Blount admired Rooney, which shaped his emotions after the game. He thought about how Rooney would walk around the locker room, stopping at each player's stall along the way to hold a conversation.

"He'd be like, 'How's your family, how you doing? Hang in there. Keep up the good work,'" Blount said. "He was such an inspiration. And we're talking about a guy who was in his seventies. He was just a guy who was a father figure. He represented stability and wisdom. And I think all those things were things I admired in him.

"So when we won our first Super Bowl and to see the Chief, man, I think when he was presented that [Lombardi] trophy, that memory of all the things that happened and all the experiences, to me, I think it epitomized what perseverance and never giving up is all about. For 40 years his team had been the doormat for the NFL. And he finally got his moment, and to witness that and to be a part of it was very special to me."

Ham remembered a nice aspect about receiving his winning check of $15,000. On the withholding stub, he found a special note that Rooney had written him. He later found out Rooney had composed a personalized note to every player on the team.

"He always took time out to do that," Ham said. "He'd jot down a note to make you feel special. Just a special, special man to everybody; I mean everybody loved the guy. I still have the stub from my first Super Bowl."

White played a stellar game, then returned to the hospital for another 10 days. One thing stuck in his craw from the experience. He'd been missing when the team picture was snapped and there was no mention of him missing in the names underneath the photograph.

"To this day I'm still upset about not being in the team picture and it not saying 'not listed: Dwight White,'" White said. "Couldn't they have said 'missing'? And I'm the guy that got out of the hospital bed. I'm the guy that scores the safety. I'm the guy that played my ass off and I don't even get the courtesy of having 'Dwight White missing.' I'm a big boy and you move on. I'm sure it was an oversight: they probably were not as efficient in the front office as they should have been. But goddamned right it hurts my feelings. I'm still pissed off about it."

Others thought about the celebration in the streets of the Steel City.

"The Burg may be in ashes," Ham said. "I wonder if there'll be a town there when we get back."

10

Super Bowl Sequel

How does a team approach a season after winning a Super Bowl, particularly after it had waited so long to win a championship?

Following their first Super Bowl victory—and for every Super Bowl win thereafter—Chuck Noll and Dan Rooney arranged to have the players' championship rings delivered by early June. If the ring manufacturer couldn't guarantee it, they could not bid on the contract. Noll and Rooney didn't want the previous year to linger.

Keeping his team motivated never presented a problem to Noll, who believed in maintaining a competitive environment, which could be perceived as cold or sensible, depending on one's point of view.

"It was competitive, there was no question about it," Noll said. "As soon as you think you've got a lock on things you're in trouble. I'm talking about as a coach, as a player, whatever, because competition is a good thing. There's always going to be somebody competing for your job, and that's the nature of it. And it's not bad. That's a good motivation."

Steelers players were not afforded the luxury of showing up at training camp with any security.

"You had to go out there and win your job," L. C. Greenwood said. "We didn't come into training camp and have Chuck say, 'OK L.C., you're my starting defensive end.' We'd come into training camp hoping that we'd be able to start or hoping that we'd be on the team."

Noll never gave the players a sense they had it made.

"And quite honestly, that was intentional on Chuck's part," Mike Wagner said. "That's how he wanted to coach. You figured out as a player you had to earn your spot. Not only every year but every week. That's just the way it goes. The key thing is, that was across the board, didn't matter who you were."

Noll intimidated people through his quietness.

"Sometimes if people aren't talking a lot you kind of are wary, particularly if they're in a position of power," Wagner said. "And I think that was one of his tools."

Noll's approach might have added anxiety to his players' lives, but it was respected.

"I think, to [Noll's] credit, he always kept that as a carrot or a focal point that 'football is not your life's work, this is just something you're doing,'" said Mel Blount, who said he never felt secure about his job despite all of his success. "He would always say, 'If you can't do this, then you need to go on with your life's work.' And I thought that was telling in the sense that it would keep players reminded that, you know what, you've got to prepare yourself for the day this passes on. You saw it in practice. You saw it in training camp. Guys would get cut or somebody would get hurt or just couldn't play football anymore. Somewhere in your subconscious, you had to know that 'you know what man, I've got to find something else to do when this is over.'"

John Stallworth believes a lot of players try to hang on to athletic careers because they don't know what the next step in their lives is.

"And I think the sooner you can prepare yourself for the next step the easier it is when the time comes to walk away from it," Stallworth said. "Certainly Chuck put it in our consciousness that there was another part to our lives, and a major part to our lives, and we need to prepare for that. I think in that preparation came some sense of I can do something else and I can walk away from [football] when the time comes."

Stallworth laughed when told Blount had never felt secure about his job.

"I will tell you as the guy who had to go up against Mel every day, I never thought anybody came along that threatened Mel's job," Stallworth said. "Mel's going to leave when Mel's ready to leave and not until that day comes."

In the end, Noll's players weren't necessarily friends with their coach, but they recognized he had managed the team in the right way.

"I think he did what he thought he had to do to put a football or a winning football team on the field," Greenwood said. "I think he handled it the way he thought he had to handle it, and I guess, kind of like the rest of us, he just ended up doing the right thing."

The 1975 Steelers certainly showed no hangover from success.

After an upset loss to the Bills in the second game of the season, the Steelers reeled off 11 straight wins with a balanced—and dominating—

display of offense and defense. Even though Joe Greene was out with a back injury, the Steelers defeated Cincinnati and twice defeated Houston to control the AFC Central Division. During a 31–17 win over Cleveland on December 7, Franco Harris became the seventh running back in NFL history to surpass 1,000 yards three times. Meanwhile, Bradshaw enjoyed his finest season to date completing 58 percent of his passes, including 18 touchdowns. Lynn Swann led the AFC with 11 touchdown catches, and Mel Blount led the league with a remarkable 11 interceptions.

The Steelers finished the regular season with a 12–2 record to win the division, holding off Cincinnati at 11–3 and Houston at 10–4. One of the Steelers' losses came in the final game of the season against the Rams, who beat them 10–3 in Los Angeles. The Rams game, which pitted two teams who had secured their places in the playoffs, played out like a glorified exhibition game.

In contrast were the Baltimore Colts, who had to win during the final weekend of the season to earn a spot in the playoffs. Facing the New England Patriots at Baltimore's Memorial Stadium, the Colts took a 34–21 contest to earn the team its ninth consecutive victory and the AFC's Eastern Division title. And for their trouble the Colts' reward would come six days later against the Steelers in the first round of the playoffs.

The Colts were feeling good about themselves heading into the play-offs. Their defensive line—composed of ends Fred Cook and John Dutton and tackles Joe Ehrmann and Mike Barnes—was affectionately known as "the Looney Tunes" and had earned the Steelers' respect for their league-leading 59 sacks.

"I know the kind of hell you go through to accomplish that kind of feat," Joe Greene told reporters when asked about the Colts' sack total. "You just don't do that sittin' down. That's playing football. That's what we call throwin' down or gettin' down. Whatever you want to name it, they were doing it."

Greene and his teammates on the Steelers' defensive line had seen their sacks total fall from 52 in 1974 to 43 in 1975 due primarily to the respect gained from opponents, who used a lot of play-action, three-step drops, first-down passes, and maximum protection to slow the Steelers' rush.

Colts quarterback Bert Jones had similarities to Terry Bradshaw. Both hailed from Louisiana, and each packed a strong arm on a large, physical body. Helping Jones lead the Colts was Franco Harris' old Penn State teammate, Lydell Mitchell, who had been the better known of the pair in college. Mitchell had finished fifth in the Heisman

Trophy balloting and established a national college record with 29 touchdowns. Despite the fact that Mitchell had gained more yardage than Harris at Penn State, Harris had been drafted in the first round while Mitchell went to the Colts in the second.

Harris' work in the pros had overshadowed Mitchell's to that point, but Mitchell had been no slouch in the Colts' backfield. After a disappointing rookie year that saw him gain just 215 yards during the 1972 season, he followed with rushing totals of 963, 757, and 1,193 in 1975 to become the first player in franchise history to gain 1,000 yards. Harris and Mitchell remained good friends and even had a bet on which of them would finish the 1975 season in second place behind O. J. Simpson for the rushing title. Harris' 1,246 won, but he openly teased he would never collect from his friend.

The Colts had balance and a threatening defensive line going for them. On top of that, Greene continued to suffer from a pinched nerve, which made way for Steve Furness to start in his place. But the Steelers still had the best corps of linebackers in football and a relentless secondary led by Blount.

"I truly think the best football player I ever had to play against, who intimidated me and the team the most, was Mel Blount," Jones said. "He was just a phenomenal cover guy. He had good size and hit harder than anybody on the football field. He was just an intimidating force. I mean he covered you better than a spiderweb. He simply occupied one half of the football field and said, 'This is my side of the field, go play on the other side and hope that you can come out successful.' And it was difficult. But Blount wasn't the only guy. They were a phenomenal team. We certainly enjoyed competing against them, but we were just outmatched man for man."

Jones laughed when asked if the Steelers had any holidays in their lineup on either side of the ball.

"There were none," Jones said. "Lynn Swann, John Stallworth, and Terry, they had some great skill players. But hey, if you scored 10 points, you won the game if you were the Pittsburgh Steelers. I mean they just dominated the football on defense."

Of note, this playoff game brought forth the "Terrible Towel" to Steelers fans. During one of Myron Cope's 11:00 P.M. sportscasts the week of the Baltimore game, he urged fans to bring gold towels to the game. The fans responded, turning Three Rivers Stadium into a sea of gold towels that taunted the Colts while encouraging the home team. And a tradition had been born.

The Colts discovered how dominating the Steelers' defense could be on their first series of the game. On fourth down the Colts punted, but the Steelers roughed the kicker to give the ball back to the Colts for four more downs. Jones' throwing arm got unintentionally kicked by J. T. Thomas during the seventh play of the game, which sent the Colts' leader to the bench for his injury to be treated. All told, the Colts held the ball for nine plays and did not make 10 yards, which told both teams all they needed to know about what the Colts could expect to endure that day.

Late in the second quarter Baltimore defensive back Lloyd Mumphord flipped Bradshaw into the air. Bradshaw hurt his right knee on the play and needed help leaving the Steelers' sideline at halftime when the injury caused him to lose feeling in his foot. But he returned in the second half and did not miss any time.

Marty Domres took over for Jones and couldn't do much, but a Harris fumble early in the third quarter led to a Colts field goal that put the Steelers behind 10–7. The Colts' lead didn't last long.

Blount locked into the fact that the Colts had been running turn-in routes throughout the game and figured they would go back to it. So when Colts receiver Roger Carr began to hook inside with the Colts facing a third-and-14 from their own 14, Blount recognized the route. Sniffing a familiar scent, he stepped in front of Domres' pass to make the interception and returned the ball to the Colts' 7. Rocky Bleier scored on the next play to give the Steelers a 14–10 lead.

A short punt early in the fourth quarter gave the Steelers the ball at the Colts' 39, which led to a 2-yard touchdown run by Bradshaw that pushed the lead to 21–10 before Andy Russell salted away the game.

Jones had just returned to the game when Jack Ham hit his arm and jarred the ball loose. Like a shortstop scooping up a ground ball, Russell recovered the fumble on one bounce and ran 93 yards for the game's final score. Russell had a bad knee and he was 35 years old, which made his run to the end zone resemble anything but a sprint. The touchdown made the final score 28–10 and made the good-natured linebacker fair game for his wisecracking teammates.

One of the better zingers came from Ray Mansfield, who noted: "I thought that [Russell] was trying to run the clock out. I thought he was trying to get the game over and score at the same time."

Jack Ham added: "I thought he might get a penalty for delay of game."

The victory over the Colts put the Steelers back in familiar territory against the Raiders in what had come to be their annual meeting in the playoffs. The game would be the fourth straight year Oakland and Pittsburgh met in the postseason.

The condition of Bradshaw, who had a sprained knee, had the Steelers concerned, but Noll was so confident that Bradshaw would be ready that he didn't give backups Joe Gilliam or Terry Hanratty extra work. And, after missing the previous week's game, Greene looked like he might play.

In the previous year's game the Raiders were held to 29 yards rushing. Once again the Steelers recognized that their efforts in shutting down the Raiders' running game would likely dictate whether they won or lost.

"If they run the football on us, I'm going to be watching the Super Bowl on television," Ham said.

The Steelers got some added help from the weather—and a fortuitous tear in the tarp covering the field at Three Rivers Stadium.

The night before the game the tarp ripped, which left the middle of the field unaffected but left the areas from the hash marks to the sidelines frozen for the game. While it's never been proven that the field's condition was anything but an accident, the Raiders suspected the Steelers had the field frozen to hamstring deep threat Cliff Branch, who averaged more than 17 yards per reception and caught nine touchdowns during the 1975 season. Having the outside portions of the field frozen over was the equivalent of shutting down the speed lane on a busy interstate. Branch would have a hard time repeating his previous year's performance against the Steelers in the 1974 AFC Championship Game when he caught nine passes for 186 yards.

If indeed the Steelers had pulled some shenanigans, it wasn't as though the Raiders hadn't been accused of pulling similar stunts. During one game Pittsburgh players experienced a marsh inside the Oakland Coliseum—despite the fact that Northern California was in the midst of a drought—that sunk their running game; punter Bobby Walden believed a deflated football was put in service when he punted against the Raiders in games at Oakland; and Oakland linemen were accused of rubbing Vaseline on their jerseys.

"The condition of the field was good until you got down to the corners of the field," Donnie Shell said. "It was a little icy then, but it was extremely cold. I remember the saliva, as I was running down on kickoffs and prevent defense, the sweat and saliva coming from my mouth froze right on my bar. The tarp had blown off the field the night before. I think that's what happened. But we had to play on the same field: neither team had an advantage."

Also greeting the Raiders at game time was a windchill temperature of minus 12 degrees. Hoping to combat the icy field, the ground crew spread a product over the field known as Sno-Flo that was supposed to work like rock salt to break down the ice and make the field manageable. It didn't work, leaving the players to complain about having their cleats crunch down on the little white Sno-Flo balls, which contributed to the football becoming slippery and hard to grip. Players might have reached for the jar of Firm-Grip, which was a legal substance in those days, except they couldn't scoop out the sticky substance used to help them hang onto the football because the stuff had frozen in the jar.

Tony Parisi once again broke out the special Canadian cleats he'd successfully debuted against the Vikings in the Super Bowl, and his wife sewed fleece-lined flaps to the players' jerseys so they could keep their hands warm.

The Steelers had one big surprise for their rivals at the beginning of the game when Greene left the sideline to take his position in the middle of the Steelers' defensive line. Though he was slowed by the lingering effects of a pinched nerve in his neck and a pulled groin muscle, Greene's presence gave the Steelers an emotional lift and helped clog up the Raiders' running game.

Throughout the contest both teams handled the football like it was greased, not frozen. Between the two teams there were 13 turnovers and countless dropped passes.

Roy Gerela gave the Steelers a 3–0 lead when he connected on a 36-yard field goal in the second quarter. The Pittsburgh kicker wasn't as fortunate in the second half, missing a 44-yard attempt and having another blocked by Oakland linebacker Ted Hendricks. Gerela wasn't the only one having difficulties, particularly in the third quarter.

Pittsburgh's Mike Collier fumbled a punt at his own 16, and the Raiders recovered only to fumble the ball back to the Steelers. On the play Jack Lambert recovered for the first of his three fumble recoveries in the game. Lynn Swann then gave the ball back after a vicious clothesline by Oakland safety George Atkinson at midfield. The Raiders recovered, Swann was sent to the hospital with a concussion, and three plays later running back Clarence Davis fumbled at the Steelers' 30; Lambert recovered. In the span of eight plays during the third quarter, each team fumbled twice.

When the third quarter ended, the score remained 3–0 Steelers.

On the second play of the fourth quarter, the Steelers called for a Harris sweep around the left end. After a jarring crack-back block by

Stallworth, Harris suddenly saw mostly open space. Only rookie corner-back Neal Colzie, starting in place of veteran Willie Brown, stood between Harris and the end zone. Colzie unsuccessfully tried to plant his helmet into Harris' chest and was swatted away like an annoying kid brother en route to the end zone.

Harris' 25-yard touchdown run pushed the Steelers' lead to 10–0.

Ken Stabler answered the touchdown by moving the Raiders the length of the field through the air in six plays. A sidearm touchdown pass to Mike Siani from the Steelers' 14 capped the drive to move the Raiders within a field goal of tying the game.

The Raiders' defense forced the Steelers to punt on their next possession, but the fumble parade continued on the Raiders' first play. Marv Hubbard coughed up the football and, once again, Lambert was in the right place at the right time and recovered. Stallworth ran onto the field with the Steelers' offense and promptly told Bradshaw he could get open on a flag pattern since the Raiders were in "Defense Two," where the cornerback rotates toward the wide receiver and the safety rotates behind him. Bradshaw called the play two plays later. Stallworth took off on the flag route and cut inside Colzie toward Tatum, the safety. Stallworth slipped but put down his hand and managed to keep his balance; the ball had arrived by the time Stallworth was upright. Colzie appeared to have a chance to intercept the pass before slipping on the frozen turf, and Stallworth hauled in Bradshaw's pass for a 20-yard touchdown. Gerela's frustrations continued when he missed the extra point.

Bradshaw had left the game after getting kicked in the head, leaving Terry Hanratty to finish out the game, which amounted to taking the snap and handing the ball off to Harris to preserve the Steelers' 16–7 lead with less than two minutes to go. And true to the theme of the game, Harris fumbled at the Raiders' 35.

The fumble led to a 41-yard field goal by George Blanda with 17 seconds remaining. Tension filled Three Rivers Stadium as the black-and-gold-clad fans cursed Gerela's missed extra point. If Oakland could somehow recover an onside kick and put the ball in the end zone, the hated Raiders would effectively steal a return trip to the Super Bowl from their beloved Steelers. If the Steelers fell on the kick, the game would be over.

Predictably, the Steelers' Reggie Garrett could not handle Ray Guy's squib kick, and Hubbard recovered the ball near midfield with seven seconds remaining. Stabler went downfield to Branch, who hauled in his second catch of the day at the Steelers' 15, and tried to get out of bounds. Blount, who wisely let Branch catch the ball rather than risk an interference call, slammed Branch to the icy turf as the clock ran out with an estimated twenty thousand fans down on the field adding to the confusion.

Steelers 16, Raiders 10, and the Steelers had earned a return trip to the Super Bowl.

11

Return to
the Super Bowl

By earning a trip to their second consecutive Super Bowl, the Steelers drew a different kind of test in Super Bowl X against the Dallas Cowboys, a team with an image and style of play contrasting the Steelers'. Though NFL Films had yet to tag the Cowboys with the "America's Team" moniker that would both immortalize the team and curse it, the Cowboys' differences could get under an opponent's skin.

"Dallas is flashy, modern, streamlined, barbecues, and big Texas egos," Dwight White said. "When I think of Dallas, I think of El Dorados and Sevilles. We have El Dorados and Sevilles in Pittsburgh, too. But the salt on the roads has eaten big holes in them."

Tom Landry had served as the Cowboys head coach since the team's inception in 1960. He had led them to back-to-back losses to the Packers in the NFL Championship Game during the 1966 and 1967 seasons and to a loss in Super Bowl V before winning Super Bowl VI to put to bed their reputation as the team that couldn't win the big one. In a game like football that thrived on human emotion, Landry resembled a coaching oxymoron. Instead of employing his team to "go out and hit somebody!" he was more prone to explaining what needed to be done in an icy, meticulous fashion. He knew football and gave the Cowboys an advantage in most games they played because of his knowledge.

Given the Cowboys' style of play—including their use of the shotgun formation, which had yet to catch on with other teams—they were entertaining, and their quarterback, Roger Staubach, had been a Heisman Trophy winner at the Naval Academy and cut the figure of the All-American boy.

"We had not done particularly well against them in regular-season games or even exhibition games," John Stallworth said. "We'd never really done well against the Cowboys, and so we knew we had a game in front of us. And we had a very good team to beat. I think we were all confident that if we played well we could beat them. But nobody was cocky that we could just go out and kick their butt. They were a team we respected. They had a lot of talent and they were well coached.

"There was also a very distinct difference in our styles. We were very much a punch-you-in-the-mouth football team, and they were finesse. And we just thought a punch in the mouth was going to win every time."

While Pittsburgh had been penciled in for the Super Bowl prior to the start of the season, Dallas' route was less expected and far more dramatic.

After compiling a 10–4 record during the regular season, the Cowboys finished second to the 11–3 St. Louis Cardinals in the NFC Eastern Division. Despite not winning their division, the Cowboys qualified for the playoffs as the wild-card team, which opened the door to some odd and exciting football.

Against the Vikings in the divisional playoffs at Minnesota, the Cowboys trailed 14–10 when Staubach hit on a prayer of a pass to Drew Pearson with 24 seconds remaining for a 50-yard touchdown pass and a 17–14 win to advance to the NFC Championship Game.

The Cowboys' next opponent was the Rams, who were favored to win and go to the Super Bowl for the first time in the team's history. The Cowboys left little suspense this time. Employing their "flex" defense, they allowed the Rams just 22 yards rushing. Staubach threw four touchdown passes en route to a 37–7 win to earn a trip to Miami for their third Super Bowl.

In the aftermath of the Steelers' win over the Raiders, doubt lingered about whether Lynn Swann would be available for the Super Bowl. Thanks to the concussion administered by Oakland safety George Atkinson, Swann spent two nights in a Pittsburgh hospital. But doubts about whether he would play weren't the only doubts circulating. Swann's whole professional career flashed before him, and he wondered if he was through.

Swann's concerns were legitimate. Once word spread that Swann's head couldn't take the abuse—thanks to Atkinson and his running mate, Jack Tatum—defensive backs would swarm around his noggin like bees around honey. Every time Swann went across the middle he would be a target. Would a career in pro football be worth such abuse? Only Swann could answer the question.

An off week was sandwiched between the AFC and NFC Championship Games and the Super Bowl, affording Swann the opportunity to recover from the blow to the head. During the first week of practices, Swann remained on the sidelines mostly, save for some light running and a few patterns to keep his timing right while doctors continued to monitor his progress. Eventually the doctors cleared him for play, but they did so while adding a caveat: if he took a big hit to the head, he might incur irreparable damage. So the decision about whether Swann would play was his.

Wind and rain caused temperatures in Miami to plummet, and the glorious Super Bowl X buildup became a miserable exercise in how to best negotiate foul weather. Sun worshippers remained inside, leaving their exotic poolside drinks in the blender while they waited for the weather to clear. The players began to feel cooped up and edgy.

Super Bowl tickets were in great demand. Countless tales circulated about people paying upward of $200 for scalped tickets that turned out to be counterfeit. Others purchased expensive packages including air travel, hotel stay, and game tickets only to discover their tickets did not exist. Local authorities estimated the total take for the con games to be approximately $1.5 million.

Football fans simply found the attractiveness of the matchup an irresistible lure. On the surface the game appeared to be a classic confrontation between the Cowboys' offense and the Steelers' defense. The Cowboys' shotgun formation could confuse even the most astute and talented defenses. And Staubach brought myriad problems the Steelers needed to prepare for in order to stop the Cowboys. In addition to being able to pass with the best quarterbacks in the league, Staubach could be elusive. While the Vikings' Fran Tarkenton had little luck scrambling against the Steelers in the previous year's Super Bowl, Staubach brought a different challenge when rousted from the pocket. Instead of scrambling, he would take off running.

According to Andy Russell, the Steelers' defense wasn't as concerned about the shotgun formation as they were about where the Cowboys stationed their people when Staubach dropped into the formation.

"They used a lot of motion, so you had to figure out where those people were going," Russell said. "They tried to flood zones with receivers, which caused you to change from defense X to defense Y, and pretty soon the ball is snapped. If you were in the wrong formation at that point you could be in trouble."

Stallworth likened Dallas' offense to a "Bill Walsh team."

"They made it harder for the defense," Stallworth said. "They kept changing the sets. So you'd see one set, you'd see another set, they kept moving it around. So you'd change the defense. It's a little more difficult that way; you'd rather be thinking about what play they're going to run and how you're going to stop it rather than thinking about what defense I'm in."

Mel Blount wasn't in awe of the Cowboys' offense, which probably cut to the heart of why he reigned as one of the best cornerbacks in the league.

"As a player, you convince yourself that this guy in front of you can't beat you," Blount said. "You look at film and you study guys, but when you line it up and buckle up the chin strap it's about what's on the inside of a guy. [You're] going to go into techniques and play the coverage and all that, but there's got to be something inside of you, driving you to compete. I never thought the Cowboys' offense was that complex. They did a lot of motion and a lot of what I call trying to fool people. But that was just basic fundamentals that you had to stick with. Most of the times the play came right back to you. You dissect it and you made the play on it."

Noll remembered being more concerned about the Cowboys' flex defense than the Cowboys' offense. The essence of the "flex" defense was to achieve containment of every gap, which they tried to accomplish by offsetting two linemen in a flex fashion to combat counters and traps. Nobody else ran the defense the way the Cowboys did, and it worked well against the run.

"I think defensively was where they were most complex, different than anybody else we played," Noll said. "We had to understand what they were doing. When we got into a formation, they had extensive scouting, and they would load up against you based on that information. We would study that and try to take advantage of that."

Super Bowl X had not become the media circus that future Super Bowls would become. Still, anything in the news—such as the status of Swann's head—proved more than topical for those covering the event. When asked about Swann, Cowboy's safety Cliff Harris told reporters: "I'm not going to hurt anyone intentionally. But getting hit again while he's running a pass route must be in the back of Swann's mind. I know it would be in the back of my mind."

Amid comments such as Harris', Swann reached a decision. Though he would not be at the top of his game physically, he mustered up his courage and decided to play in the game and, basically, to continue his career. He refused to be intimidated.

But turning one's talents off and on isn't necessarily an easy thing to do. Swann did not look sharp at practices, dropping passes and looking stiff and reserved. Fortunately for the Steelers, Swann finally regained his form.

Miami's Orange Bowl hosted a crowd of 80,187 for Super Bowl X, while another 80 million viewers watched at home, composing the largest TV audience in history at the time—which explained how a commercial minute of television could have climbed to $230,000. A record number of press credentials, 1,735, were issued, and CBS's pregame had swelled to 90 minutes. Even Hollywood could see what a piece of Americana the Super Bowl had become. Paramount's major undertaking of 1976 was a movie titled *Black Sunday*, a thriller dealing with assassination plots and terrorism, including a helicopter running into a blimp at the Super Bowl. Crowd shots and some on-the-field action were filmed during the actual game.

Appropriately, the punch-'em-in-the-mouth vs. the flashy matchup began with the Cowboys putting their trickery on display. On the opening kickoff former Steeler Preston Pearson fielded the kick and handed off to Thomas "Hollywood" Henderson, who would have scored on the reverse had Roy Gerela not roll blocked him out of bounds around midfield. Despite the big return, the Cowboys couldn't convert their field position into points.

When the Steelers got the ball they wanted to control the tempo of the game, so they pounded Harris into the line on four of their first five plays before they had to punt from their own 40-yard line.

Bobby Walden took his eyes off the ball and dropped a snap that hit him in the hands. The veteran punter bobbled the ball, never getting off the punt. Dallas tight end Bill Joe Dupree, who played on the special teams, brought down Walden at the Steelers' 29, where the Cowboys took possession.

Staubach got to work and connected on a 14-yard pass to Pearson crossing the middle, and he scored to give the Cowboys a 7–0 lead after just four minutes and 35 seconds had clicked off the clock. A significant side note about the touchdown: it was the first touchdown scored in the first quarter against the Steelers all season.

Mike Wagner cited a checkoff that he did not hear for making Pearson's touchdown possible.

"To Bud Carson's credit, this was a play that we saw them run three or four times during the season and they always ran it the same way," Wagner said. "It was a series of shifts and motions out of a certain formation. So if you saw it and you could follow all the shifts and adjustments, you knew every time they were going to throw the ball to Drew Pearson over the weak side.

"Here I am playing strong safety in that formation. We go through a couple of days' practice watching this film, and I go to Carson and say, 'Hey look at this. We have J. T. Thomas and me sitting here in a strong zone in a Cover Two, basically we're playing them.' I said, 'You've got two guys with no wide receivers in these two zones. They're flooding the weak-side area. They're clearing out our weak corner, our weak backers, our middle backer.'"

Wagner suggested to Carson that Wagner chase Pearson across the field and as soon as Thomas saw Pearson in motion Thomas would fall into the spot Wagner vacated.

"This was a complicated coverage because they did so much shifting," Wagner said. "Because during that shifting motion we'd change our defense two, maybe three times. We're calling audibles for our secondary and our linebackers. The first time they ran it Drew Pearson scored a touchdown and it was my fault because we were trying to get to that coverage and I didn't hear any checkoff. I was worried that J.T. or some of the players didn't get it. So I didn't run over there. I told the coaches it was my fault."

Bradshaw and the Steelers came right back at the Cowboys, driving to the Cowboys' 7 by alternating running plays between Franco Harris and Rocky Bleier, and they got a lift from a nifty catch by Swann, in which he leapt along the sideline to grab a pass against Dallas cornerback Mark Washington. Swann's play, which has been an NFL Films staple ever since, saw Swann control his body in miraculous fashion to land one foot inbounds and then another, even when his momentum wanted to carry him out. The catch employed some of the moves Swann had learned while a student of ballet, and he gained a much-needed confidence boost. He would say later that he'd never played a game in which he felt so loose. The high-flying play covered 32 yards and put the Steelers in position to show the Cowboys how two could play the game of deception.

Facing a third-and-1 at the Cowboys' 7, Bradshaw concluded the Cowboys would be anticipating more of Harris pounding the line, so he called reserve tight end Randy Grossman's number. The Steelers lined up in "Play 333," a three-tight-end formation Noll often employed when the Steelers were deep in their opponent's territory; he used guard Gerry Mullins as his extra tight end. A red flag went up for the Cowboys' defense as soon as they recognized the formation from which the Steelers had a tendency to run. After faking a block, Grossman released and took a diagonal path toward the end zone where he found himself open. Bradshaw tossed him the ball, and the score was tied at 7.

The drive had been a confidence builder for the Steelers, who moved 67 yards in eight plays, and Bradshaw had completed the only two passes he had attempted.

Toni Fritsch kicked a 36-yard field goal to give the Cowboys a 10–7 lead in the second quarter. After the Steelers stalled, Staubach began another drive from his 48. Six plays later, the Cowboys were at the Steelers' 20, where they met the Steel Curtain at its best. Robert Newhouse tried to go off left tackle and was stopped for a 2-yard loss. Then Staubach was sacked on successive plays. L. C. Greenwood went first, tackling Staubach for a 12-yard loss, then Dwight White followed suit, tackling the Cowboys' quarterback for a loss of 10. After a Dallas punt, the Steelers had the ball at their own 6 with almost four minutes left in the half.

Swann's encore followed, and though this catch would be different, it would prove to be equally mystifying when he and Washington went up for a jump ball at midfield. Swann tipped the ball before falling to the Orange Bowl's turf. Both players were down on the field, but Swann never lost his concentration and managed to recover enough to make the 53-yard catch. In eight plays, including Swann's grab, the Steelers drove to the Dallas 19 with 32 seconds remaining to set up a 36-yard field-goal attempt by Gerela that would have tied the score at 10.

Gerela had suffered bruised ribs tackling Henderson on the opening kickoff and had trouble kicking the rest of the day. He missed the field goal, and the Steelers went into the locker room trailing 10–7.

In addition to the three points they didn't get, the Steelers received additional bad news. Joe Greene would have to sit out the second half because of a pulled groin muscle. Steve Furness would fill the gap as he had for much of the season, once again personifying the depth of the Steelers. Most teams could not suffer the loss of a player who had talent the magnitude of Greene's and hope to win.

Looking for some sort of spark, the Steelers appeared to get the break they needed when J. T. Thomas intercepted a Staubach pass early in the third quarter and returned it 35 yards to the Dallas 25. When the Steelers' offense stalled, Gerela was called upon to try a 33-yard field goal. Once again he missed, bringing about one of Super Bowl X's more celebrated moments.

Harris taunted the Steelers kicker by patting him on the helmet following the miss. Jack Lambert, who was on the field-goal team, didn't find any humor in the Cowboys safety's act and slung him to the ground.

"No one can be allowed to intimidate us," Lambert later said. "We're supposed to be the intimidators."

The officials stepped in, but before Lambert could be cited for a penalty he allowed a smile, which was totally out of character for the Steelers' linebacker, and the situation was defused.

Accounts of the game have mistakenly credited Lambert's action for waking up the Steelers when just the opposite was true.

"I thought it was completely insane and I went over to Lambert and chewed him out," Russell said. "Because, I said, 'Jack, we can't afford for you to get thrown out of this game for doing that; that's silly. I mean, come on.' I just thought it was ridiculous, told him not to do things like that, but that was his nature. He was a feisty character and he went with his gut. I was trying to think about how we didn't want Lambert to get thrown out of this game, which could have happened. It didn't take much to get thrown out of games for fighting. I know a lot of the announcers claimed that was an inspirational moment for us. No way. It was the reverse of that."

Lambert's performance remained strong; he would finish the game with 14 tackles on a day that saw the Steelers record 7 sacks.

Dallas held the 10–7 lead until three minutes into the fourth quarter when they faced a fourth-and-13 situation at their own 16 and were forced to punt. The Steelers put on a 10-man rush with Dave Brown and Reggie Harrison lined up over the Cowboys' center.

Harrison, who played football for the University of Cincinnati before joining the NFL as a member of the St. Louis Cardinals, had gone to the Steelers in 1974. A running back, his primary duty was to back up Franco Harris, which left his only playing time on special teams.

At the snap of the football, Harrison charged past the center's left shoulder and was met by a blocking back, whom he basically ran over. Suddenly he had an unobstructed path toward Cowboys punter Mitch Hoopes, who had just taken his first step. Harrison raised his arms and continued to charge toward the ball. Even after the game, Harrison wasn't quite sure where the ball hit him; the only certainty was that the ball ricocheted off him and out of the end zone for a safety to cut the Cowboys' lead to 10–9.

The Steelers received the Cowboys' free kick following the safety and drove into Dallas territory. This time they came away with three points by virtue of a 36-yard Gerela field goal to take a 12–10 lead.

On the Cowboys' next possession, Staubach attempted a first-down pass to Drew Pearson that was intercepted by safety Mike Wagner, who returned the ball to the Dallas 7. After the game Staubach said: "I didn't even see Wagner. He wasn't supposed to be there. I bet Golden Richards [wide receiver] was wide open, but I didn't see him either. Golden was Wagner's responsibility. Wagner just guessed, and guessed right."

The coverage was the same coverage keying on Pearson that Wagner had botched earlier in the game.

"And to this day, Roger Staubach continues to say that I guessed on the pass I intercepted in that game, that I shouldn't have been there," Wagner said. "They ran the same motion and I just ran to that area—didn't play it safe—and I saw the football. My biggest concern was catching the ball. And of course they're saying how can the strong safety be 40 yards deep, he's supposed to be on the weak-side flat. Complete opposite."

Wagner never completely explained what had happened on the play while he still was an active player.

"It's the kind of thing when you're playing during your career you don't make a big deal out of it because we might play the Cowboys next year," Wagner said. "And that's exactly what you'd want them to think, that you're guessing. This is the kind of strategy Bud Carson brought to our team."

Four plays after Wagner's interception, Gerela kicked an 18-yard field goal and the Steelers, with eight unanswered points, had a 15–10 lead late in the fourth quarter.

The Cowboys were hardly in panic mode. They had taken the Steelers' best shot and trailed by less than a touchdown with more than six minutes remaining in the game. The Cowboys' offense failed in their next possession and had to punt.

The Steelers took over at their own 30 and moved the ball to the 36, where they faced a third-and-4 with just over three minutes remaining.

Bradshaw read a blitz.

Feeling like he could continue to beat Washington, Swann broke his route and took off down the middle of the field, where he found himself facing single coverage. Washington didn't get any help from the Cowboys' safeties, and Bradshaw was more than happy to exploit the Cowboys where they had left themselves exposed. He let the ball fly just when tackle Larry Cole leveled him with a helmet-to-helmet hit. Bradshaw suffered a concussion on the play and never saw his pass fall into Swann's hands for a 64-yard touchdown.

"We thought we might be able to slip in a few long passes during that game," Noll said. "We hit some of them and missed a couple just barely."

Swann would say that Cliff Harris tried to intimidate him on one occasion by telling him he'd been lucky because Harris had just missed him with a hard shot and that Harris planned to go after him when he went across the middle. Swann opted to take the aggressive response in the war of words and told Harris to go for it and that if anybody was going to get hurt, it would be Harris.

Gerela's kick hit the upright and fell through to give the Steelers a 21–10 lead with just over three minutes remaining in the game.

Staubach came storming back from his own 20, hitting Charles Young for 7 yards, Drew Pearson for 30, and, finally, Percy Howard for a 34-yard touchdown to cut the lead to 21–17.

A failed onside kick gave the Steelers the ball at the Cowboys' 42 with one minute and 47 seconds remaining. The Steelers ran the ball three successive plays, and the Cowboys called timeout after each, leaving the Steelers faced with a fourth-and-9 situation at the Dallas 41.

Throughout the afternoon the Steelers had troubles with their punting game. Rather than risk a blocked punt or a long return, Noll decided to run the ball on fourth down, which in essence meant he'd decided to place his trust in the hands of old reliable, his defense.

Bleier gained two yards on fourth down and the Cowboys took over at their own 39.

Stallworth did not second-guess Noll's decision.

"I think the thought was he didn't want it to get blocked and run back," Stallworth said. "He was betting on his defense."

Wagner, who would be on the field as part of the unit that had to succeed for the Steelers to win, remembered thinking, 'Wow, [Noll] has really lost confidence in the punt team. But I'm saying to myself, number one, we have a great defense and we've got to do this one more time and this is what you want.

"When I think about it, at the end of the day, it was like a dream, a defensive back's dream. You want to be in the Super Bowl and you want to have the ball being fired at you to win the game. Of course you don't want to give up the winning score—that's always the biggest worry of a defensive back, blowing the game late. But that's what happened. All of a sudden, there's Roger Staubach scampering around the 40- or 50-yard line throwing the ball into the end zone. So it's sort of good news/bad news. From a secondary standpoint, Chuck had tremendous confidence in our front four, our linebackers, and our secondary to stop them."

Once again, the dangerous Staubach got back to work, running around left end for an 11-yard gain before passing to Preston Pearson for another 12 to put the Cowboys at the Steelers' 38. Time was on the Steelers' side. The Cowboys had no timeouts, so they had to either get out of bounds on a completed pass or score. Otherwise time would run out. Thus, the Cowboys began a series of deep passes, bringing to mind Staubach's "Hail Mary" pass to Drew Pearson that had won their playoff game against Minnesota. Could the Cowboys' leader pull out another victory with a miracle pass? Or would the Steelers' defense prevail at the end like it had against Oakland?

Staubach's first long one went to Drew Pearson and was overthrown; the second one to Howard fell incomplete. Glen Edwards stepped in front of Staubach's third attempt to make the interception and returned it to the Steelers' 33 as time expired to preserve the Steelers' 21–17 victory.

Even without Greene in the second half, the Steelers sacked Staubach a Super Bowl–record seven times. Swann caught four passes for 161 yards and a deciding touchdown to earn MVP honors.

And Noll's reasons for deciding to go with his defense rather than punt were explained.

"The move left them with no timeouts and needing a touchdown to win," he explained. "If they had needed a field goal, then it would have been different. But we had them in a must-pass situation, and I like for my defense to have a team in that kind of spot. Our defense did just what we thought it would do. They came up with a pass interception. I would prefer to turn a situation like that over to the defense instead of taking a chance on getting a punt blocked."

Noll was asked if he was worried at the end about Staubach doing to Pittsburgh what he had done to Minnesota, to which Noll answered he was not. When asked to elaborate on why not, he replied: "We're not Minnesota."

Indeed, the Steelers were not Minnesota, as evidenced by their second Super Bowl win in two tries. And talk of a dynasty had never been louder.

12

The Quiet Years

The NFL was living large entering the 1976 season. Two new teams, the Tampa Bay Buccaneers and the Seattle Seahawks, joined the league via expansion, and the league basked in its success, much of which had been achieved over the previous two seasons through the enormous popularity of the Steelers.

In the Steel Dynasty's prime, the 1976 and 1977 seasons would be remembered as the quiet years. Even though the Steelers had the same talent and savvy they had always had, different little nagging things like injuries, bad breaks, and being marked men knocked the team off kilter.

When opposing teams lined up to play the Steelers, they saw bull's-eyes on the backs of the two-time Super Bowl champions.

The Steelers opened their 1976 campaign on July 23 against the College All-Stars in the 43rd annual College All-Star Game at Chicago's Soldier Field. With the Steelers holding a 24–0 lead in the third quarter, rain appeared suddenly and soaked the field. Then, just as quickly as the rain appeared, the crowd of 52,895 stormed the field and had a play day on the slippery AstroTurf. The players waited underneath the stands, but the game was canceled when the security people could not clear the field. This bizarre contest would mark the final game of what had once been a prestigious tradition; the game was never resumed.

While the Steelers beat up on the College All-Stars, an indicator that everything might not be seashells and balloons came on opening day of the 1976 season and was delivered by the Oakland Raiders.

A national television audience watched while the Steelers and Raiders battled in Oakland. Late in the first half Lynn Swann took off down the right side of the field before cutting toward the middle; George Atkinson, Swann's old adversary, covered him on the play that turned out to be a broken play when Bradshaw scrambled and eventually threw a pass to Franco Harris, who took off running up field. Approximately 15 yards away from Harris, in an area totally removed from the action, Atkinson charged Swann from behind and used his forearm to strike a blow to the back of the unsuspecting receiver's head.

Swann dropped like a collapsed card table.

No officials saw the play, so no penalty was assessed. But a national television audience had seen the play in living color, and it had played out like Rambo clubbing baby seals.

Swann had another concussion and would miss the next two games, and the NFL had a public relations disaster.

Pete Rozelle's New York office heard from a nation of football fans regarding Atkinson's hit while the commissioner reviewed films of the hit.

"I've seen the replays [of the hit]," John Stallworth said. "When it actually happened, I'm on the field too, so I didn't actually see it in real time. But it was a kind of devastating blow. I remember thinking that they, the Raiders, felt like that was the only way they could cover him, that they had to be very physical with him and maybe even stepping over the line. And in doing that, that was the only way they could cover him. Desperate men tend to do desperate things, I guess. And I think they were desperate to try to stop him from being effective in that football game."

Chuck Noll went berserk. After the game, he told reporters: "You have a criminal element in all aspects of society. Apparently we have it in the NFL too. Maybe we have a law-and-order problem."

Noll's comments did not sit well with Al Davis and Atkinson. Atkinson filed a $2 million slander suit against Noll, but according to Noll, Davis bankrolled the suit.

"I remember everything about [the incident]," Dan Rooney said. "The Raiders actually put Lynn Swann out of the game. And it was a real problem because we needed him. It really caused us a lot of problems that particular day, so after the game the next day, Chuck just said that Atkinson and some of the Raiders were part of the criminal element in the National Football League. Well Davis saw this as a chance to really create problems for us. And he did. He sued us."

A league rule existed that one NFL team couldn't sue another team in the league.

Davis "hadn't broken that yet," Rooney said. What they did they had to do, *Atkinson v. Noll*, but in reality it was Steelers against the Raiders."

The suit went to trial in July 1977.

In the aftermath of the incident, Swann once again had to confront the idea that headhunters would take aim for him, but he went on.

"I'm sure that crossed his mind," Stallworth said. "I will tell you, though, that I never saw a change in the way he played. I never saw that there was an opportunity for him to jump—whether in a crowd or alone—jump up and use his athletic ability to catch the football that he did not do that."

After their opening-day loss to the Raiders, the Steelers lost three of their next four games—including losses to Minnesota, Cleveland, and New England, who beat the Steelers 30–27 in the third game of the season.

"We had some good games with the Steelers, and we beat them in 1976, and [Steve] Grogan was a second-year quarterback in his first year of starting," remembered Steve Nelson, who played linebacker for the Patriots. "Russ Francis was our tight end, and Russ made some big plays."

Despite the loss, the Steelers still had the Patriots' respect.

"The way I always looked at the Pittsburgh Steelers is the Pittsburgh Steelers were what we wanted to be," Nelson said. "We thought we had a very talented football team. And we knew the Steelers were the team we eventually had to beat [to get to the Super Bowl]. And we just could never get it done."

New England safety Tim Fox came into the NFL in 1976 and remembered how motivated the team had been to play the Steelers.

"They had been a powerhouse for so long when we went into Pittsburgh that year," Fox said. "We thought we had a pretty good football team. Talk about being up for a game. When we beat them we got a lot of confidence from knowing we could play with a team like them. They were the standard.

"They were just very, very good athletes. They caught the ball and they ran the ball, which set everything up. You had to respect them so much. They had everything going for them."

The Patriots ran a 3-4 defense and followed the universal philosophy most teams employed when trying to stop the Steelers' offense.

"We wanted to have Bradshaw beat us," Nelson said. "We didn't want Franco Harris to beat us. So we loaded up on the run. Their offensive linemen were kind of atypical in that they were shorter and lighter, but very quick. Mike Webster and all those guys, they did a lot of trapping inside. To beat them you had to shut down Franco Harris.

"We could match up on the outside because we had Mike Haynes and we had Raymond Clayborn [at the cornerback positions]. On the edge we could match up with them. We always had a hard time stopping Harris."

Nelson called Harris a special back.

"He always ran to the tight end side, so we'd slant to the tight end," Nelson said. "Just try to put more bodies on that side of the line. And [Rocky] Bleier was a good player, and certainly made some plays, but he kind of made plays because Franco Harris was next to him.

"Franco was very patient and he also had very quick feet. He was a big man. He didn't have the horsepower like John Riggins had or Earl Campbell; he had very quick feet, very light feet. He had the ability to bounce from hole to hole. You really had to have a disciplined front where you had all your gaps covered. You had to remain patient because he was going to remain patient. You couldn't try to make many real plays; you just had to play team defense because eventually with his ability to cut back and everything, he'd find the soft spot in your defense. But we felt very comfortable playing them if we could stop Franco and have Bradshaw, who was athletic and had a couple of great athletic receivers, try to beat us. [Bradshaw] could run and everything else, but our number one thing was stopping Harris."

Stopping Harris allowed opposing defenses to dictate the flow of the game.

"If they were able to run the ball on you then their defense was on the sidelines and their defense would come out fresh," Nelson said. "You never got in a situation where you were tiring their defense. We tried to win first down and get into situations where Franco was not a threat to beat us."

Though the Steelers got off to a 1–4 start in 1976 and did not escape last place until the ninth week of the season, they won their final nine games to capture their third-consecutive Central Division crown and fourth title since 1972. While the offense sputtered, thanks largely to Bradshaw suffering neck and wrist injuries that caused him to miss four games completely and play in just one half of four others, the defense flourished.

"I think the 1976 Steelers team was the greatest defensive team in league history," Paul Zimmerman said. "If you just look at what they did. Bradshaw gets hurt and Mike Kruczek goes in at quarterback and they shut out, what, five teams? Look at some of the records at what some of the quarterbacks did against them. You see a lot of five for nineteens in there."

Dan Pastorini, who played quarterback for the Houston Oilers during that period, offered a sarcastic laugh when asked about the Steelers' defense.

"Well, let me put it this way," Pastorini said. "When they tore down Three Rivers Stadium, I left a lot of DNA on that field, so I was not sorry

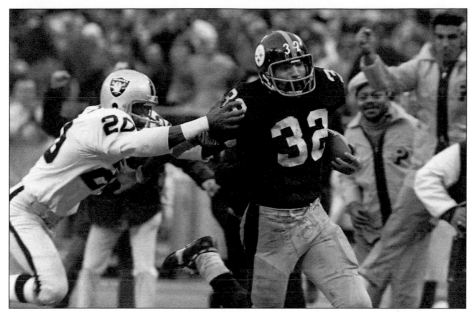

Franco Harris scores on one of the most famous plays in Steelers history, "the Immaculate Reception." On December 23, 1972, Harris scooped up a deflected pass and ran it 42 yards in the closing seconds to beat the Raiders 13–7 and advance to the AFC Championship Game.

NFL experts have called the Steelers' 1974 draft the greatest of all time. With two of their first four selections Pittsburgh landed wide receivers Lynn Swann (right) and John Stallworth.

Hall of Fame center Mike Webster (No. 52) was also taken in the 1974 draft, as was ferocious linebacker Jack Lambert (inset).

Free-agent safety Donnie Shell, an eventual five-time Pro Bowl selection, also joined Pittsburgh in 1974. *Photo courtesy of Getty Images.*

Running back and Vietnam War hero Rocky Bleier, elevated from taxi squad to special teams to reserve in three previous seasons with Pittsburgh, earned a starting role in 1974.

With all the pieces in place for the 1974 season, Pittsburgh advanced to Super Bowl IX in New Orleans, where their defense dominated the Minnesota Vikings in a 16–6 victory on January 12, 1975. Here L. C. Greenwood (No. 68), Ernie Holmes (No. 63), Joe Greene (No. 75), Mike Wagner (No. 23), and others celebrate sacking Minnesota quarterback Fran Tarkenton for a safety.

Owner Art Rooney (center, in dark suit) joins the team in prayer after their first Super Bowl win.

Quarterback Terry Bradshaw (left) and coach Chuck Noll pose with the Super Bowl trophy following a parade through downtown Pittsburgh on January 13, 1975.

Lynn Swann makes a spectacular catch during Super Bowl X against the Dallas Cowboys on January 18, 1976, in Miami. The Steelers won 21–17 for their second consecutive NFL championship.

John Stallworth celebrates after scoring a touchdown in an AFC playoff game against the Denver Broncos on December 30, 1978. The Steelers went on to win Super Bowl XIII 35–31 over the Dallas Cowboys for their third championship.

Terry Bradshaw celebrates a touchdown pass in Super Bowl XIV, which helped take his Steelers to a 31–19 win over the Los Angeles Rams and their fourth championship. Later, he posed with his MVP trophy (inset).

to see that stadium go down. And there were very few times, I can only recall two times in nine years, when I walked off that field after the game. They were a pretty tough football team."

When Pastorini retired in 1983, his medical chart, according to his own accounting, included: 16 concussions, 12 broken noses, a broken cheekbone, a broken sternum, 38 broken ribs, a broken tibia, a broken metatarsal, and three transverse processes.

"I'll tell you what, I can tell you when a storm is coming," Pastorini said.

To his recollection, many of the injuries were inflicted by the Steelers' defense.

"I know for a fact the three transverse processes were on one sack in 1972 on the first pass of the game," Pastorini said. "Joe."

"Joe," of course, was Joe Greene. For all of Pastorini's bumps and bruises, he said the Steelers were not a dirty team and even today he has special feelings toward Greene.

"There were times during my early years when we were 1–13 and we had to play those guys twice where we just got blown out," Pastorini said. "He could have ended my career several times, and he chose to hug me to the ground as opposed to nailing me and burying me into the ground. I think there was respect and I appreciated it, and as fierce as he is on the field, he was probably one of my all-time favorite people in the game to play against. He was a gentleman, he was fair, and he was tough."

Zimmerman said the 1976 Steelers defense "had the greatest collection of talent ever assembled on a defensive unit."

"They had 10 out of their starting 11 who made the Pro Bowl," Zimmerman said. "And the 11th, the guy who didn't make it, was the most feared of all of them, Ernie Holmes.

"I mean they had a perfect combination of talent. Add to that they had Bud Carson's system and their players were smart. Their linebackers, Ham, Lambert, and Russell, were really smart. So they had a series of calls where they would make calls on the go. They would have had a lot of fun with a Peyton Manning, because it would have been, who can make the last call?"

The opposing quarterback would call an audible at the line of scrimmage, and the Steelers would counter with an audible. If the quarterback adjusted, the Steelers adjusted accordingly. If somebody went in motion, a Steeler would follow.

"And they said they always had the last call," Zimmerman said. "That was Bud Carson's philosophy and system, and when you've got intelligent minds, you can do that. So you've got this incredible collection of talent playing at a very intelligent level; to me that produced the greatest defense ever."

Pastorini said the Steelers defense had no weaknesses.

"They could play you straight up," Pastorini said. "They'd do their double zone and double man, just challenge you to run the football. Nowadays, double zone, you run the football and pump it in there. Back then you had to beat that front four."

Jack Ham is generally considered to be the best pass-defending linebacker in NFL history. What made Ham different? He credited his success to anticipation, understanding passing lanes, jumping routes, and understanding what the quarterback was looking at in their zone or man-to-man coverage.

"Calculating the risks is important when you're jumping a route to go for the interception when you know you have deep help over the top," Ham said. "Reading the quarterback's eyes, again, anticipating a lot of times, and I had one of the fastest times in 10 yards both in college and at Pittsburgh.

"For a linebacker that's a real big asset to have because that's where you make or don't make plays. That burst you have to the football for a tackle to break up a pass play. Or break on a ball for an interception or whatever. And I had a lot of confidence in my ability there. And going back to football being a team game, we had those four maniacs up front, with Joe Greene, Ernie Holmes, Dwight White, and L. C. Greenwood— you've got a pass rush. So you could anticipate the ball coming out quicker. And you understood that with the reputation of our front four. So you kind of enjoyed playing that passing game. I didn't rush the quarterback all that much because at times we had blitz packages. But for the most part if you've got that kind of rush from your front four, boy it sure makes it a lot easier to make plays because you know that ball is coming out of there pretty quick."

While Ham is considered the best pass-covering linebacker of all time, Lambert isn't far behind.

"Having Lambert allowed [Bud Carson] to do things with his defense that were unheard of," Andy Russell said. "Bud had him covering the tight end all over the field. He'd assign him the first back coming out of the backfield, which was a big deal. The middle linebacker normally covered the second back, which was cake. Covering the first back was something the middle linebacker just didn't do."

Lambert also possessed an innate ability to meet at the ball and a toughness seldom seen. "The guy lived to play football," Greene said.

"He didn't like you if you had on a different colored jersey from the black and gold," Greene laughed. "He didn't like half the guys with the same jersey on as him. He had a great attitude. I loved it."

Behind the linebackers the Steelers had a defensive backfield consisting of Mike Wagner and Glen Edwards at safety and J. T. Thomas and Blount at the corners. All of the four could hit, and Blount ranks as one of the all-time best corners.

"Mel had all the attributes you needed back there," Stallworth said. "He could play a very physical ballgame with his size and strength, and Mel had the quickness and speed to run with anybody in the league. Cliff Branch with the Raiders, he was probably one of the fastest receivers in the league, and Mel's game plan against him was just to be very physical with him. I remember one game we played against the Raiders when Mel jammed Branch at the line of scrimmage and actually lifted him off of his feet. And when he lifted him up Branch's legs were still moving. It was hilarious. But that was Mel. I never ceased to be amazed at some of the things he could do on the football field. It just seemed like he was effortlessly doing things. Long stride and he's naturally strong. He didn't lift a whole lot of weights, and he was quick. He just had an internal drive that would kick in and brought along with it the focus he needed to be very good at what he did. Mel was extremely confident in his abilities to shut people down. He could shut you down. He knew it, and he knew that you knew it. So he just played the game that way."

Nat Moore believed Blount's tall and rangy build served him well.

"I played against him a lot," Moore said. "The big thing about Mel Blount was his build and those long arms. If you ever let him [get] his hands on you when he was trying to jam you, back when they could jam you all over the field, he would destroy you. Because he had such great leverage as a tall corner, you wanted to get him moving his feet lateral so that you can try and turn him around. If you got him moving his feet where you made him cross over, which is basically any defensive back, you've got him beat. But a guy who was tall and rangy like Mel, what you found was it was more difficult for him to recover. But if he got his hands on you, you could forget it, it was over."

Pastorini called Blount the best cornerback he ever played against.

"He used to drive me nuts," Pastorini said. "It was like he knew what I was thinking before I thought it. That whole defense was like that."

Greene reigned as the unquestioned leader of the defense and the team.

"We had a lot of leaders, but Joe really stands alone," Donnie Shell said.

Ham offered a disclaimer that he believes leadership can get blown out of proportion. Nevertheless, to him, Greene was the team's leader.

"I mean, Joe Greene was a leader on the football team, he was a great player," Ham said. "I have a hard time believing somebody can be a leader and not be a quality football player, and he was that. I fed off the plays he made on the field. And I think that's where the respect comes that you have for a player like that. I think it's more the play. I think the term leadership is an overused term—especially at a professional level. But by example he was a leader, so I drew from that."

Though Greene filled the role as the team leader well, he believes his role was a reflection of Noll.

"To tell you the truth, I paid close attention to what the head coach was saying in the meetings," Greene said. "I heard what he said to the press. And not only me, but all of us, we kind of reiterated that to our teammates in the locker room. And it was just supporting the coach. Not because it was the right thing to do—it was because we didn't know anything different to do. I don't want to say we weren't intelligent enough to have our own thoughts, but we knew that the common goal was to win."

Noll basically circled the wagons when he had the ball during the 1976 season and handed over the fate of the team to the defense.

"We always told the offense, just don't turn it over and we'll take care of things," L. C. Greenwood said. "That was probably the greatest season we had because we held all those teams scoreless. And it was just our objective to do that. That was our overall best defensive effort. We were dominating anyway, and we just went out and pretty much destroyed the teams we played.

"We just tried to show everybody we were the defending Super Bowl champs, we didn't have a quarterback, and our defense was the backbone of our football team. So we went out there to prove that. And I think that along the way we just got pretty fortunate that we were able to control the football games offensively and defensively because we scored touchdowns, we knocked down balls, we intercepted balls, we recovered fumbles, [and] we did everything we needed to do to give our football team a chance to win."

And the Steelers' defense changed.

"We started being more aggressive defensively," Shell said. "We had Joe Greene, L.C., Dwight, and Ernie, so we didn't blitz very much. But then we began to put in some blitz packages and began to turn up the heat a little bit. Add to that our attitude. We thought that nobody could score against us. We just got on a roll."

Greene allowed that 1976 could have been the peak season for their defense, and they did blitz more. Then he laughed and added: "We were very, very good during that stretch."

For the healthy Steelers remaining on offense, the 1976 season wasn't the most enjoyable.

"That was an awful year," Stallworth said. "As a receiver it could really beat you down. There were games when we didn't throw the ball more than two or three times. So Swanny and I had a plan." Stallworth laughed about the collaborative effort put forth by Swann and him. "One game we threw two or three passes and he caught one and the other ones were incomplete. We sat next to each other on Tuesday to watch the game film with all the rest of the offensive players, and when Swanny caught the pass we both stood up and clapped."

The reaction by the no-nonsense Noll was predictable.

"Chuck's lips are thin already, but they got a lot thinner," said Stallworth through his laughter, "one straight line across his face."

Kruczek helped trigger the turnaround on October 17 against Cincinnati in Three Rivers Stadium. Subbing for Bradshaw, the rookie quarterback's assignment was simple: hand off the ball to Franco Harris and Rocky Bleier. Kruczek pulled off the plan masterfully. Harris carried the ball a team-record 41 times as the Steelers won 23–6 and then ran the streak to nine consecutive wins by season's end.

The ball-control approach might have been ugly, but it blended perfectly with a Steelers defense that played better than ever. And the offensive line never played better.

"We had a running game that was working primarily because of our offensive line," Bleier said. "Bradshaw gets hurt and the mentality switches. We're running the ball. We're shoving it down people's throats. And we're winning."

The Steelers overpowered Miami 14–3 at Three Rivers during their winning streak. Jim Langer credited the Steelers' defensive line for setting up the entire defense's success. And any talk about the Steelers' defensive line always began with Greene.

"Joe was always a friendly guy," Langer said. "He was always smiling. He was always yucking it up out there. And one of the great things about Joe was he's always thinking. And with the great players you couldn't assume anything. They were players who were thinking. They were trying to outsmart you. You were trying to block then and they're trying to make it look like they were going one way and end up going the other. Joe's a very smart player and they worked very well together as a defensive line.

Of course he had the great ability, the great quickness, the great hands. The only thing I tried to do was get into him and tried to occupy him as long as I could. The worst thing you could do with Joe was to not touch him, which could happen quite easily. I just had a lot of respect for how he played the game. You never saw quit in Joe's eyes. If you happened to get a good block on [Joe Greene], he'd give you credit right on the field. And if he happened to give you a hard time, he'd just kind of chuckle when he went by and hit you on the ass. I just had great respect for him."

Greene and company protected the linebackers.

"Their whole linebacker corps was predicated on getting protection from that line, Ham and Lambert, those guys, they were all over that field," Langer said. "You'd knock them down and they'd get back up and keep on going. It was a scheme, a whole philosophy that you were fighting when you played the Steelers. A lot of teams don't play with that kind of unity, and you could tell it with the Steelers. The only thing I have to say about the Steelers is it was a class operation—great players on the field and great players off the field. They were winners."

The Steel Curtain defense did not permit a touchdown for 22 quarters, recording three consecutive shutouts, not allowing a touchdown in eight of the last nine regular-season games, and totally blanking five of its final eight opponents; they outscored the opposing team 342 to 138. During the final nine games they allowed just two touchdowns and 26 points. Included in this run of defensive terror were 35 sacks and 28 takeaways, and they held five teams to fewer than 200 total yards.

The Steelers moved into a tie for first in the Central Division with a 42–0 win over Tampa Bay—a win that saw Harris surpass the 1,000-yard rushing plateau for the fourth time. They clinched the division with a 21–0 win over the Oilers in the season finale when the Raiders defeated the Bengals.

While the Steelers' passing attack barely registered a pulse, the running game worked. Harris finished the season with 1,128 yards rushing, and Bleier had 1,036, making them the second pair of running backs on the same team to surpass the 1,000-yard barrier in the same season.

"Of course I always joked that Rocky was the only 1,000-yard rusher who never changed directions," said Andy Russell with a chuckle.

The Steelers traveled to Baltimore for the first game of the playoffs to face the team they had beaten on their previous season's march to the Super Bowl. Bert Jones remembered having some keys to what the Steelers might do on defense.

"Strategically we could play with them, but there weren't many places to exploit," Jones said. "The only thing that we had any success with was getting presnap reads, crazy things. If Jack Lambert put his right hand on his side it meant he was blitzing. If Jack Ham put his right foot in front of his left foot when he was on the outside, that meant he was coming. If J. T. Thomas was looking directly at the wide receiver and not inside that meant it was two-man [coverage]. So we had to do things strategically when we knew what they were doing, which was not all the time, in order to be successful. Look, we didn't match up to them. We had to strategically beat them if we were going to beat them."

According to Mike Wagner, former NFL quarterback Billy Kilmer told him during a golf outing that the Redskins knew exactly what the Steelers coverage was and what front they were playing, and they called the perfect play but still couldn't beat them.

"At the end of the day, it still comes down to football," Wagner said.

While the keys the Colts had picked up on the Steelers probably helped some, the Steelers found a key to the Colts' offense that likely helped the Steelers more.

"Wednesday before we played the Colts [Steelers defensive line coach] George Perles comes busting into our meeting and he's going nuts," Wagner said. "He says he can't believe it, but they'd been watching film of the Colts' offense and every time they ran a pass or a run the center would have either one hand or two hands on the ball. We thought it was a joke. It was just a habit he had, like grade school football. But that's the way it worked out."

Jones and Lydell Mitchell—who rushed for a Baltimore club record of 1,200 yards in 1976—were the main ingredients to a Colts attack that led the AFC with 417 points scored. Whether the key picked up about the Baltimore center affected the game is unknown, but with Bradshaw playing quarterback for the Steelers the Colts were crushed 40–14 at Memorial Stadium. Bradshaw riddled the Colts for 264 yards passing for three touchdowns while completing 14 of 18 passes.

Obviously Baltimore fans were disappointed by the lopsided defeat, but it turned out to be a blessing. Minutes following the game, a man piloting a small plane crashed into Memorial Stadium's upper deck between sections 1 and 2.

"We were watching the second playoff game on TV in the locker room," Bleier said. "And as we were getting dressed and ready to leave they cut into the broadcast and went to Baltimore where they showed what had happened. We never heard [the crash]. There's a case of

153

things happening for a reason. If that game would have been close, a lot of people might have gotten hurt because they still would have been in the stadium."

Having hit their peak in the first-round dismantling of Baltimore, the Steelers appeared as though they might just win their third consecutive Super Bowl. Only the Raiders stood in the way of the Steelers reaching the pinnacle of professional football again. But the Steelers had major problems.

Among these were the Raiders, a splendid football team that had gone 13–1 during the regular season before beating the Patriots 24–21 in a controversial game in the first round of the playoffs—and they would be playing in Oakland-Alameda County Stadium.

"I looked at the Raiders as being the bullies on the block," Greene said. "They'd beat you up whether you were in the bed sick, if you were crippled, or standing up healthy. It didn't matter with them. They were going to beat you and it didn't change how they thought about you. Initially in my playing days, they used to beat up on us pretty good. Then we came of age, to a large extent because of the competition with them. You knew how you had to compete if you were going to win."

Next problem for the Steelers was their hobbled offense.

Though Harris had gained 132 yards on the ground against the Colts, he'd left the game in the third quarter with bruised ribs. Bleier also left the Colts game with a sprained toe, Frenchy Fuqua pulled a calf muscle, and Roy Gerela aggravated a groin pull. Reggie Harrison had the dubious distinction of being the Steelers' only healthy back going into the game against the Raiders, leaving Chuck Noll to figure out some way to cope with his depleted backfield. He came up with a one-back alignment where he replaced the second back with a slot or motion tight end in Randy Grossman.

Oakland feasted on the new alignment.

"We tried to put in a new offense in a very short time," Stallworth said. "We were not at all used to it. There was confusion in the huddle. What were we doing? Looking back on it I feel like we would have been better suited to stay with the offense that we had. Because we could have executed it better. We were in disarray to some extent. And with the new plays and formations it was like, 'What do I need to do on this one?' And it wasn't just a tweak here or a tweak there. In some cases it was wholesale changes."

A blocked punt and an intercepted pass led to a 10–0 Oakland second-quarter lead. Bradshaw managed to cobble together a touchdown drive with 10 minutes left in the half, but Ken Stabler quickly led the Raiders up the field for a touchdown and a 17–7 halftime lead. The Raiders added a touchdown in the second half to make the final score 24–7 and end the Steelers' season.

The waning moments of the Oakland game made for one of Wagner's favorite recollections.

"There's like 30 seconds to go in the game and our defense was back on the field," Wagner said. "I can't remember the linesman's name, but it was a fella who'd been in the league a long time and this was his last game. For whatever reason, we're in the defensive huddle and he sticks his head in and says something to the effect, 'Hey guys, I just want to tell you you're one of the greatest teams I've ever seen.' And Lambert unleashes on him with this [torrent] of words, just like, 'What the hell are you doing? Can't you see we're trying to win a football game? Get the @#$% out of here.' I was looking at the referee and he realized he'd just made a major mistake in his life. Emotion got to him. I just looked at Jack and shook my head."

Although the Steelers did not advance to the Super Bowl, Greenwood fondly remembered the 1976 season.

"It was actually a great season because it was fun going out there on Sunday and doing the things that we did," Greenwood said.

Legislation against the defense continued prior to the 1977 season when the rules committee passed a rule outlawing defensive linemen from striking an opponent above the shoulders or making a head slap.

"A head slap would knock you silly," Langer said. "It would literally stun you. If you happened to get whacked on the side of the head it would momentarily stun you. That was the object.

"L. C., Joe, those guys, they would do that. They kind of noticed on film if they could do it or not. If they sensed they had a young guy who wasn't aware about how to stop it, they would get their hands up and then whack him."

Steelers players understood the motivating force behind the continued rules changes.

"I just thought it was to get more offense at the time, I didn't really know," Greene said. "I didn't think it was fair. There was a certain facet of people in the league office that thought the population wanted to see offense. So it was slanted that way."

Don Shula joined the competition committee in 1975 and admits the committee's emphasis was to make the game more wide open.

"The whole philosophy of the committee and the league was to open up the game and let the stars shine," Shula said. "Let the great players play."

155

The committee would meet once a year in preparation for the league meetings. At the league meeting the committee would present their findings and work to the owners, who would vote on the recommendations of the committee. To get a measure passed the committee needed to have an approval by two-thirds of the ownership.

The head slap "was just a real advantage for a defensive lineman," Shula said. "Actually it was unnecessary roughness to slam the other guy in the helmet coming off the ball. It was just a dangerous type of maneuver."

Shula said the rule was implemented for the sake of offensive football, "to enable the offenses to have the opportunities to make plays."

"That helped give the quarterback time to throw the football," Shula said. "[Before the change] big defensive linemen would be in the quarterback's face, creating the possibility of injuries or knocking a star player out of the game. Again, the goal was to make the game as exciting and open as you could without drastically changing the nature of the game."

The Raiders, who went on to win the Super Bowl against Minnesota, continued to nag at the Steelers during the summer of 1977. That's when *Atkinson v. Noll* went to court.

"Geez, I pushed that out of my mind," said Noll when asked to recount the episode. "That was Al [Davis]. Al and me were on the same staff in San Diego. I knew Al very well. And he was trying to bring a [slander] case against me when I called Atkinson part of the criminal element, because what he wanted to do was maim you, knock you out of the game. Al was behind the lawsuit."

The Steelers stood behind Noll. Rooney's insurance company tried to get the team to settle with Atkinson for $50,000, but Rooney also had concerns about the welfare of the NFL. All of the league owners, save for Davis, were united. Rooney felt strongly that Noll had to win to be exonerated and to keep the league from being hurt by a wild-card like Davis.

The trial was held in the San Francisco Federal Building beginning July 11.

"We had a very, very fair judge," Rooney said. "We went there with the idea that we were right and we were honest and that the people [in that area] were honest and that they would see it. So we did not challenge one person [in jury selection], but there was one woman that was there and the judge said to her, 'You live in Oakland; are you a Raiders fan?' She said, 'Yes I am. I have season tickets with the Raiders.' And he said, 'Do you think it would be fair to have a complete jury like yourself?' She said, 'No,' and he said, 'You're excused.'"

The timing of the trial caused problems for the Steelers, who were getting ready to begin training camp.

"They brought Chuck Noll out there as one of the witnesses, and we were starting training camp," Rooney said. "So we had to petition the judge to let Chuck come back and get the camp opened up and then come up. And he did that. It was a real distraction for us. And then I ended up being the guy there that was fronting the case for us. Because Chuck was back running training camp. I was there. We had a great lawyer; James Martin McGuiness was his name."

Pete Rozelle was brought in to testify, and Atkinson's attorney rolled out footage of other savage NFL hits. The Steelers brought in a lot of their players to testify, including Ham, Bleier, Russell—who had retired prior to the 1977 season—and Bradshaw.

"We thought, 'Boy, this Russell is going to be terrific; he is really going to be the best witness in this whole thing because he's bright, he knows what he's doing,'" said Rooney, offering a brief chuckle. "Well, he was terrible. And the reason he was terrible was because he was smart. He tried to vie with their lawyers. They'd ask him a question and he'd start to try and outthink them, this and that."

Bradshaw saved the day.

"When Bradshaw got on the stand, he was just like he is, he was happy-go-lucky," Rooney said. "He kidded around. Answered their questions right on with what he thought. He made the jury laugh at different times. He was great. He was just outstanding."

Final arguments were heard July 22. The jury met for four hours and rendered a verdict of no slander, no malice, and no damages for Atkinson.

"We won it," Rooney said. "But I thought the fact we won it in San Francisco, in the Bay Area, was a tremendous thing."

Standing up to Davis proved to be a victory for the Steelers and the NFL, allowing the Steelers to direct their full attention to football.

Like any dynasty that experiences a hiccup during its run, questions began to permeate the Steelers' world. Had the team gotten old? Was complacency running rampant after so much success? Could they find the old magic to claim yet another Super Bowl?

Not helping matters were the holdouts of Lambert, Blount, and Holmes during training camp. All three eventually signed before the season began, but the episode helped divide the team and turned some Steelers fans sour.

Shell called the 1977 season "our distraction year."

Doubts surrounding the 1977 team increased after a 2–1 start. In a 27–10 loss to the Oilers on October 9, Bradshaw suffered a broken wrist and Kruczek went out for the season with a shoulder separation.

Bradshaw returned with his wrist in a cast to lead the Steelers to wins over Cincinnati and Houston, but he threw five interceptions in a 31–21 loss to Baltimore.

The Steelers won five of their last six games to complete a 9–5 season and clinch their fourth straight division title. Included in the victories was a 30–20 win over the Seahawks in their 12th game of the season.

"We played the Steelers in our second season," said Steve Largent, who played receiver for the Seahawks. "If you'll remember the expansion franchises, Tampa and Seattle, the first year we played all the NFC teams and the second year we played all the AFC teams. And Tampa had just the reverse.

"The second year was the year we played the Steelers. They were winning Super Bowls every year, had the Steel Curtain and Lambert, the whole gang, Bradshaw and Swann, all the great players that are now in the Hall of Fame. But I'll never forget, we were playing them at Three Rivers and there was a TV timeout. Here we were, our second year in the league; I don't even know that I needed to shave every day at that point. But I looked through our offensive linemen over at the huddle of the Steelers during this TV timeout and there they all were—L. C. Greenwood, just the whole gang over there. I knew every single name, and they're all sitting on their helmets. You know, I was brought up where that's not kosher at all, you never sat on the football field, and here they were, it was like they were on the beach during this timeout just relaxing, telling stories. And here we were, we were nervous as could be playing the great Pittsburgh Steelers, and of course we never had a prayer."

Largent remembered being intimidated by the Steelers and that they were a physical team, but he also added, "They were always a class act."

"They never had a reputation of being a dirty team," Largent said. "They didn't talk trash. Take Mel Blount. He was always kind of the class act on a very classy team. He would hit you as hard as he could and help you up. And I always admired that kind of sportsmanship. They were very professional, which is what I observed when I played on some Pro Bowl teams with their guys. And that's what really impressed me about them. They came to work and you know, they worked hard, and they treated it like a business. But they were very professional in my opinion about the way they approached the game. That always really impressed me."

The Steelers brought an intimidating aura to the field, but reporters found the team engaging.

"Noll had the most open locker room I'd ever seen," said Paul Zimmerman, noting that reporters could always walk into the locker room, even the coaches' offices. "You could do it; it was friendly. Of course there were a lot fewer people around. Not these assholes with their mini cams and their sound bytes and all that shit.

"I remember walking in there one time and there were some Chinese nuns in there interviewing Lambert about something. These strange people, a guy with an apron on came in and delivered a pizza and stuck around. Noll just didn't care. It was outside the realm of winning and losing. And everybody talked. Everybody was a personality. I remember talking to Terry Bradshaw about [his second wife and champion figure skater] Jo-Jo Starbuck. And he's telling me how they found Christ together and all this stuff. And Terry Hanratty's sitting in the corner laughing his ass off. After Terry gets through, [Hanratty] says, 'Come over here a second. I bet I know what he was telling you about, Ice Palace Sally.'"

Zimmerman laughed.

"They were all great talkers," he said. "They were all funny. It was a pleasure to cover that team, oh God."

Zimmerman's nine-year-old son, Michael, loved the Steelers, which led to the *Sports Illustrated* writer taking his son to a game as a reward for making good grades on his report card.

Zimmerman laid out the rules for his son. After the game he would introduce him to anybody he wanted to when they were coming out of the locker room. Then Zimmerman went into the locker room to do his job.

"I'm in the locker room and all of a sudden I see him against the wall, kind of huddled over there," Zimmerman said. "And I knew what happened. Art Rooney Jr., who has the biggest heart in the world, got him in there. I said, 'All right, that's OK' and I knew who he wanted to meet, Jack Lambert. He was his favorite player."

Lambert and equipment manager Jack Hart were jawing, using some colorful language. Once their exchange died down, the Zimmermans approached.

"Jack, this is my son Mike," Zimmerman said. "He likes to watch you play."

"Are you a good boy?" Lambert said. "You do your homework? You listen to your father?"

"Yes," Michael said.

"OK, then I'll shake your hand," Lambert said.

When Michael Zimmerman prepared for bed that night he spoke to his father.

"He said to me, 'Daddy, he was just the way I wanted him, he was perfect,'" Zimmerman said. "If Jack would have been jolly, a guy like Terry, it wouldn't have been right. This was perfect."

Zimmerman got to know the Steelers pretty well. When asked what made Noll different from other coaches, Zimmerman chuckled. "He knew a lot about wine," Zimmerman said. "He and I were wine buddies."

Noll had a taste for Beaulieu Vineyard's Private Cabernet. "That was his wine," said Zimmerman, recalling a conversation with Noll where Noll told Zimmerman he could not find the 1974 Private Reserve at the state stores. "So I told him I'd get him all he wanted for $10 a bottle," Zimmerman said. "He said, 'Bring me a case the next time you come out.'"

Zimmerman bought a case of the wine prior to his next trip to visit Noll and the Steelers, but he experienced trouble trying to get the wine on board an Allegheny Airlines flight and had to check the case with his bags. When the flight landed, Zimmerman stood waiting at the baggage claim and smelled his package before he saw it.

"There was a spreading stain [on the case]," Zimmerman said.

He grabbed the case of wine and headed to the Steelers practice, where he placed the case in the equipment room so he could give it to Noll after the practice.

"So after practice I tell him what happened, you know, 'Allegheny, I don't know how many bottles are broken,'" Zimmerman said. "I'm apologizing and I'm feeling shitty. And Jack Hart is watching this operation, so we open the case and I'm thinking please god, just one bottle. And only one bottle was broken. And Noll holds up one bottle and he says, 'There it is, the Private Reserve.' Jack Hart says, 'Eleven bottles of Private Reserve; one bottle, injured reserve.'"

Zimmerman laughed at the recollection, noting, "Noll lived a totally different life outside of football. Lived a real life.

"There's a lot that's very strange about him. He was totally outside the normal. First of all, he had [a higher] IQ than any of the other coaches. Second of all, he liked the things they only heard about. Classical music, he was interested in crustaceans, deep-sea marine life. He really had an interest in life outside of football."

If any Steelers player had a breakout year in 1977, Stallworth was the guy. The perception had always been that Swann was the number one receiver and Stallworth number two. After 1977 they were viewed as equals. In his fourth season in the league, Stallworth doubled his previous best for number of catches with 44 while scoring 7 touchdowns and averaging 17.8 yards per catch.

"In my early years Swanny was number one—that's who Bradshaw was throwing to," Stallworth said. "But Bradshaw developed over time. In the early years Bradshaw was very much one-sided; he used to throw the ball to the right side come hell or high water. My thing was to somehow get him to turn the other way. 'Look over here—I'm open! I'm open!' But he had a very good rapport with Lynn and it was working. If it hadn't been working I'd have had a big gripe. I could take it to somebody and say, 'Yeah, we need to do this.' But here it is, it's working, Swanny's catching the ball having great years. And we're winning football games."

Stallworth did experience the occasional low moment.

After one particularly frustrating game, which the Steelers won, Stallworth went to the Steelers' facility to work out in the weight room on a Monday even though it was an off day for the team. While he was working out, Noll walked into the room.

"John, how are you doing?" Noll said.

"I'm pissed off," Stallworth said.

Puzzled, Noll queried the receiver: "What are you pissed off about?"

"I caught one pass," Stallworth said.

"Well John, you caught one pass, but we won the football game," Noll said.

Stallworth looked Noll in the eyes. "I'd like to think we could do both," he said. "I'd like to think I could catch more passes and we could still win football games."

Noll laughed at the remark then turned and walked away.

When reminded of the story, Noll chuckled.

"Stallworth could never get enough passes," Noll said. "If you threw it to him on every down it wouldn't be enough."

Stallworth said Noll put "some things" into the system that made Bradshaw look to his side more often.

"At that time we'd draw up pass plays, even numbers to the right, odd numbers to the left," Stallworth said. "And all the pass plays were even numbers. Meaning your progression was going to start on that side, that was going to be the strong side. After that instead of all 60s, I saw 61s; instead of 90s, I saw 91s; instead of 62s, I saw 63s. So I think Chuck and [offensive coordinator] Tom Moore started to put more things into the game plan that dictated Bradshaw start on [Stallworth's] side."

161

Stallworth and Swann had their own private competition, which Stallworth believes helped motivate both.

"For me as a receiver, having Swann there did that," Stallworth said. "There's no question in my mind. Having that direct competition with him catching passes, great great passes, great catches, in big games, made me want to do that. So we sort of battled each other in that regard. We weren't disrespectful and we never did anything detrimental to the other in the pursuit of goals and furthering of careers; we just helped fuel each other to want to do more. You just wanted to make a bigger catch in a bigger game than the one the other guy made."

Stallworth believes that spirit of competition existed at many positions on the team. He also believes the pressure to win was evenly dispersed.

"I think the fact we had so many folks on our team that could take the load on any given game, on any given Sunday, made you relax a little more," Stallworth said. "Sometimes when you are the guy, there's a lot of pressure to be the guy every Sunday. We felt relaxed in there. If Franco wasn't doing that well, or the offensive line wasn't really clicking, we felt like we could throw the football and, I think, vice versa. And if the offense on a given Sunday was not up to scoring 25 or 30 points, we knew we had a defense that with 10 points you could win a football game."

Running the offense, of course, was Bradshaw, who carried the label of being less than blessed with a lot of smarts. Since his playing days ended Bradshaw has been outspoken about how sensitive he was to the "dumb" label, but as a player he internalized his feelings.

"Once you get that label, boy, you're in deep shit," Gregg Bingham said. "And he wasn't dumb. Keep in mind he had the ability. Probably the reason that [label] got started was because he had a tremendous arm. And he would throw into double coverage and get away with it. A guy like [Cleveland quarterback] Brian Sipe didn't have the arm Bradshaw had, so Brian Sipe would have to be more calculating and play his own game rather than Bradshaw's. Terry would throw into double coverage a lot, and then the media would say, 'Well, there's a dummy throwing into double coverage,' but he did it because he could. No, Terry Bradshaw was not a dummy."

Ray Oldham recalled Bradshaw taking him under his wing when he joined the team prior to the 1978 season and treating him to a great deal of hospitality, which afforded Oldham the opportunity to get to know the Steelers' quarterback.

"I don't know about wounded feelings," Oldham said. "Everybody teased Brad. Brad played off it, too. Brad plays off of it today. They always kidded Brad about how dumb he was. That's kind of the way Bradshaw was. Brilliant man, he's fooled a lot of people over the years. And you know what. He's just down to earth and simple, one of the greatest friends I'll have. I love him to death. I spent a lot of quality time with him while I was there. He's a smart guy or he wouldn't be where he is today."

Oldham said he was sure some of the dumb label stemmed from the fact that Bradshaw was from the South. "I am sure some of it was," Oldham said. "But it went right off his back like water off a duck's back. Like, 'Hey, if they think I'm dumb, let 'em talk. They still have to line up and play me. Let 'em talk about how dumb I am. Let 'em talk about how stupid I am. Guess what? They still have to play.' And he just beat 'em. I think it was motivation for Brad. I think it was motivation for him to go out and show them what he could do."

Bill Bergey said Bradshaw got a horrible rap that came from the coaches. "Everybody thought he was this Louisiana Tech hillbilly, redneck," Bergey said. "And they pretty much thought he was stupid. Even in our game plans, 'not a very smart quarterback, will do dumb things' and all of that. However, he was going through his learning process. And of course rookies are going to make mistakes. But I thought it was very unfair he was labeled a dummy because I thought he was very smart. Excellent, excellent quarterback. All I know is, every year I played against him at Cincinnati, every year he got better and better. And he just developed into a great quarterback. I know that he and Chuck Noll had a lot of tough times with one another. But I always respected and revered the guy. I just always thought he was a top-notch quarterback. I always had the utmost respect for the guy."

In the first round of the 1977 AFC playoffs, the Steelers traveled to Denver to play the Broncos in Mile High Stadium.

Under new coach Red Miller, the Broncos were known for their "Orange Crush" defense, tagged as such for their bright orange jerseys and hard-hitting play. Earlier in the season the Steelers had lost to the Broncos 21–7 in Denver. A return trip to Denver for a Christmas Eve contest against the Broncos put the Steelers up against a team that had gone 12–2 en route to their first championship of any kind, the AFC West title. More than seventy-five thousand fans jammed into Mile High hoping for the improbable to occur against the Steelers.

Miller instilled a Pittsburgh-like mentality into his team, whose creed had been for their defense to carry their offense. By the end of

163

the second quarter the Broncos clung to that philosophy, but it appeared it would be only a matter of time until the Steelers prevailed. While the score stood tied at 14 at the half, the Steelers' offense had controlled the ball for 20 of the 30 minutes, outgaining the Broncos 183 yards to 44.

Greene got frustrated with Broncos guard Paul Howard, who had held him on way too many plays for Greene's liking. When holding wasn't called after several incidents, Greene landed a punch to Howard's chest—which went unseen by the officials. Two plays later center Mike Montler got a hand inside Greene's face mask, prompting Greene to punch Montler as he had Howard. That time Greene received a 15-yard penalty, all of which served to stir a pot full of bad blood between the two teams. Miller and Perles nearly squared off to fight when the teams headed to their respective locker rooms at half-time.

The game had advanced to a 21–21 tie in the fourth quarter when Jim Turner kicked a 44-yard field goal to give the Broncos a 3-point lead. Broncos linebacker Tom Jackson then intercepted a Bradshaw pass and returned it 32 yards to the Pittsburgh 9 to set up another Turner field goal. Jackson intercepted another Bradshaw pass—Bradshaw's third interception of the day—to give the Broncos the ball at the Pittsburgh 33. Broncos quarterback Craig Morton then found Jack Dolbin on a 34-yard touchdown pass to make the final score 34–21.

And seemingly in an instant, the Steelers were two years removed from the Super Bowl. Had the team lost its magic? Could they recover? Was there a sense of desperation that their dynasty had run its course?

"I don't think there was desperation," Stallworth said. "In 1974 and 1975 we won it all. In 1976 we had the injuries. Then in 1977, we were trying to sort of get it back together after those injuries. So I don't think we were frustrated. I think we felt that there were very clear reasons why we didn't get it done during those two seasons between."

13

Return to Excellence

Despite the fact that the Steelers had not won a Super Bowl in two years, the team remained the poster child for dominating defenses. And NFL executives insisted that their fan base preferred wide-open, offensive oriented games, which perpetuated the trend toward the competition committee striving to weaken defenses. So the legislation against defense continued prior to the 1978 season.

For almost a decade the Steelers' pass rush had managed to successfully charge past offensive linemen like water speeding through a busted dam. What better way to handicap said charges than to give offensive linemen more liberty in the blocking techniques they used? After the 1977 season, linemen were licensed to extend their arms and open their hands during pass blocking.

"Hands could be fully extended, arms just like today," Jim Langer said. "You wanted your arms blocking out. Guys who could bench 500 pounds, that's what they did that for, so they could arm-chuck somebody. You wanted to try and keep that guy away from your body. As far as run blocking, you didn't block with your arms in the old style, arms folded."

Paul Zimmerman cited the rule change for giving offensive linemen a big boost.

Offensive linemen "gained a big advantage from that one, because no longer did they have to tuck their heads and duck," Zimmerman said. "Before that you had guys who would just go punching left-right into the backfield. That was a very profound thing."

"Things weren't done selfishly for anybody on the committee," Don Shula said. "We did it for what we thought was best for football. It was done before I got on the committee and done after I was on the committee."

Asked how dominant defenses were at the time, Shula said, "There were good offenses, too."

"But the whole emphasis was to try and make the game as exciting and open as possible and as safe as possible," Shula said.

In other words, defenses such as the Steelers' needed to be tempered.

"Our surveys showed us that fans liked more scoring," said the late Don Weiss during a 2001 interview. "Plus there was a general feeling that the best athletes in the league, who were wide receivers and really remarkable athletes, were so hampered by the way defenses played, getting held up at the line of scrimmage and what not. Before we changed the rules, you could chuck them at any point on the field and many of them just weren't physical enough."

Blount was more specific in his opinion about the origin of the changes. "I think they were trying to slow down the Pittsburgh Steelers because we just really were on top of the league, dominating games," Blount said. "It wasn't one particular individual, it was just position by position we were better than people, starting with our front four, our linebackers, our cornerbacks, and the same on offense. We were just better than people. The league is really interesting in that if they can't catch up with you they try to legislate things to make it more even. And it still happens today. That's why they come up with the rules committee and all the rules changes. Try to make people with less talent competitive."

Zimmerman remembered how the Steelers smothered offenses at that time.

"Guys like Mel Blount, who was kind of a butcher out there, played that double zone so he didn't have to run with the player all the way down the field," Zimmerman said. "He just hammered [the receiver] at the line.

"The game was being so smothered by defenses, particularly by the Steelers, that they had to do something. It was done in pieces, but [the changes] were done to air mail the football and make passing easier."

In addition to the rules committee's studying of statistics and fan surveys, Weiss said the media had an influence on the changes.

"We measured media coverage very closely," said Weiss, a former Associated Press reporter. "We had a lot of respect for what they were writing, particularly columnists. And we would take those pieces and we'd make regular mailings to the clubs and keep them apprised about what they were saying because we thought they represented what the press thought of our game."

Zimmerman agreed that the media had an effect on NFL rules and continues to do so.

"I think you've got a triumvirate—fans, media, rules change people," Zimmerman said. "I think fans indirectly influence media, which pretends to be a spokesman for the fans. People changing the rules [pay slight attention to that]. Although sometimes if you go a little too far, they react like nobody's going to tell them what to do. Sometimes the change you want to affect takes a few years longer because they react against the media. Everybody hates the media."

However, Zimmerman begs to differ with the idea that the NFL competition committee is responsive to what the fans want. "Could you please tell me when the last fan survey was taken and who took it?" Zimmerman said. "That's a Tex Schramm thing. Tex Schramm, who was a promoter. His being in the Hall of Fame is absolutely obscene. He was a T-shirt salesman . . . and Tex Schramm's theory was fans love scoring, you've got to give them scoring. Fans, number one, like to see their own teams win, no matter how they win. They can win a 3–0 game and they love it. Fans love anything that's good, that's well played. [That is] unless you talk about idiots who are flipping the dials and, if they see scoring, they might hold it another five minutes. And I think that's the perception the league has always had—that you lose the fans unless you give them a lot of scoring, cheap touchdowns, cheap thrills. [I say] take a survey, then tell us about that. But they don't do that. Why bother? That takes money and work."

In addition to the blocking change, the rules committee made a further attempt to free receivers to run their routes with few obstructions. The rule change stated that defenders were permitted to maintain contact with receivers in a five-yard zone beyond the line of scrimmage, but contact was restricted beyond that point. To most this rule came to be known as the "Mel Blount Rule."

Nick Buoniconti said the five-yard bump rule had legs long before Blount's influence.

"We were instrumental in getting the rule changed because we played the playoff game [in 1973] against Cincinnati, and Isaac Curtis never got off the line of scrimmage," Buoniconti said. "[Linebacker Bob] Matheson pounded him, I pounded him, we got [tight end] Bob Trumpy out of the game early. We're the ones who caused that five-yard rule where you couldn't touch the receiver after he got five yards beyond the line of scrimmage. And that was called the 'Isaac Curtis rule' because Paul Brown bitched and moaned about it so much and for so long that they finally changed the rule. So we were a great part of that.

167

"It was not the Mel Blount rule, believe me. You go back and trace the history of how that got changed and you'll find that it was Isaac Curtis in our playoff game could not get off the line of scrimmage. Paul Brown got it changed in the competition committee."

Nat Moore, who had been a college running back at Florida and was used to contact, said he never had a problem prior to the rule change and actually felt like the change hurt his game.

Prior to the rule change "you were able to take advantage of [a defense's] aggression," Moore said. "Once the rules changed, what you started to get was more and more zone defense where guys could actually sit back and watch the quarterback and it made it where you didn't get as many big plays. You caught more square-ins for 14-, 15-yard gains versus having a guy trying to jam you and the safety gets caught out of position and now it's a touchdown.

"Basically as they changed the rules it took away, especially for us smaller receivers, the opportunity to take advantage of guys trying to jam you and push you around the field. What happens is, if you're not known as a receiver who blocks and gets after people, then guys are willing to take the cheap shot on you because they don't have to worry about taking the payback. I grew up in an area where that's what it's all about. Therefore, when I had an opportunity to block guys who had to go get the football, now it's my time to deliver the punishment, and I took advantage of it."

Like Moore, John Stallworth said playing in the environment prior to the change never bothered him.

"From a size standpoint, I matched up very well against the guys I was playing against so it came down to a very physical thing," Stallworth said. "I was very capable of being very physical with them. So that wasn't an issue with me. I think the loosening up of things may have benefited the smallish kind of guy more than it did for me. Of course, you've got to realize I grew up in the National Football League going five days a week against Mel Blount. So everybody else was a piece of cake after that."

While the rule known as the "Mel Blount Rule"—or the "Isaac Curtis Rule," depending on how one views history—was created to prevent a Mel Blount from dominating a game, the rule did little to curtail Blount's talents.

"The scary thing about that [rule change], Mel was so intimidating with his brute force, yet he was still the best cover man in the league, so it really didn't affect him," Bert Jones said. "He was just phenomenal. He would rock your jock, yet he could sit in your hip pocket like he belonged better than a wallet. He just was phenomenal and he intimidated everybody who played on the field."

Blount spoke about how he played prior to the change.

"You could jam a guy as long as the ball wasn't in the air. You could jam him all the way down the field," Blount said. "I was always a physical cornerback, big for my position, and I had good feet and was quick, had a lot of speed. So it was really to my advantage, the rules back in those days. You'd just get up in a guy's face and get physical with him and you ran with him. You couldn't shove him once the ball was in the air. Then in 1978 they changed the rule where you could only jam the guy within the five yards from the line of scrimmage. I don't think it really hurt me. It might have taken something away from some of the other players on the team. But I just had the ability to run with people and I had good, quick feet for a guy my size. And I think that was an advantage."

Given the stage of the life of the Steelers' dynasty, the argument can be made that the rules changes—while aimed at taking away the dominance of defensive teams—actually helped the Steelers' overall team. Because so many of the Steelers' players were comparable in age, their physical skills began to diminish—though slightly—in a collective fashion. Meanwhile, the Steelers' offense was in the process of making the transition from a run-it, punt-it offense to more of a wide-open attack.

"I think the rules changes hurt the Pittsburgh Steelers' defense, but [they] opened up the floodgates for our offense," Mike Wagner said. "It was frustrating. When they changed the rules the game became fast-break football. Between the 20-yard lines it was fast-break football, it was so easy to move the football—like it is today. The hard part is the red zone when the passing zones compress, when the defenses are able to better cover some of the receivers. When our defense in the middle seventies began giving up more points per game, our offense started putting up more touchdowns per game."

Bradshaw had matured, and Stallworth and Swann were well seasoned, which allowed Bradshaw to exploit opposing teams' pass defense.

"That rule change sort of gave us the opportunity for Bradshaw to open it up a little bit more," Stallworth said. "To move away from what we had typically done the last three or four seasons when we had run the ball so much. It just played into our hands. Our defense was still a very good, solid defense, and the rule change slowed them a little bit. But it allowed us on offense to pick it up just a little bit more."

Amid the fruit of the Steelers' blossoming offense were new uses for Stallworth, who rarely went down where he caught the ball because of his ability to run with the football. So the idea was to get the ball into Stallworth's hands any way possible.

"We had some quick screens, short passes, and reverses that would get me the ball and give me the chance to run with it," Stallworth said. "I don't know if they put in anything new to the offense; it was just saying this particular play suits John's ability; let's let him do this play. Let's put this into the game plan for him, more than they had in the past."

Bradshaw had his best season in 1978, throwing 28 touchdown passes and leading the AFC in passing; few defenses had an answer for the Swann-Stallworth tandem. And Franco Harris had yet another 1,000-yard rushing season.

Veteran defensive back Ray Oldham came to the Steelers prior to the 1978 season to give them some added depth when J. T. Thomas was discovered to have a blood disorder and missed the entire season.

"Everybody wanted to play for Mr. Rooney," Oldham said. "He was one of the greatest team owners I've ever been around."

Oldham immediately noticed that the Steelers owner seemed to know everybody on the team.

"He'd come in the locker room and he always wore his top hat, smoking a big old stogie—I mean that thing was about a foot long," Oldham said. "He'd always come out, every day. And he'd watch practice."

Tight end Bennie Cunningham ran a square-out pattern toward the sideline on Oldham's second day of practice, resulting in Oldham breaking up the pass but hitting Rooney and knocking him down in the process.

"He had smashed that cigar all the way down, and I picked Mr. Rooney back up," Oldham said. "I'm like, 'Mr. Rooney, Mr. Rooney, I'm sorry.'"

Rooney examined the new addition to the Steelers.

"Great play, Ray Bob," Rooney said. "Welcome to the team."

Rooney stuck the smashed cigar back into his mouth, straightened his topcoat, put his hands behind his back, and continued walking.

"I'm thinking, I just got here and I'm going to get cut," Oldham said.

Oldham saw Cunningham at a golf tournament in 2004, and they reminisced about Oldham's collision with Rooney.

"Bennie said, 'I thought you were gone,'" Oldham said. "Bennie and I were both laughing about that."

Steve Courson also joined the Steelers in 1978 as a rookie guard out of South Carolina. Several players providing background information for this book alleged widespread steroid use among the Steelers offensive linemen, whom one of the players described as having "freaky" bodies due to their steroid use. Though claims about the Steelers linemen using steroids cannot be substantiated, Courson admitted to using anabolic steroids during his weight training regimen in a May 13, 1985, *Sports Illustrated* piece where he alleged that 75 percent of NFL linemen were on steroids, while 95 percent had probably tried them.

Rules changes and their impact on playing defense aside, the Steelers continued to make life miserable for opposing offenses in 1978. Guile and savvy had supplanted whatever the defense might have lost in the way of physical advantage due to aging.

"I remember playing against them at Three Rivers [actually in New York in 1978], and Jack Ham punches me in the gut after the play," said Mickey Shuler, at that time a rookie tight end with the Jets out of Penn State. "I'm like, well, so much for Penn State. From that point on I was trying to kill him."

Shuler paused to laugh.

"Now realize, they were at the end of their careers when I first played against them," Shuler said. "And I'm a rookie, so I'm going 90 miles per hour. Here I am going against two legends in my mind. Lambert has like no teeth and he was skinny, wasn't nearly as big as I thought he would be. They knew how to try to intimidate, and they knew how to play all the way up to the bell, and maybe just a hair beyond—I think that was their thing. It was just funny. I didn't stop until after the whistle from then on."

The Steelers defeated the Jets 28–17.

For the season they held eight opponents to 10 points or less, allowing the fewest points in the league (195 in the first 16-game season).

The Steelers streaked to seven victories before losing to Houston 24–17.

The Oilers had supplanted the Raiders as the Steelers' biggest rival by 1978. Bum Phillips coached the team that had powerful running back Earl Campbell.

"Well, you know, there was a lot of respect between those two teams," Gregg Bingham said. "I played against Mike Webster in college. I went to Purdue and he went to Wisconsin, so I guess we might have had about 15 or 16 years together. We went way back, Mike and I did. He was quick, tough, strong, and mean—he was the total package."

Bingham discussed the problems the Oilers faced when lining up against the Steelers' offense.

"We never thought Lynn Swann was the great receiver there," Bingham said. "We thought it was John Stallworth. And to be quite frank with you, I played them twice a year, so I guess I played against them about 26 times counting the playoffs. Playing John Stallworth we wanted to double him and single Lynn Swann."

The danger of double-teaming Stallworth came in Bingham having to cover Bleier one-on-one out of the backfield, which led to complications pertaining to the Steelers' trap play.

"The problem is [Bleier] takes three steps to the outside linebacker and you can't tell if he's going out for a pass or blocking and you have to take two steps with him, which puts you right on the trap block," Bingham said. "It always put me with heat in the kitchen. It was very difficult on me because either Franco had the ball or my guy was out in the flat and I had to cover him. It's a very difficult read. Our defensive coordinator used to always say to me, 'We're going to put you in the hot box again' because it's extremely difficult coverage on me."

Houston defensive end Elvin Bethea enjoyed the rivalry with the Steelers, "because you knew if you got past them you went to the Super Bowl."

"I always respected them, Joe Greene, L. C. Greenwood, Terry Bradshaw," said Bethea, who recalled the Oilers beating the Bengals to help the Steelers clinch the division title in 1977.

"The year we beat [Cincinnati] down here to knock [them] out of the playoffs, the Steelers went to the playoffs as the Central Division champions, [and] they sent us all Samsonite briefcases," Bethea said. "We had something going between the two teams."

Bethea believed the key to stopping the Steelers was keeping Bradshaw under control.

"The key thing you knew, Terry was tough physically—he had good size on him for a quarterback—Bradshaw wasn't easy to bring down," Bethea said. "You had to get a blind shot. The only way to get to Terry was from his blind side because he could scramble, he could move. There were a few good shots where I got him and he just got up and shook it off. That's why I said he was one of the tougher quarterbacks. He's taken some good shots. But he was a tough all-around player. He started a generation of big quarterbacks. He could move out there, very agile with his feet, which most people I'm sure didn't think. I remember people always talking about how he wasn't the smartest quarterback. But to me, I can tell you, he was. He was one of the smartest and toughest I ever played against. And I felt like he was the key. If you stopped him, you stopped the Steelers."

The Steelers won the rematch with the Oilers, 13–3, at Houston en route to a 14–2 record, the best in the NFL. Both teams knew they were likely to meet again in the playoffs.

But first, Pittsburgh hosted Denver on December 30 in the divisional playoffs in a rematch with the team that had eliminated them from the playoffs the previous season.

Harris had two second-quarter touchdown runs of 1 and 18 yards to put the Steelers up 16–3. The Steelers' defense forced the Broncos to go to Norris Weese at quarterback in the second quarter in place of the less mobile Craig Morton. Weese managed to complete a few passes to set up Dave Preston's 3-yard touchdown run that cut the Steelers' lead to 16–10. But that would be it for the Broncos, who could do nothing against the Steel Curtain defense while the Steelers' offense thrived.

Bradshaw threw fourth-quarter touchdown passes of 45 and 38 yards to Stallworth and Swann on an afternoon when Stallworth could do no wrong.

Highlights from Stallworth's 10-catch day included a leaping 22-yard number that set up Harris' second touchdown and his final grab when he went up in the end zone with Broncos defender Steve Foley on a 45-yard jump ball. Stallworth came down with the ball and deftly touched both feet in bounds for a 26–10 lead.

The Steelers dominated on both sides of the ball and came away with a 33–10 victory. Meanwhile, in Foxboro, Massachusetts, the Oilers took care of business with a 31–14 dismantling of the New England Patriots to earn another shot at the Steelers.

Houston had shown the versatility that made them a team capable of beating the Steelers. Campbell ran for 118 yards, Pastorini threw for three touchdowns, and the Oilers' offense held the Patriots to 83 yards rushing.

Oilers coach Wade Phillips was forever telling his players that the road to the Super Bowl went through Pittsburgh. If the Oilers wanted to reach the big game, they would have to go to Three Rivers Stadium the first week of January and beat the two-time Super Bowl Champion Steelers in the AFC Championship Game.

Rain and freezing temperatures transformed Three Rivers Stadium into a wintry tomb for the Oilers, who were destroyed by the Steelers 34–5. The Steelers' defense lived up to Phillips' praise when he equated going up against their unit to eating an ice cream cone on a hot summer day. "Before you get it all in your mouth, it gets all over you."

Though the two teams shared 11 first-half fumbles, the Steelers managed a 17-point knockout punch in 48 seconds late in the first half to take a 31–3 lead. With 30 minutes to go, Phillips and company understood the harsh reality: the Steelers would be the only team taking a road from Pittsburgh to the Super Bowl.

"You couldn't get any kind of footing," Pastorini said. "It was cold enough where you couldn't feel the ball. I mean, I've played in colder games at Cleveland on a clear day. It was just that slush. I remember seeing Terry Bradshaw run one time, and he went down and slid for 20 yards on the turf. Just wasn't the best playing conditions. Had we been able to get that game in the Astrodome, it might have been a different story. But you're playing Pittsburgh up there, lousy conditions, those fans. It was pretty hard to hear yourself think up there."

Houston planned to saddle up Campbell and hope that he could do well enough to set up the play-action pass.

"They pretty much stuffed Earl," Pastorini said. "Then we got to a point where we had to play catch-up and we couldn't hang on to the ball. We had turnovers that cost us. The game got out of hand and the Steelers were not a team to fall behind against. They were a tough team to come back on."

Pastorini threw four interceptions while Campbell fumbled three times and gained just 62 yards.

"They always shut down Earl in Pittsburgh," Bethea said. "I don't know why. It was cold. That game they shut Earl down and once we were out of it, it was all about catching up."

By virtue of the win over the Oilers, the Steelers had earned another trip to the Super Bowl where they would play the Cowboys, who had just defeated the Rams 28–0.

14

Cowboys Rematch

If the NFL had a wish list for Super Bowl XIII prior to the 1978 season, the pairing they would have selected to meet in Miami's Orange Bowl would have been the Steelers and the Cowboys.

The Cowboys were the defending champions after beating Denver in the previous year's Super Bowl, giving them two titles for the decade. The fact that the Steelers also had two titles meant the winner of the Super Bowl could stake a legitimate claim to being the team of the 1970s.

The Cowboys had a different team from when they lost to the Steelers in Super Bowl X. Among the upgrades was Tony Dorsett, the 1976 Heisman Trophy winner from the University of Pittsburgh. Dorsett's speed added another dimension to the Cowboys' offense; he rushed for 1,007 yards during his rookie season in 1977 and 1,325 yards in 1978.

The Cowboys went to Miami riding an eight-game winning streak, including a 27–20 win over Atlanta in the divisional playoff followed by their thrashing of the Rams in the NFC Championship Game. Staubach passed for two touchdowns against the Rams, and the Cowboys' defense picked off five passes. During the season the Cowboys' defense had allowed an NFC-leading 107.6 rushing yards per game; Pittsburgh's defense had allowed an AFC-leading 107.8 rushing yards per game.

The Steelers also had evolved into a different team since Super Bowl X—particularly on offense. Bradshaw could stretch any defense with the strongest arm in football, and his main targets, Swann and Stallworth, were the most dangerous receiving tandem in the NFL. The pair worked together to give defenses fits. Lined up on opposite ends of the line, one would go deep while the other dragged across the middle. If the defense committed to one, Bradshaw went to the other.

Each team had stability in their personnel—both had signed 42 of the 45 players on their roster out of college—and each team was filled with talent as personified by the fact that 10 Steelers and nine Cowboys made the Pro Bowl.

"You had two great football teams there, and I think when you look back at those two football teams that's one of the greatest Super Bowl matchups," Ray Oldham said. "The talent on that field was the same. Landry brought that talent up. You had a lot of great players out there. That was an equally matched game.

"I don't think we were ever worried about Dallas from a standpoint other than the fact Roger Staubach had a way of getting points on the board. We were never concerned that they had one weapon that was going to beat us. Dorsett might if he broke a long run. But you've got to remember, when you've got Joe Greene, L. C. Greenwood, and you've got Lambert and Ham, when you've got a secondary like we had, you're not real concerned about the [other team's] offensive threat. We went into every game—especially the Super Bowl—the same. Building a game plan around their tendencies and being able to say, 'let's just play our normal game and we'll win.'"

One department where the Cowboys ruled—thanks to linebacker Thomas "Hollywood" Henderson—was in the war of words. During the 14 days of pregame hype leading up to the game, Henderson became the most active mouth in Miami. He called Jack Lambert "a toothless chimpanzee" and "Dracula." Cunningham was out, prompting Henderson to call his replacement at tight end, Randy Grossman, a backup who "only plays when someone dies or breaks a leg." Henderson saved his best for Bradshaw, whose alleged lack of intelligence prompted him to note: "He couldn't spell *cat* if you spotted him the *C* and the *A*."

Bradshaw tried to shrug off the remarks by saying, "Sure it hurts to be called dumb. But the only way to get rid of a reputation is to show everybody they're wrong."

Upon hearing Henderson's remarks about his quarterback, Noll remarked: "Empty barrels make the most noise."

The Friday before the Super Bowl, Noll watched the perfection displayed by his team and cut short the practice.

"We were incredibly ready, and [Noll] didn't want to ruin it," Donnie Shell said.

Noll wasn't the warmest of men in the locker room, but occasionally he would allow his dry sense of humor to slip through. Prior to the start of the game, Oldham sat at his locker wrapping white tape around his shoes to spat them, a practice he'd followed since his college days. Just when he was finishing, Noll walked by and noticed Oldham's shoes.

"Ray Bob, what the hell are you doing?" Noll said.

"Spatting my shoes like I've always done," Oldham said.

"That's like putting whitewalls on a dump truck," said Noll as he moved on.

An old-school echo howled through the Orange Bowl when George Halas went to midfield in an antique car for the ceremonial coin toss. Halas had achieved NFL fame on multiple levels, but he was primarily known for being one of the NFL's cofounders in 1920 and for being the coach of the Chicago Bears.

The Cowboys won the toss and elected to receive, moving the ball from their own 28 to the Steelers' 34 before they tried a double reverse that Drew Pearson fumbled. Steelers tackle John Banaszak recovered at the Steelers' 47. Further Cowboy frustration came from the fact that Pearson was supposed to pass the ball to tight end Billy Joe Dupree after he'd taken Dorsett's handoff. Dupree had been wide open and might have scored had the pass been thrown.

Bradshaw quickly moved the Steelers up the field and capped a seven-play drive by finding Stallworth in the corner of the end zone for a 28-yard touchdown that gave the Steelers a 7–0 lead.

Dallas defensive end Ed Jones recovered a Bradshaw fumble at the Pittsburgh 41 with one minute remaining in the first quarter. Two plays later Tony Hill caught a Staubach pass at the Steelers' 26 and hugged the sideline all the way to the end zone to tie the game at 7 and chalk up the first first-quarter touchdown scored against the Steelers' defensive unit all season.

Early in the second quarter Bradshaw lost the ball again. After brushing past Harris, Bradshaw fumbled, but he managed to pick up the ball before Henderson collared him, which afforded linebacker Mike Hegman the opportunity to strip loose the ball and run 37 yards for a touchdown to put the Cowboys in front 14–7.

Two minutes later Bradshaw took the snap at the Steelers' 25 and looked for Swann deep on a post before finding Stallworth short at the 35. Stallworth turned what should have been a 15-yard gain into a 75-yard touchdown when he broke free from cornerback Aaron Kyle's grasp and slanted across the middle of the field until he found the end zone.

"Nobody ever caught John from behind," Noll said. "He had those long strides, whether it was game speed or whatever. I used to tell him he was scared." Noll laughed. "That wasn't the case."

When the Cowboys got the ball back they went to their two-minute drill and took the ball to the Steelers' 32 before Blount intercepted a Staubach pass intended for Pearson. After the game, Staubach said of the interception: "Of all the passes I've thrown, this one will haunt me the longest."

Much of Staubach's frustration stemmed from the fact that Blount had not been where he was supposed to be. To this day Blount ranks the interception among the top two of his career.

"I was supposed to go to the deep one third," he said. "But I saw Mike Wagner deep and I also saw Drew Pearson coming across the middle deep. So instead of me dropping back to the deep one third, I didn't go exactly deep. Staubach never saw me, because he knew from watching films that's the way we played. He expected me to stay deep third. I came off and started moving toward the reception area where I anticipated Drew Pearson to receive the ball, and I stepped in front of him and made the interception. That was a huge play. And then to tack on to that, Billy Joe Dupree clotheslined me and they tacked on a 15-yard penalty. That was huge."

Blount's interception gave the ball back to the red-hot Bradshaw with time running out in the first half. With 33 seconds remaining, Bradshaw displayed his passing touch by lofting a seven-yard touchdown pass to Bleier to give the Steelers a 21–14 lead at the half.

Bradshaw burned the Cowboys' highly touted flex defense for 253 yards through the air in the first half, but the torrid scoring pace lapsed to a crawl in the third quarter when the Cowboys scored the only points of the quarter on a 27-yard field goal. But the one that got away during the third quarter would haunt the Cowboys.

Thirty-eight-year-old tight end Jackie Smith retired from the St. Louis Cardinals following the 1977 season due to a problem with his neck. For the length of his career, Smith had been considered one of the best tight ends in the NFL. Unfortunately for Smith, who was elected to the Hall of Fame in 1994, his personal success had never been accompanied by team success with the Cardinals. So when the Cowboys needed a backup tight end in 1978, Smith forgot about the dire forecast for what might happen if his neck took the wrong kind of blow, and he joined the Cowboys hoping to get a chance to play in the Super Bowl. When the Cowboys indeed reached the Super Bowl, Smith's decision to take a chance looked as though it might have a happy ending. Instead the NFL's grandest stage would shape Smith's lasting legacy in another direction.

With little time remaining in the third quarter, the Cowboys faced a third-and-3 at the Steelers' 10. Landry called for a set using an extra tight end, which gave the impression the Cowboys planned to run. Dorsett went into motion, which made a pass to him in the flat a distinct possibility, or Staubach could have handed off the ball to the lone half-back, Scott Laidlaw. Instead Staubach dropped back to pass and spotted Smith open in the middle of the end zone. He directed a pass toward the veteran tight end, but what looked like a sure game-tying touchdown became an incomplete pass when Smith could not hold on to the foot-ball. Frustrated, Smith flung his body against the ground like a toddler throwing a tantrum. Staubach turned his head in frustration, and even the sedate Landry grimaced at the touchdown that didn't happen.

Shell still doesn't know why Smith was so open.

"Somebody missed their assignment I guess," Shell said. "[Staubach] threw it and in all fairness to [Smith], that was a tough catch. He was wide open and I think Staubach threw the ball low and he had to go down to catch it. But the great ones still make the great catches; tough catch because it was a low catch."

Oldham was on the field in the nickel package as a fifth defensive back and spotted Smith all alone.

"I was on the outside, I was bumping and running, I think it was Tony Hill or Drew Pearson at that time," Oldham said. "I know they went in motion and something happened. And there was a bump off or something and Jackie was wide open. This guy's been an All-Pro forever. Nine out of ten times he would have caught that ball in his hands. And that ball hit him right on the shoulder pads and bounced straight off.

"When I saw him I just thought he was going to turn his hands and catch it like a snowcone right at him. But he didn't; he tried to catch it cradling it in his arms. And he kind of stumbled a little bit. That was a horrible field—and I think that's what kind of got him. When he turned around he started stumbling about the time the ball got there. It hit his shoulder pads and just bounced off. He'll go down as being one of the greatest tight ends in history, but no one will ever remember anything about him except that play. And that's sad."

Staubach accepted some of the blame by telling reporters he "took a little too much off the ball" when he threw it. Though Staubach's gesture was noble, Smith offered no excuses. He said he dropped the football, simple as that.

The Cowboys kicked a field goal to cut the Steelers' lead to 21–17.

Early in the fourth quarter the Cowboys found themselves on the wrong end of a judgment call that led to the Steelers' fourth touchdown.

Bradshaw correctly read a safety blitz from his own 44 and threw the ball down the field in Swann's direction. Cornerback Benny Barnes and Swann collided on the play, and the pass fell incomplete. From the Cowboys' sideline the play looked like a classic no call, while the Steelers agreed with the call made by field judge Fred Swearingen, who called Barnes for tripping and placed the ball at the Dallas 23.

The Cowboys claimed Swann ran across the back of Barnes' legs and tripped to the ground. Naturally, Swann said the official made the right call. Three plays later Bradshaw stepped to the line and noticed a gap on the left side, prompting him to call Harris' number; the Steelers' running back burst through the left side of the line. Charlie Waters recognized the opening and ran toward the gap to try and stop Harris. But just when Waters reached the hole he collided with an official, leaving Harris untouched as he scampered 22 yards to the end zone to cap the eight-play, 84-yard drive.

Holding a 28–17 lead, the Steelers received an unexpected gift on the ensuing kickoff.

Roy Gerela's plant foot slipped when he approached the ball, resulting in a squib kick. Randy White stood in the middle of the field preparing to block when the kick came to him. Not helping matters was the cast worn by Dallas' All-Pro defensive tackle to protect his fractured left thumb; White scooped up the ball. The Cowboys' contingency plan in the event of such a kick was to lateral the ball to one of the deep backs. But White had taken so long to field the ball that he couldn't do anything else but grab the football and gain as much yardage as possible. Future NFL coach Tony Dungy tackled White and forced a fumble that Dennis Winston recovered at the Cowboys' 18 with almost seven minutes remaining in the game.

On the next play Bradshaw saw Swann angling across the middle of the field and sent a spiral in his direction. Swann left the ground and glided in the air like a paper airplane to haul in the 18-yard touchdown pass that gave the Steelers a 35–17 lead.

Believing the game was over, players on the Steelers' sideline erupted in a celebration. But the Cowboys offered no give and immediately got back to work by marching 89 yards in eight plays to score on a 7-yard Staubach pass to Dupree with more than two minutes remaining.

Trailing by 11 points, the Cowboys tried an onside kick. Dungy bobbled the ball and the Cowboys recovered at their own 48. Nine plays later Staubach completed a 4-yard touchdown pass to Butch Johnson with 22 seconds left to make it 35–31.

Could the Cowboys find enough magic to successfully pull off another onside kick? The thought haunted Oldham, who stood on the front line ready to receive the kick.

"I knew they were going to kick an onside kick at that point," Oldham said. "I was on the side where I knew they were going to kick it. Rocky Bleier and I were standing side by side, and that's where they were going to kick it, to us. And the only thing I remember was saying a prayer, 'Please don't kick it to me. Because I'll drop it and I won't get a Super Bowl ring. It will be on national TV and I'll drop it.'"

Bleier, Oldham, and the remainder of the Steelers' "hands team" stood on the Dallas 45 waiting for the kick.

Bleier confessed to experiencing the same thoughts as Oldham.

"We were teammates, not heroes," said Bleier with a laugh. "I was right in the front. I'm thinking, are they going to drill this kick toward me? They'll probably sort of bounce it. And if that's the case, then I'm going to let it go through and have our backup guys pick it up and I'll just throw a block. Then they dribble it.

"My first thought was they can't do anything before it goes 10 yards, so I'll just jump on it before it goes 10 yards. And it was just a roller. [After he recovered the ball] that was the toughest hit I got that whole game."

Oldham joined the pile once Bleier had the football.

"I fell on top of him, and I just remember saying, 'Thank you Rocky, we got a ring buddy,'" Oldham said.

Bradshaw took a knee, time expired, and the Steelers were the first NFL team to win three Super Bowls.

MVP honors went to Bradshaw, who completed 17 of 30 passes for a record 318 yards and passed for four touchdowns, another Super Bowl record. Bradshaw's passes had proved to be a soothing tonic for the Steelers on a day when their running game produced only 66 yards against the Cowboys' flex defense.

After the game Bradshaw's message to Henderson, who later admitted to having sniffed 1½ grams of liquefied cocaine during the game, was simple. "I can spell *win* if you give me the *W* and the *I*."

15

One Last Time

Jack Lambert once commented that quarterbacks should wear dresses. Coming from the Steelers' ultimate warrior, the comment never fails to draw laughter. However, the continued tweaking of the rules to allow offenses to have a better chance to succeed probably cut to the heart of Lambert's remark, which was made in the frustration of such rules. In 1979 came the competition committee's passing of the rule that whistled a play dead once a quarterback was in the grasp of a defender.

"People don't want to see the third-string quarterback playing," said former NFL media director Jim Heffernan, who defended the rule. "No question the league wanted to protect the quarterback. They didn't want to lose the stars to injury. The quarterbacks are the Clark Gables of the league."

Don Weiss said the league did not want to single out the quarterback by making special rules to protect him. "But he is an integral part of the game," Weiss said. "Maybe the most integral part."

Paul Zimmerman did not share Weiss' complimentary stance about the NFL's competition committee or the role of the quarterback that Heffernan and Weiss expressed, and he offered an example of his frustration.

"Every year at the league meeting the competition committee has a meeting with the press," Zimmerman said. "We're going back over 20 years now, when Don Shula and Tex Schramm headed the competition committee and I was Johnny One Note. There was one rule I thought was so outlandishly bad that something had to be done about it and that was the rule where a defensive linemen's legs could be taken out from behind within the legal clip zone. It was absolutely brutal. And I used to raise my hand, the same litany, I said, 'Easy rule, no cutting unless you're face up.' And everybody would groan. Tex Schramm would say, 'Oh my god, there he goes again.' And I said, 'Easy rule, no cutting unless you're face up.' It's like training seals. You don't want to make it too complicated.

"Finally, Shula gets a hold of me after one of the press conferences and says, 'What the @#$% is wrong with you? You want to cripple all of our quarterbacks? We've got to slow those guys down.' I said, 'Don, did you really play defense? Were you a defensive player or did I get that wrong?' About 10 years later they changed the rule. . . . They've finally come around to understand that it's dangerous. And the only way that changes is if you have more defensive coaches on the competition committee. Because it's all self-serving and it's all opportunistic."

The collective age of the veteran Steelers would be the only splash of doubt clouding the forecast for the 1979 season; 10 of the team's 22 starters were age 30 and older. Such doubts were quickly forgotten when the team's effort mirrored the previous season's. Simply stated, the Steelers had become artists of the game of football; it seemed that the men in gold and black had mastered every facet of the game.

Four consecutive victories opened the 1979 season. After the Steelers dominated the Oilers 38–7 in the second week Elvin Bethea said: "They are the best team I've ever played."

In the fifth game of the season the Steelers traveled to Philadelphia to play the Eagles. The Steelers turned the ball over on their first four possessions of the second half en route to their first loss in 13 games dating back to the previous season.

The Eagles and Steelers did not play each other often during the regular season, but they regularly played during the exhibition season, and the script usually played out the same.

"[They] had Hall of Famers everywhere," said Jerry Sisemore, an offensive lineman for the Eagles. "It was like, let's don't call any time-outs. Keep the ball, stay in bounds, and the first one that can get on the bus gets the sandwich. Get out of town without getting killed. It was pretty amazing."

Sisemore said the Steelers had developed a fairly healthy disrespect for their intrastate rivals.

"In the exhibition games, we were like, this is a pride deal, we would swing hard, and we beat 'em a couple of times," Sisemore said. "In fact that 1979 year when we beat them in Philadelphia during the regular season, they could not stand that. They could not believe that. Couldn't believe we were on the same field as the almighty Steelers."

The Steelers rebounded against Cleveland the next week before they lost to Cincinnati thanks to nine turnovers. Impressive victories followed over Denver, Dallas, and Washington. A 20–17 loss to Houston in a Monday night game on December 10 was the last blemish on the Steelers' record. Beating the Steelers gave the Oilers hope they could finally hurdle the Steelers to get into the Super Bowl.

"It was like we had won the Super Bowl that day," Bethea said. "Because we knew that was the team we had to beat to get to the Super Bowl. The fans went crazy. We just knew we had arrived."

Bum Phillips even allowed himself to enjoy the win.

"Bum always took one game at a time," Bethea said. "So when we won, Bum celebrated with us. We were dancing. Bum was dancing. [Oilers owner] Bud Adams came in and the music was playing. The locker room was like we'd just won the Super Bowl. We had a lot of character on our team plus we had characters. We had a lot of outcasts from other teams, we just piecemealed, put together a team that played over our heads on Sundays."

Unfortunately for the Oilers, the Steelers took a 28–0 victory over the Bills at Three Rivers Stadium in the final game of the season. Franco Harris compiled his seventh 1,000-yard rushing season, tying Jim Brown's NFL record, and the Steelers' 12–4 record earned the team its sixth consecutive AFC Central Division title. The Oilers finished at 11–5 to make the playoffs as a wild-card team. Translation: if the opportunity to play the Steelers arose once again, the game would take place in Pittsburgh.

The Steelers faced Miami in the first round of the playoffs. Even though the Steelers were getting a little long in the tooth, they maintained their aura.

"They were just a team that walked onto the field similar to the way the Dolphins did when I first got to Miami," Nat Moore said. "You didn't wonder if you were going to win, you expected to win. You had that persona that said, 'Hey, we're the best team on this field.'

"When we went up there to play them in the [1979] playoffs, the one thing that I did see was we had some younger players that were in awe of the way the Steelers were coming on the field. It was kind of strange. When you start to look at Mike Webster and that offensive line racing to get on the field to go against our defense. . . ."

The Steelers entered the game banged up. Jack Ham had an injured ankle, tackle Jon Kolb had an injured shoulder, and Mike Wagner had a bad hamstring, causing all three to miss the game and leaving the

Steelers without the services of three All-Pros. But the incredible depth of the team once again showed through as tackle Ted Petersen, linebacker Dirt Winston, and free safety J. T. Thomas filled in nicely for the wounded.

The Steelers scored three touchdowns in the first quarter on drives of 62, 62, and 56 yards to effectively kill any possibility of a Miami upset. When the final gun sounded, the Steelers had a 34–14 victory.

Houston traveled to Pittsburgh the following week for the AFC Championship.

"We thought we could beat them," Bethea said. "The year before I didn't think I'd see another playoff or have another chance to get to a Super Bowl. But that year we had felt we had played well enough to match them and that we could go up there and take them on."

Near the end of the third quarter, the Oilers trailed 17–10 when Dan Pastorini found receiver Mike Renfro in the right corner of the end zone for what appeared to be a six-yard touchdown. Replays showed Renfro's catch to be legitimate, but the ruling on the field said Renfro did not have possession. The Oilers had to settle for a field goal.

"Mike Renfro, we thought that one play would get us back in there, and the referee said it wasn't a touchdown," Bethea said. "And later on we found out that it was a touchdown."

Pastorini said even today everybody believes Renfro made a legal catch.

"Including every referee that's ever seen a replay of it," Pastorini said. "If you look back in history, instant replay came about the next year because of that play. I think the importance of instant replay to this day stems from that football play. It certainly changed that game, but I don't know if it would have changed the outcome. They were a great football team. We might have just wakened a sleeping giant. But we were turning around our momentum right there. We didn't score on the play, and it seemed to take the wind out of our sails."

The Steelers went on to win 27–13 to advance to their fourth Super Bowl. In the end, Pastorini surmised the Steelers were just a better football team.

"There's no question about it," Pastorini said. "We were kind of overachievers who were always playing above our heads to get where we were. We were pretty good, and a lot of people thought those two games in 1978 and 1979 were really the Super Bowls because people felt the Houston Oilers and the Pittsburgh Steelers were the two best teams in the NFL, which I have to agree with."

The controversy about Renfro's catch put a damper on the victory for Joe Greene.

"Absolutely, I was disappointed," Greene said. "On the field I told the officials to give it to them. Why did I say that? Think about it, it's been, what, 26 years since that game and we're still talking about it. It had nothing to do with whether we were going to win the ballgame or not. It's just like when Jackie [Smith] dropped the ball in the Super Bowl, it had nothing to do with whether we were going to win the ballgame, because when that catch became in question it questioned the ballgame, whether we were going to win it or not."

Even with the disappointment of the questioned play, the Steelers looked forward to facing the Rams in the Super Bowl. The Rams' road to the Super Bowl had many bumps and wrong turns en route to capturing their seventh-consecutive NFC Western Division championship. Chaos ruled in the Rams' organization dating back to before the 1978 season.

Chuck Knox coached the Rams from 1973 to 1977 before leaving to coach the Buffalo Bills, prompting Rams owner Carroll Rosenbloom to hire longtime NFL coach George Allen, who had coached the Rams from 1966 to 1970. After the Rams lost their first two preseason games, Allen was fired by Rosenbloom and replaced by Allen's offensive coordinator, Ray Malavasi.

Malavasi had been Knox's defensive coordinator and had undergone quadruple bypass heart surgery early in 1978. The Rams went 12–4 under Malavasi in 1978 but got hammered by the Cowboys 28–0 in the NFC Championship Game, adding to the belief that the Rams were an underachieving team lacking heart. On April 2, 1979, Rosenbloom drowned while swimming off Golden Beach, Florida, and his widow, Georgia, took control of the team. Meanwhile, Malavasi returned to the hospital in the spring of 1979 to receive treatment for hypertension.

During the 1979 regular season the Rams had outscored their opponents by a mere 14 points, and they had been humiliated 30–6 by Dallas and 40–16 by San Diego. And what would a Rams season have been without a quarterback controversy? Pat Haden began the season as the number one signal caller before breaking a finger. Veteran Bob Lee and rookie Jeff Rutledge had their turns behind center before Vince Ferragamo returned from a broken hand to emerge as the team's starter. The third-year quarterback from the University of Nebraska took over in time to lead the Rams to four wins in their final five games, which proved to be good enough to eclipse the 8–8 mark of the New Orleans Saints.

"Turned out everybody wanted me to be the starting quarterback," Ferragamo said. "I'd had a lot of success in the preseason. It was pretty much a known fact that I was ready to play and wasn't playing because Pat was there. We had good chemistry when I went in, and everybody was ready for me to come in—the players were, management wasn't, but the players were. And they responded. I became the starter thereafter, and we went on a winning streak. We ended up winning our division, went to play Dallas, then Tampa Bay."

Once in the playoffs, the Rams edged Dallas 21–19 then beat the Tampa Bay Buccaneers 9–0 on three Frank Corral field goals.

The Rams' 9–7 record was the worst record for any team ever reaching the Super Bowl, and by reaching the Super Bowl the Rams became the first team from the NFC West ever to take part in the title game. The roller-coaster season couldn't have been a health boost for Malavasi, who remained on medicine to treat his hypertension.

While the 10-point line favoring the Steelers reflected the lingering perception that the Rams lacked heart, the team had several things working in its favor.

For starters, the game would be played in Pasadena's Rose Bowl, which essentially made the game a Rams home game. Discounting the home-field advantage was the feeling by Rams players that their fans were the most fair-weathered bunch in all of sports.

Another plus for the Rams came in the fact that the Steelers were aging.

"Early on, 1974, 1975, 1976, we could play defense that was really truly stifling," Greene said. "In 1978 and 1979, we did play some stifling defense, but it was kind of hit-and-miss at times. Sometimes we didn't; other games we did."

They had all the knowledge and the aura gathered from an amazing run, but they were slowing down. Even the Steelers' players understood how aging had taken its toll.

"I could feel it," Greene said. "Nagging injuries, had a harder time recovering after games. Wasn't as quick, wasn't as fast, wasn't as strong. And plays that I was making in the past I wasn't making anymore."

But motivation never presented a problem for the Steelers.

"Wearing the black and the gold, that was motivation," Greene said.

Perhaps the most significant challenge the Steelers faced stemmed from the Rams' coaching staff, which included former Steelers coaches Lionel Taylor, Dan Radakovich, and Bud Carson, who had left the Steelers for the Rams after the 1977 season.

"There was no question they knew everything we would do," Noll said.

The familiarity the Rams coaches had with the Steelers removed any element of surprise for the Steelers.

"If they know what you're going to do it comes down to execution," Donnie Shell said. "We were a running team, and people used to put eight men in the box and we would still run the ball. We knew it was about believing in what we were doing and getting it done. A mentality of, 'no matter what they do against us—because they know the plays—we just have to execute.'"

Even if the Steelers managed to execute every play perfectly, Carson felt optimistic.

"We beat them [in Los Angeles] the year before that [in 1978]," Carson said. "We were a good football team too. We had good personnel. At that point I thought we were a better defense than Pittsburgh to be honest with you. We beat them [in 1978], and I felt like we'd beat them again.

"I knew basically everything they did and how they did it. The parts I didn't know were the automatics. They had a lot of those and they would change from game to game. You had to really be very careful that your presnap look did not give away defenses where they could take advantage of it."

Carson recognized the type of team the Steelers had transitioned to over the years.

"The pass very definitely did become a bigger part of their offense," Carson said. "As Bradshaw grew, they grew."

Carson's confidence spilled over to the players he coached on defense.

"Bud came in the first day after we beat Tampa and he was all fired up," said Rams linebacker Jim Youngblood. "He said, 'We can beat them. I know we can beat them. We've done it before with the same personnel. We can beat them.'

"Once we started watching films of the Steelers, I knew we could beat them, too. If I'm going to play I want to play the best. And at that time the Steelers were the best. I knew we could beat them."

Among the Rams' starters on defense was Jack Youngblood, one of the best defensive ends in football who had broken his leg in the playoff game against the Cowboys.

"I got it caught on the turf," Jack Youngblood said. "My leg was planted up against somebody's body on the ground and I got bumped from the inside. I couldn't get my foot up fast enough [to avoid getting injured] and snapped the fibula."

Team doctors told Youngblood his leg was already broken, so continuing to play wouldn't make the injury worse.

"They said the only thing playing would do was keep it from healing by being on it constantly," Youngblood said. "They said if I could manage the pain and deal with that, and still play at a reasonably high level, then it was up to me."

But there was little Youngblood could do to dull the pain.

"You can't shoot a bone, it's just going to hurt," Youngblood said. "You take the aspirin and pain killers to try and dull the pain, but you're not taking anything that would compensate for it."

In his mind playing was the only option.

"I wanted to go out and compete in those games because you never know from one year to the next if you were ever going to have that opportunity again," Youngblood said.

Jack Youngblood also bought into Carson's belief that the Steelers could lose.

"We believed," Jack Youngblood said. "Bud had us playing in a team format; it wasn't so much about individuals but how everybody played together. And we knew that we could match up helmet-to-helmet with their guys—their first line against our first line—and it wasn't any big deal.

"The thing that I remember was that we were the big underdogs. As a football team we didn't believe that. The core of us didn't and we knew we could go in there and play with them. We just didn't have the quarterback who could take that game and take charge of that game like Terry [Bradshaw]."

Once a young team trying to break into the NFL's elite, the Steelers were now the NFL's best—champions accustomed to winning. When pressed, Chuck Noll allowed that this Steelers team was the best to date. Rams backup quarterback Bob Lee wondered out loud how the Steelers had managed to lose four games. But Ferragamo felt confident. Part of the Rams quarterback's confidence came from being prepared. Not only did Carson and company help the Rams' defense get ready for the Steelers, they also helped the offense.

"Basically, with their knowledge of the game, they took our best plays, or incorporated the plays we would run best, from some of those plays coming from Pittsburgh," Ferragamo said. "They knew how to put plays in that could defeat almost any defense, and that's what we'd run."

Ferragamo gained additional confidence knowing he would have protection.

"I didn't pay much attention to the great Steel Curtain defense as far as what they would present with their pass rush because we had a great offensive line," he said.

The NFL honored Art Rooney by asking him to make the ceremonial coin toss prior to the game. The Rams won the toss and elected to receive the kickoff in front of a record Super Bowl crowd of 103,985 in the Rose Bowl.

"I was ready for that one," Ferragamo said. "That was a game you dream about playing in. Butterflies, you're going to get butterflies. That's what gets you ready to play. All the preparation and you're going to play in the Super Bowl. That's the game you live to play. I always liked to go out and play in a big game."

After stalling on their first possession, the Rams punted. Eleven plays later the Steelers took a 3–0 lead on rookie kicker Matt Bahr's 41-yard field goal.

Bahr followed his field goal with a weak kickoff that got only as far as the Rams' 41. Then something strange began to happen on the manicured turf of the Rose Bowl: the Rams ran the ball down the Steelers' throats.

"I didn't think [the Steelers] would lose, because I didn't think the Rams were any good," Paul Zimmerman said. "Turns out they were good. They ran on the Steelers. They pushed them around up front. That was what set the tone."

Wendell Tyler ran a sweep around left end that covered 39 yards to lead an eight-play scoring drive culminated by Cullen Bryant's 1-yard touchdown late in the first quarter to give the Rams a 7–3 lead.

"We marched to our first score; it was just a power run by Cullen," Ferragamo said. "The way our offensive line was playing that day it just gave you an air of confidence. After that it was like, 'This game is our game. We can win this game.' And so that push and that line and Cullen Bryant just driving in there to score that first touchdown was really exhilarating. People didn't even expect us to score a touchdown in that game."

The Steelers answered quickly. Larry Anderson, who set a Super Bowl return record that day with 162 yards on five kickoffs, gave the Steelers good field position after taking Corral's kickoff 45 yards. Bradshaw then put on a quarterback clinic in which he alternated crisp passes with runs into the Rams' line. Harris went around right end for a 1-yard touchdown on the ninth play of the drive to make the score 10–7 with more than 12 minutes remaining in the second quarter.

But the Rams' defense stiffened, turning away the Steelers on three consecutive possessions. During the same space of time the Rams got field goals of 31 and 45 yards to take a 13–10 lead at the half.

"Nobody on our team thought we would lose that game even though we were behind at the half," Dwight White said. "But we also knew the Rams were playing well and we had our work cut out for us."

Given the nature of the Steelers' dynasty, they found themselves in an odd situation where the offense was playing well but the defense looked vulnerable.

The Steelers received the second-half kickoff, and Bradshaw connected with Swann on a 47-yard touchdown three minutes into the third quarter to regain the lead, 17–13. Rams free safety Nolan Cromwell, one of the NFL's best at his position, appeared to be in perfect shape to knock down the pass to Swann, but he only managed to touch the ball before Swann hauled in the pass.

A jubilant Steelers sideline breathed a little easier after Swann's touchdown. However, the celebration and the lead were fleeting.

Three plays after getting the ball back, the Rams found themselves on the Pittsburgh 24 thanks to a 50-yard strike from Ferragamo to Billy Waddy. What happened next could be attributed largely to the knowledge of the Rams' coaching staff and their familiarity with the Steelers' tendencies.

Lawrence McCutcheon swept wide and the Steelers chased in hot pursuit only to watch in horror when the Rams' halfback planted and threw to Ron Smith for a touchdown.

"It was called a halfback sweep pass," McCutcheon said. "I was looking at film of Pittsburgh at that time and they were a team of very aggressive corners and safeties. Once they recognized you were running a sweep they had a tendency to really rush the line of scrimmage. We felt that the halfback pass would be a great play under those circumstances. It was. It worked just like we thought it would and resulted in a touchdown."

Ferragamo said the play was a reaction to the Steelers' defense being "a little bit overwhelming."

"We were able to trick them," Ferragamo said. "We used trickery and it worked. They bit on the run because we like to run the football, and the pass was wide open."

Corral's extra point went wide left to leave the Rams' lead at 19–17 with 10 minutes remaining in the third quarter.

The Steelers began their next possession from their own 26 and advanced the ball to the 44 after two plays. Cromwell's misfortune continued on the next play.

Bradshaw threw deep to Swann, and Cromwell found himself in position to make the interception. Instead the ball sailed through his hands and dropped to the turf.

"After I dropped the ball, I looked up and saw where everyone was," Cromwell told reporters. "I felt sick. There was one Steeler in front of me and he was blocked. I just took my eyes off the ball. We could have been nine points ahead and that might have changed the result."

Of all the plays that happened during that Super Bowl, Jack Youngblood best remembers Cromwell's missed opportunity. "As you look back—and I've been asked this question a lot of times—the things you remember for the most part are the failures or the mistakes, or something that didn't quite go right," Jack Youngblood said. "The successes were expected. To this day I still can visualize Nolan Cromwell. We had the Steelers backed up, and Bud had called the right defense. Nolan obviously read the play, stepped in front of the pass, and it hit him dead between the numbers. There was nobody in front of him except me. And when I spun around to see where the ball went, it hit Nolan right in the numbers. You throw that ball to him a hundred times and he catches 99 of them. It just wasn't meant to be. Lady Luck was not smiling."

The Steelers did not capitalize on the drop. And during the same series they lost Swann after Bradshaw threw high to Swann going across the middle and Rams cornerback Pat Thomas made him pay. The hit knocked out Swann, who experienced blurred vision when he regained consciousness and didn't return to the game, leaving the Steelers with but one deep threat in Stallworth.

Bradshaw was intercepted again after leading the Steelers inside the Rams' 20 with one minute left in the third quarter.

At that point the chances for a Rams upset were looking more believable. The Rams were leading, and the Steelers' running game wasn't working and their defense looked tired. Bradshaw had been accurate for the most part, having completed 12 of 17 passes, but he also had thrown three interceptions. Meanwhile, Ferragamo had completed 11 of 16 and had not been intercepted.

The Rams had the ball at their own 17 when the third quarter ended. Showing their spirit, the Rams sprinted to the other end of the field like high school sophomores. The veteran Steelers took their sweet time walking to change ends.

"We were real excited," McCutcheon said. "We were two- or three-touchdown underdogs, but we felt that we were playing well at that time—had won six of the last seven games. We came into the game with a lot of momentum and confidence and felt we had a chance to win the game. At that point we thought we had them on the ropes."

Believing they had put away perhaps the best team in football history might have been detrimental to the Rams.

"It had happened to me before," Ferragamo said, "when you think you've got the game put away and all of a sudden things didn't turn out that way. That happened to me in college against Oklahoma. Anything can happen. I just think that the experience factor offensively hurt us a little in a big game like a Super Bowl. It was our first appearance there. That has somewhat of an effect."

Part of the Steelers' frustration trying to run the football came from the Rams' ability to defense the trap. The Rams had an outstanding front four of defensive linemen and three quality linebackers, which allowed them to play a 4-3 defense when many teams had gone to a 3-4 due to not having enough quality defensive linemen. The talent of the group, and the fact that they had been schooled well on their responsibilities by Carson, allowed them to play straight up against the Steelers' offense on most plays.

"You play your responsibility no matter what front they were in," Jack Youngblood said. "Because our front seven could handle any running plays as long as you played your responsibility. That sounds simplistic, but that's what we believed and we believed it to a point where we stopped people by doing that."

Throughout the game, the Rams had effectively taken away the short pass, prompting Noll to talk to Bradshaw.

"You're not going to pick your way down against the Rams," Noll told him. "Go for the big play."

If a big play was coming, Stallworth needed to be the guy.

"I remember double coverage on every play," Stallworth said. "Very seldom did I see single coverage. We knew what it was going to be, so it was going to be sort of an inside, outside sort of game. A lot of things to disguise that double coverage, but it amounts to the same thing, they gave it different looks to try and confuse us a little bit. I remember the running game wasn't working very well because they knew what we were going to do.

"But I remember the double coverage. And the thing that we knew going in was because of the coverages they played it was going to be the big plays that were going to get them. We were not going to complete a whole lot of short intermediate routes against them."

Three minutes into the fourth quarter the Steelers went to a play they'd practiced all week tagged "60 prevent slot hook-and-go." Noll sent in the play and Bradshaw wanted to change it. He had sound logic given that the Steelers had tried the play repeatedly during the practices leading up to the game and it had not worked once.

"When a play doesn't work it's hard to have much confidence in it," Stallworth said.

Still, Stallworth talked Bradshaw into going with the called play as the Steelers faced third-and-8 at their own 27.

Stallworth lined up as a slot receiver and headed up the field with Rams cornerback Rod Perry on his right. Approximately 10 yards past the line of scrimmage he faked a hook route when he reached the safety, Eddie Brown. Brown, who should have been helping Perry, bit on the fake. Stallworth went deep and Bradshaw laid the ball perfectly into the streaking receiver's hands just past the leaping Perry.

"I remember seeing [Perry's] hand getting close just when I was about to catch it," Stallworth said. "He almost made a great play."

Instead the Steelers took a 24–19 lead when Stallworth caught the ball 40 yards past the line of scrimmage and scampered to the end zone with no company.

Perry had expected to receive help on the play, but it never arrived. Brown had gotten confused thinking the Rams were in a dime package—six defensive backs—instead of a nickel—which used five—so he went for the outside receiver instead of Stallworth in the slot.

"I've got a lot of sour grapes about that one," Carson said. "First of all, Lynn gets knocked out so there's only one guy you've got to cover, Stallworth. We basically were doubling him every time they went to three wide receivers; he's the guy you had to double.

"The game plan after Swann went down was pretty simple: double Stallworth. The big play Stallworth caught down the middle for like 70 yards, we had him doubled. Both of our safeties were playing under him. We had a guy who was supposed to play over him and cover deep, play under. Just a tremendous, tremendous freaking mistake we never made. We played that defense over and over and we'd never made that mistake, but we made it. And Stallworth catches the football. We had Perry underneath him in perfect coverage, and we don't have the safety over him covering on the top side. He catches the ball, runs it in. It's a big, big mistake."

Familiarity works both ways, and Noll remembered one particular tendency Carson had.

"Knowing Bud, he always wanted to get you in a third-and-long situation," Noll said. "He was going to play it for the possession pass. So every time we got in third-and-long [against the Rams] we went deep." Noll smiled. "You don't have to have a high percentage on the long ones; complete a couple of those and you're in good shape."

Having the mind-set they were going to throw long, the Steelers had to bait the hook.

"Again, they would make sure they jumped on your short routes," Noll said. "So we'd try to give them the picture of things we normally did in possession [situations] and go deep and Terry would find them. And that was Terry's strength, his ability to go deep and accurately. Terry did that exceptionally well."

Ferragamo continued to show an unexpected poise on the next Rams drive. With more than eight minutes remaining, the Rams began at their 16 and progressed to the Steelers' 32.

"We were driving the ball down the field, probably one of our better drives," Ferragamo said. "We were moving the ball consistently and with great ease. That particular play was called and, again, inexperience keeps coming back that entire Super Bowl. They called a play we hadn't practiced that was a play we used during the preseason. We called it a switch."

On the switch the flanker and split end switch assignments.

When the Rams broke the huddle with the play-action call made, Ferragamo struggled to remember what to do on the play.

"I showed a lack of experience there," Ferragamo said. "I should have known if I had any questions, I could call another play that I knew how to run—again, my first year at the helm. With a little indecision and not knowing the correct assignment, coming back throwing that ball, you're not focusing, you're not thinking. Not visualizing the play correctly. What happened was the result of a bad play."

Ferragamo threw to Smith, and Lambert came from nowhere to make the interception.

"My inexperience in underestimating the range of Jack Lambert was one of the things that hurt us," Ferragamo said. "He could cover a lot of ground because he was so big with those long arms. And he was tall. He could cover a big area back there. So they could depend on certain things. Especially when they were in a deeper alignment."

Ferragamo offered an ironic chuckle when pointing out that the NFL Films' version of the play shows Billy Waddy open deep on the play.

"Everybody thinks Billy Waddy was open on the play streaking up the field on a post route," Ferragamo said. "He really wasn't open. Little do they know the cornerback was right there. You see the highlight film, [Waddy] is holding his hand up like he's wide open. You don't see the cornerback in the frame of the picture. Guy's running like he's wide open and the cornerback was right behind him. I guess they use that for the drama thing."

Lambert, who made 13 tackles during the game, had been emotional for most of the game in trying to wake the defense before taking over by making the critical interception. The Steelers had the ball at their own 30 with 5:24 showing on the clock and managed to gain just three yards on the first two plays. Then they went for the jugular when Bradshaw recognized that the Rams were in the same coverage for the third-and-long situation.

Once again Bradshaw found Stallworth. This time the completion went for 45 yards and put the Steelers at the Rams' 22. On third down Bradshaw threw to Smith in the end zone and Pat Thomas was called for interference, giving the Steelers the ball at the Rams' 1. Harris went off tackle and into the end zone to give the Steelers an insurmountable 31–19 lead with 1:49 left.

Carson still regrets the outcome of the game. "We had them but let them get away," he said. "All they had left was Stallworth, and we blew the coverage. We should have gotten that one. If ever a Super Bowl was thrown away it was that one. I don't know what happened. We knew a lot about Pittsburgh. Just didn't work out.

"You had to give Pittsburgh a lot of credit, and nobody has really heard me crying about the things I'm crying about now. But we had that botched coverage and then we screwed up offensively after that. We lost a game we should have won. To Pittsburgh's credit, they came back and won it, but it's the toughest one I've ever lost, and I've been in a lot of them."

Greene credited the Rams for playing with a lot of heart and intelligence.

"Throughout the game they read our blitzes well, they ran the ball well right at us, and we just seemed to be missing something in the first half," Greene said. "I remember it seemed like we were kind of sleepwalking out there. They were prepared for that game and you had to respect what they did."

Going into the game Jack Youngblood felt like they could win the game if they didn't allow the big play. "But we didn't stop the big play and we lost," Youngblood said. "The play that Stallworth caught the football on was just a tremendous play by John. It wasn't that we made a mistake, it was John made a great play.

"That was Chuck's confidence in what Terry could do with the passing game. He was predominantly a ball control type of an offensive coach. But I think he realized he had a big arm in Terry and had two pretty good receivers out there."

Shell said the Steelers had never felt threatened by the Rams, though they probably should have.

"Really they should have beat us," Shell said. "They had our coaching staff out there. They knew all of our plays and everything. They were able to run the ball. But we knew that and we still beat them."

Epilogue

In 1980 the Steelers went to camp carrying the slogan "One for the Thumb," meaning they'd run out of fingers on which to wear their many Super Bowl rings. But their thumbs would have to go bare.

Thanks largely to injuries, the Steelers finished third in the AFC Central with a record of 9–7 and did not make the playoffs.

"The 1980 season took on a personality of its own," Rocky Bleier said. "Guys were tired. And it was tough. It was tough to keep that edge, that edge you need to win, because it's a fine line, a step here, a misplay there, keeping that fire of wanting to be the best."

In the rearview mirror of this Pittsburgh Steelers team was the wake of a dynasty.

From 1972 to 1979, the Steelers went to the playoffs eight times, capturing six consecutive AFC Central titles, and Chuck Noll became the only NFL coach to win four Super Bowls.

Twenty-two Steelers played in all four Super Bowl victories.

"The reason we won was not because we were so close and so committed," Andy Russell said. "It was because we were so talented. We had 13 guys in the Pro Bowl, or some such number. I mean, how can you not win? We had an All-Star team."

No team before or since has achieved similar excellence to this rare team. The Steel Dynasty truly was the greatest dynasty in NFL history.

More than 25 years after playing quarterback for the Rams in Super Bowl XIV, Vince Ferragamo believes his team lost to the best team in pro football history.

"The Pittsburgh team from the seventies is probably the best of all time," Ferragamo said. "Cumulatively, between offense and defense and special teams, and the coaches and owners, I put them up against any team. Joe Montana [49ers of the eighties], Pittsburgh would win. They not only had the power and the grit, but they had the flash and the great talent and athletic ability of Bradshaw's arm. Franco Harris and Rocky Bleier could power at you.

"Defensively they had no weaknesses. They could cover. Mel Blount, J.T. Thomas, from one side to the other, everybody was a Hall of Famer. And they had so many Hall of Fame guys, like the old Green Bay Packers. I can't really compare them to Green Bay because that was before my time. But the Vince Lombardi era would be the only team to probably give them a run. Could anybody else beat them? I don't think so. As good as Bill Walsh and Montana were, they wouldn't have been able to beat them. Pittsburgh would have found a way to win. They could throw the deep ball, so they would beat San Francisco."

Dwight White believes the Steelers were special for more than just winning the games.

"Yes, we won a lot of games," White said. "But I don't think that's what developed a fan base and almost a cult following that we had then and even to this day have. It wasn't so much that we won a lot of games, but it was the way we won the games. You knew that when you came into Pittsburgh, what you wanted to do was get out of here alive. You're going to lose the game, but you want to get out of there alive, because these guys really beat you up. It ain't even close. It's like you're history, hello dead man. That was sort of a cocky, braggadocios kind of way, but for Pittsburgh, a place everybody wiped their feet on, that was a damn good feeling for some people to have a turnaround. Payback is a bitch. And I think that's what people in Pittsburgh were feeling. They were all out of Appalachia, nasty, dirty-faced coal miners and smutty-faced steelworkers, the water's brown and the sky is brown, and that's the way it really was here then. This ain't Fort Lauderdale, this ain't Hilton Head. I just think Pittsburghers took great pride in who they were. Self-esteem is a helluva thing. We played a great part in that self-development here in Pittsburgh."

Some people will tell you that pro football isn't such a complicated game. You line up. He hits you in the mouth; you hit him in the mouth. The tougher guy wins. It's the people, the athletes, who make the difference. There's some truth in that view, but there's a lot more to playing in the NFL.

"One of the things that was so strong and so powerful about our football team was the leadership from the head coach was constant," Joe Greene said. "There weren't any peaks and valleys; it always was on an even keel. You know, you do these things you win, if you don't you won't. Chuck Noll gave us all the same kind of treatment. He respected us as players and as individuals. But he didn't put his arms around us and hug us or he didn't celebrate when we came off the field after a good play. But we knew he knew that we knew he had a good plan."

It was a plan resulting in nine Hall of Fame inductions—Joe Greene, John Stallworth, Lynn Swann, Terry Bradshaw, Franco Harris, Jack Ham, Jack Lambert, Mike Webster, and Mel Blount all have busts at Canton— and a plan that brought a defense so smothering that the NFL had to adjust its rules.

In today's NFL players make more money, and under today's rules it is difficult for any team to form a dynasty—even though the New England Patriots have managed to change that perception by winning three Super Bowls in four seasons.

"When I look back, I wouldn't trade my experience from the seventies from where I came and what the game did for me for anything in the world," White said. "It was a different time, a different day; we made some decent money, but as Chuck would say so many times, 'You've got to get prepared for your life's work.' So all of us, no matter how successful or spectacular our careers were, you knew in the back of your mind you had to find something else to do after the game. A lot of us began to prepare. Probably made us more well rounded than some of these guys who have this warped view of success and [don't understand the] values that people develop from working and getting in traffic every day and raising families, paying a mortgage, and worrying about making ends meet, etc.

"Today a guy can make in one season what most people won't make in a lifetime. Life is more than money, and success is more than playing in the NFL."

Added Bleier: "If you asked any of [his Steelers teammates] would you rather have the money or would you rather have played on a team that won four Super Bowls, I would say, when they searched their souls, they would prefer to be right where they are, a part of that dynasty."

Index